MOUNTAIN MADNESS

Scott Fischer,
Mount Everest &
a Life Lived on High

ROBERT BIRKBY

CITADEL PRESS
Kensington Publishing Corp.
www.kensingtonbooks.com

CITADEL PRESS BOOKS are published by

Kensington Publishing Corp.
850 Third Avenue
New York, NY 10022

Copyright © 2008 Robert Birkby

All Kensington titles, imprints, and distributed lines are available at special quantity discounts for bulk purchases for sales promotions, premiums, fundraising, educational, or institutional use. Special book excerpts or customized printings can also be created to fit specific needs. For details, write or phone the office of the Kensington special sales manager: Kensington Publishing Corp., 850 Third Avenue, New York, NY 10022, attn: Special Sales Department; phone: 1-800-221-2647.

CITADEL PRESS and the Citadel logo are Reg. U.S. Pat. & TM Off.

First printing: February 2008

10 9 8 7 6 5 4 3 2 1

Printed in the United States of America

Library of Congress Control Number: TK

ISBN-13: 978-0-8065-2875-5
ISBN-10: 0-8065-2875-3

MOUNTAIN
MADNESS

For All the Bruces

"Scott had one adventure after another after another. Most of us have an occasional big adventure, but it's not this continuous series. Who does that? Nobody. Most of us are so conservative. But not Scott."
　　—Stacy Allison, the first American woman to climb Mount Everest

"It's all so doggone fascinating, the whole lot of it, isn't it? In terms of what we did and where we are now, it was just perfect. Of course, it would have been good to have fewer people die along the way. . . ."
　　—Wesley Krause, climbing partner and Mountain Madness cofounder

"You're either cruisin' or you're bummin'. Cruising's a lot more fun, so you might as well cruise."
　　—Scott Fischer

Contents

Introduction

IT'S A CLEAR, cool Nepalese morning and Scott Fischer is showing me the skyline of Mount Everest where he will be taking the last steps of a remarkable life. He and I are atop Kala Patar. At 18,000 feet it is higher than any mountain in the contiguous United States, but here in the heart of the Himalaya it is little more than a rocky bump encircled by some of the most spectacular peaks on the planet—Pumori, Nuptse, Lhotse, Ama Dablam. Guidebooks call Kala Patar a trekkers' peak within the abilities of anyone able to hike steep terrain and manage the rigors of backcountry travel, and I am pleased to have made it this far. Scott barely broke a sweat as he led the way, and while the views in every direction are stunning, his gaze turns, as it always has, toward Everest.

I had assumed that because mountains of the Himalayan Range are all huge, they would balance one another and negate some of the largeness of scale, but I was wrong. The peaks near Everest are stupendous in size, dragging the landscape straight up into the sky and giving new meaning to my sense of vertical if only because there is so much here that is so far from being anything else.

The clarity is as extreme as the elevation. There is no haze, no smog, not even much atmosphere to soften the soaring uplift of rock and ice. Edges are sharp, clean, and precise. The landscape is devoid of color save for dark stone and dazzling snow, as if a crisp black and white photograph had been set against a luminous blue sky. This is terrain without compromise, topography that is distinct, absolute, and overwhelming in its immediacy. Rising above it all, a full two miles higher than where Scott and I are sitting, the immense tilted pyramid that is the final height of Everest dominates even the giant mountains nearby. It is as though we are staring at the sun.

Scott is completely at ease here, and lets me know he is pleased I've come along. I have known him long enough to understand we are both more content in wilderness than we could ever be in a city, but I don't share his willingness to risk so much to climb so high, especially when I see what is involved now that he has yet again come right up against Everest. The mystery of his motivation is as compelling to me as are the mysteries of the mountains themselves, perhaps because I recognize that I have limits and Scott seems never to have reached his. I remind him now and then that I intend to be playing the piano well into my eighties, and for that I'll need a full complement of fingers. I'm not about to lose any to frostbite simply for the sake of standing atop the world's tallest peak. I know that Scott respects my choices in this regard, but it's obvious that he is hearing a very different soundtrack inside his head than the keyboard works of Beethoven, Chopin, and Brahms.

We dig through our packs and pull out a lunch of goat cheese, Nepalese fry bread, and a couple of chocolate bars. Far below us near the toe of the Khumbu Icefall we can see dozens of red, yellow, and blue dots, the tents of Everest Base Camp where this spring's expeditions are preparing to send climbers toward the top of the world. As we eat, Scott points out the route he will be taking through the jumbled seracs and crevasses of the Icefall into the lofty valley of snow called the Western Cwm, then up the Lhotse Face at the head of the Cwm to the South Col, the pass at 26,000 feet of elevation between Everest and its neighbor Lhotse. From there they will set out for Everest's Southeast Ridge and follow it to the summit. It's the way that Edmund Hillary and Tenzing Norgay climbed Everest in 1953, and the first successful American expedition a decade later.

Scott doesn't realize the significance of where he is guiding my eye. He can't know that he is pointing out the line of travel where, as leader of a team signing on with his Mountain Madness adventure travel company for a chance to reach the top of Everest, he will climb out of relative obscurity and into a storm of controversy. All of Scott's clients will return safely, but in what would quickly become known as the 1996 Everest tragedy, Scott and seven climbers and guides with other expeditions will perish in the ferocious winds and rarified cold of one of Earth's most beautiful but inhospitable places.

Coverage of events unfolding that spring on Mount Everest transformed the obscure pursuits of high-altitude mountaineers into the story of the moment. It made the national news, the covers of *Newsweek* and *Time*, and was featured on the television programs *Nova* and *Nightline*. Books were published, most notably Jon Krakauer's *Into Thin Air* and Anatoli Boukreev's *The Climb,* each author providing an eyewitness assessment of what had happened on the mountain. A made-for-television movie shrank the story to fit the small screen, and an IMAX film expanded it again to provide panoramic perspective. Millions of armchair mountaineers devoured the details and second-guessed every word, every step, and every breath of thin or bottled air.

The glare of worldwide attention buffeted Scott as severely as had the Himalayan weather, but nearly all the publicity was focused on that last Everest expedition, Scott's final forty days. In print and on film he seemed to have materialized atop Everest fully formed, as if it were natural for a man to appear without prelude at 29,000 feet above sea level. Scott was presented as a caricature of himself, his strengths and shortcomings selected and shaped to heighten the drama and forward the narratives of others. Little was said about the forty years that had led up to those final forty days of his life. Little was offered about who Scott Fischer really was or about what had caused him, of all people, to be there, of all places.

After Scott died, for some it was too painful to think about what had happened in the Himalayas; for many it was all they could do. His friends were stunned that following decades of significant alpine achievements and outrageous escapes from almost certain disasters, Scott had finally encountered difficulties he had not been able to overcome even with the sheer force of will that had always gotten him through. Some were angry with Scott for leaving his young children without a father. Others were furious with the media for revealing so little about him, or for assuming so much. All felt a profound emptiness, a void in their lives that had once been filled by Scott's exuberance, energy, and infectious good cheer.

Those who knew Scott well have gradually come to see him again in the larger context of his entire existence rather than simply in his loss on Everest. Over beers in town and around camp stoves in the high country, friends and fellow climbers recall with pleasure the adventures they shared with him, and they do little to disguise how much they long for the freedom and expansive possibilities they had enjoyed when Scott was in the lead and shouldering back the boundaries of what was possible and what, at least up until that moment, was not.

I have felt much the same way, especially if I happen to open the storage box I long ago pushed under the basement stairs and come upon spiral-bound notebooks with NEPAL or MOUNT ELBRUS or KILIMANJARO scribbled on the covers. Inside I find a few forgotten rupees, rubles, or Tanzanian shillings, perhaps a photograph or two, a frayed ticket stub from Aeroflot or Royal Nepal Airlines, and my penciled report of yet another Scott-inspired Mountain Madness adventure. When I finish reading one journal, I put it down and open another.

Now and then in my current travels I run into people I had known in the Fischer days, or I dial the telephone numbers of members of Scott's family who were good friends and have become distant only because time and topography have eased us apart. We begin talking about Scott and soon the stories are pouring out.

Craig Seasholes, a friend of Scott's and a fellow mountaineering instructor, told me recently about a dream he'd had soon after Scott died. In the dream, Craig is sitting on a bench on the deck of a boat in the middle of Puget Sound, the same small cruise ship he'd taken a few days earlier to attend Scott's memorial service. The door to the ship's cabin opens and Scott steps onto the deck. He sits beside Craig and they ride together for a few minutes, the waves lifting and lowering the ship as it makes good speed through the Sound.

"Wasn't that great!" Scott suddenly says.

"The memorial service?" Craig asks. "Is that what you mean?"

"No, man," Scott tells him. "Life! The adventure! The whole thing! Wasn't it great?"

He smiles at Craig and puts his hand on his shoulder, then stands and walks back to the cabin door. "Just great," he says again, and is gone.

As I listen to Craig's story and as I read the journals, I feel the familiar stirring to equip myself for one more extended expedition, only this time instead of a backpack and hiking boots my gear will be a fresh notebook and a good pen. Rather than a wilderness destination, I find myself compelled to journey back in search of Scott Fischer. I want to revisit those who knew him best, study the trip accounts, and examine the photographs. I'm eager to travel deep into Scott's life to better understand what it was that motivated him, that caused him to inspire so many, and that ultimately led him to die alone in a place as close to the sky as anybody has ever been.

Most of all, though, I want more of the life, the adventure, that whole great thing. I want to feel again what it was like to be sitting with Scott on Kala Patar, basking in the sunshine and the friendship and the views, finishing the last of the cheese and chocolate and noticing that the afternoon is beginning to slip away. I pick up a small stone as a souvenir and drop it into my pack, effectively reducing the elevation of Kala Patar a tiny fraction of an inch. Scott laughs and tells me if everybody did that, the Himalayas would disappear and he would have nowhere left to climb. He doesn't collect any rocks, though I doubt that his decision is premised upon preserving the elevation. The summit stone he is determined to pocket lies quite a bit higher than mine.

It takes us an hour to descend the slopes of Kala Patar and rejoin the trail alongside the Khumbu Glacier. My tent is pitched near a Sherpa village a few miles down the valley. Scott is headed the other way, wanting to reach Everest Base Camp in time for dinner with some of his buddies who are guiding clients on the mountain for their own adventure travel companies. With a grin and a wave he sets off up the trail, moving away from me and toward Everest with fast, powerful strides.

I return his farewell gesture and shift the weight of my pack on my shoulders. It is the last time I will see him in the mountains, our last adventure together before he becomes woven into Everest lore. The way that we had come is in shadows now, and a chilly wind is blowing across the glacier. As I begin hiking down the Khumbu, I hear and feel the crunch of frozen snow beneath my feet and notice the impressions that the lugged soles of our boots had left in the shallow drifts when we had traveled this way early in the morning. Scott's footprints are still clear enough to follow. Their outlines give me a good idea of the very long way that he had come, and of the long way back I will have to travel if I am to find him again, even as his steps are disappearing beneath skiffs of blowing snow.

CHAPTER 1

Olympus

In truth, if you want to find out about a man, go for a long tramp with him.
—Stephen Graham, *The Gentle Art of Tramping,* 1927

EVERYONE WHO KNEW him has their Scott Fischer stories. Mine begins the evening he convinced me to climb Mount Olympus. He was in his midtwenties and the speed of the passing seasons was only beginning to make him edgy that there wouldn't be enough time to scale all the big peaks and make a life for himself as a mountaineer. It was before I had climbed much of anything at all, and a dozen years before Scott would reach the summit of Everest.

"He's pretty intense," my girlfriend Carol whispered.

Intense? The man who walked through the front door of the Seattle house that summer evening in 1982 might as well have been an adventure hero right out of central casting. Scott was just over six feet tall with broad shoulders and a narrow waist, his chest and arms stretching the fabric of his knit shirt, a muscle twitching in his square jaw. Beneath a tousle of blond hair his eyes shown with a pale blue iridescence, and his smile, full but also a little shy, filled the room with an energetic presence even greater than his physical size. He gave Carol a warm hug and reached out to shake my hand, the smile never leaving his face.

Carol and Scott's wife Jeannie had become friends six years earlier as students at Northwestern University. By chance the four of us had moved to Seattle at about the same time, and soon we were sitting down to get acquainted over a dinner of Dungeness crab from

Puget Sound and white wine that we had purchased, not because it was from a Washington state winery, but because it had been in the least expensive bottles on the grocery store shelf. New enough to the Pacific Northwest to be without appropriate utensils for the local cuisine, we cracked the crab shells with pliers, a carpenter's hammer, and a pair of Vise-Grips, then dipped the sweet meat into melted butter. Jeannie was as blond and strikingly attractive as her husband, and as we ate she told us about her new job as a flight engineer aboard the Alaska Airlines fleet of jetliners based at Seattle's SeaTac airport. "Flying third seat," she called it, the entry-level position in the cockpit. She was determined to advance to co-pilot and then captain, a career path that had led her and Scott to the Northwest. The fact that Seattle was surrounded by mountains was just fine with her husband.

Scott poured more wine for everyone and regaled us with several stories of his alpine exploits. In recent months he had taught outdoor leadership courses in Wyoming, climbed the highest peak in South America, and led an expedition to the top of Alaska's Mount McKinley, the tallest mountain in North America. He was organizing a climbing trip to the Soviet Union and had an invitation to work a few weeks on a commercial fishing boat in the Bering Sea. Then there were his plans for an adventure travel company. "We take clients anywhere in the world they want to go," he said as he reached for more crab. "It's called Mountain Madness."

My own adventures had been more horizontal in nature, mostly in the form of extended bicycle journeys and long backpacking trips. As the crab shells piled up and we opened another bottle of wine, I shared the highlights of what I had done, including summers leading trail-building crews in the mountains of northern New Mexico and a recent hike of the Appalachian Trail, going solo the 2,000 miles from Maine to Georgia. Scott was interested in my accounts of constructing backcountry trails, but mostly he wanted to hear all about my Appalachian journey, quizzing me on the duration of the hike and the discipline to continue walking for five months straight. Even as I told the story, though, I sensed that my wanderings had been tempered by a caution every bit as strong as the confident abandon with which Scott seemed to approach mountaineering.

Toward the end of the evening, Scott suggested that we all climb Mount Olympus, the highest peak in Olympic National Park across Puget Sound from Seattle. "Just a couple of days," he told us. "It'll be a cruise!" Jeannie and Carol reminded him they had work schedules to keep. I, on the other hand, had left a teaching job in Missouri to hike the Appalachian Trail and then had moved to Seattle to give writing a try, which meant my calendar was nearly as unencumbered as that of a man determined to make a career out of being a mountaineer.

I confessed that while I was very much at ease in the backcountry, serious climbing was new to me. I liked hiking up mountains that had trails all the way to the top, but the idea of going where ropes and ice axes were necessities made me nervous. Scott dismissed my concerns with a wave of his hand. "Don't worry, we'll do good," he said, and somehow I was convinced we would.

A few mornings later, sunlight slanting through the branches of Douglas fir and western red cedar splayed across the scratched windshield of Scott's rusty maroon Dodge Dart as we sped along the narrow highway curving around the top of the Olympic Peninsula, the Dart's speedometer needle climbing well above eighty. "That's Dart Units, not miles an hour," Scott shouted over the howl of the engine and a Joni Mitchell tape blaring through the static of a stereo long gone mono, "but when the speedometer gets into the higher D.U.'s, the Dart's really moving!"

Scott slapped the steering wheel in time with the music and rocked back and forth as if urging the vehicle forward. I kept him supplied with a hot slurry of coffee and cream poured from a dented metal Thermos that had been rolling around on the floor below the backseat. The cup from the top of the vacuum bottle was all but hidden inside the grip of his hand.

"The Dart's made up of pieces from a couple other Darts," Scott said. "I had one in Alaska when I worked up there leading mountain trips and doing some commercial fishing." He glanced over at me and laughed. "I don't know where the other one is now, but this is the Dart that makes oil."

"It does what?" I asked, not sure I'd heard him.

"Every time I check the dip stick, there's more oil than before."

"Really?"

He shook his head. "Hey, I don't understand it either, but I'm not complaining."

We had been moving since before dawn, crossing Puget Sound aboard the Washington State ferry *Walla Walla* and then driving at the speed of many Dart Units into a forest that, as we neared the Pacific Ocean, became so dense and huge it felt as though we were motoring through a dark green tunnel. When we reached the trailhead parking lot deep in the Hoh Rain Forest, we pulled our packs out of the Dart's trunk and loaded them with a tent, stove, sleeping bags, and other camping gear that I knew well from my own back-country trips, then lashed on the crampons, ice axes, harnesses, and a coil of climbing rope that Scott had brought along. We laced up our leather boots, lifted the heavy packs to our shoulders, adjusted the padded belts to put most of the weight on our hips, and walked up the muddy trail. Crowded on either side by giant ferns and by the head-high trunks of fallen trees, the first miles of the route rose gently, and we found it easy to talk as we hiked.

Scott told me about growing up in New Jersey. He'd played a little football, found the usual ways to get into minor bouts of adolescent trouble, and had felt no real sense of direction until he had seen a television program about mountain climbing in Wyoming. "That was it," he said. "I knew right then what I was going to do." He had been teaching mountaineering courses and setting off on climbing trips ever since.

I asked him how he was managing to mesh his wide-open lifestyle with his wife's much more structured schedule. It was something I was struggling to figure out myself, the urge to disappear into the backcountry for a few weeks or months at a time yet still building a relationship with a woman wired into the corporate world and showing increasing interest in the less-mobile pursuit of having a family. "Jeannie knows I'm a mountain climber and that's what I'm always going to be," Scott said. "We talked about that before we got married."

We stopped for a moment's rest and I leaned over to ease the pressure of the pack straps on my shoulders. Scott offered me a handful of raisins and nuts, and I asked him what it was about climbing that he found so inviting. "I try to be graceful," he told me. "That feeling of doing everything right, that's what I like. That can be as good as reaching the top." He described the mountains as a stage upon which to practice a mastery of motion even if there is no audience but the empty sky. His answer sounded rehearsed, and I suspected he had repeated his explanation of what he did with enough regularity that the message had become honed just the way he wanted it to come across.

"There are people who see some of the climbing I do and they say, sure, you can do that because you're so strong," he continued. "Well, I am, so they got that part right, but what they don't realize is how much effort it takes to stay tough. You've got to be smart about it, too, and not let your mind make a promise that your body can't keep."

We started hiking again. "You ever do that?" I asked. "Make one of those promises and then not keep it?"

He thought awhile, almost as if the question had no resonance for him. Then instead of answering, he told me about falling into a glacial crevasse on a mountain in Wyoming. He had ricocheted off the cold, wet walls and slammed onto a gloomy shelf of ice, dislocating his shoulder. "I'd heard somebody say it was a safe glacier, no crevasses, so I was crossing without roping up," he said, "which is real stupid." His partners had crept to the edge of the abyss and peered in, doubting he was even alive. "I saw their silhouettes way up there against the sky, and I shouted, *Oh, yoo-hoo! I'm down here!*" They lowered nearly the full length of a 120-foot rope. Scott tied the end around his waist and they hauled him into the sunlight. His companions bandaged his wounds and tried to reduce his dislocated shoulder, but he was so muscled that it was impossible for them to pop the bone back into place. It took three days on foot and then on horseback and then driving more than a hundred miles of rugged back roads to reach the nearest clinic where a physician could deal with his injuries.

There had been other falls, too, he told me. "For a while people were calling me the fallingest man in climbing, but I'm pretty sure I'm done with that now," Scott continued. "I'm twenty-six years old. The best Everest mountaineers are in their thirties and early forties, and I still want to be around then."

Oh good, I thought, I'm on my first real mountaineering adventure and my guide is not only compelled to climb Mount Everest, he has until recently been famous for falling. Suddenly I wasn't so much worried about reaching my thirties and early forties as I was hoping I might just make it back to Seattle.

By the end of the day we had hiked sixteen miles to the upper reaches of the Hoh Valley. The forest had fallen away below us and we found ourselves across a glacier from Mount Olympus, the snow on the mountain turning a luminous pink and then deepening shades of red as late afternoon turned into evening. In the chill of the gathering darkness we pitched Scott's tent on a patch of bare earth, fired up my camping stove, and stewed a pot of potatoes, carrots, and onions. I reached for my bandanna to use as a hot pad to adjust the position of the pot on the burner, but Scott beat me to it by lifting the pot with his bare hands, oblivious to the heat. We ate dinner, cleaned our kitchen gear, and put everything away. After we crawled into our sleeping bags Scott took out his contact lenses and put on a pair of glasses with very thick lenses, then we played chess with magnetic pieces on a little folding chessboard he had brought along. Illuminating the moves with our headlamps, we discovered we were perfectly matched in the ineptitude of our chess strategies.

The next morning dawned clear, the cold air full of promise and of the sense of distance that lay between us and the parking lot and the crowded world beyond. The 200 inches of annual rainfall that caused the vegetation farther down the Hoh Valley to grow to astounding size also ensured that Mount Olympus is perpetually draped with snowfields and glaciers, and in the early light I looked across at the cracked ice of the glacier and the steep snow slopes on the far side. The mountain was big, craggy, and topographically complicated. If I had been backpacking by myself or with Carol, this would have been the turnaround point of the trip and I would have been fully satisfied. For Scott, though, the hike had been a necessary trudge to get to the real beginning of the adventure as the trail ended and the gradual rise of the valley floor collided with terrain that was much more dramatic.

We brewed a pot of coffee for Scott and a cup of sweetened tea for me, then split a breakfast of oatmeal, which we ate right out of the pan. After I had scoured the pan with snow from the edge of the glacier, we put the day's ration and some extra clothing into our packs and stowed everything else in the tent. Scott cinched a climbing harness around me and double-looped the end of the waist belt back through the buckle, then showed me how to strap the sharpened teeth of a pair of metal crampons onto my boots. His levity of the previous day had disappeared, replaced by a quiet seriousness as he explained how I should form a figure-eight knot in the end of the rope, then clip an aluminum carabiner to my harness and then into the loop of the knot. He secured the rope's other end to his harness and handed me an ice axe, instructing me to stay far enough behind him to keep the rope between us tight, and our tiny expedition set off across the glacier.

I stepped onto the ice and followed Scott as he made his way around the ends of crevasses or found places where the cracks in the glacier were narrow enough to jump across. The points of my crampons cut into the ice and gave me sure footing, but if Scott had fallen into a crevasse I'm not sure I would have had a clue what to do. He was probably no more protected with me roped to him than if he had been traveling solo. My entire knowledge of glacier travel consisted of the recent understanding that if I dropped into a crevasse I should yell, "Oh, yoo-hoo!" and wait for somebody to pull me up. That may have been Scott's thought, too, that he had absolute confidence in his own glacier-travel skills but that tethering me to a rope would make it easier for him to drag me out of any difficulties that might engulf me. As I stepped over another narrow crevasse, I found his approach most interesting, especially after his story of the previous day about not taking glaciers for granted.

We untied from the rope when we reached the far side of the glacier. Scott coiled the line and secured it to his pack, then led the way as we started up a steep snowfield, kicking the toes of our boots into the snow. "Use the rest step," Scott told me, demonstrating how he locked his knee and paused a moment before stepping up. "Your bones take your weight and not your muscles," he continued. "You can keep going for hours." A couple of those hours brought us near the top of a hump of the mountain called the Snow Dome. From there we followed an ascending ridge across broken terrain to the summit block of Mount Olympus, a tower of stone jutting a hundred feet out of the snow.

Scott studied the rock above us, his face filling with a joy matched by the trepidation I was feeling. While I saw all the places I might fall, he seemed to imagine nothing but opportunity. "I'm not very comfortable with this," I told him, but even as I was suggesting that I wait where I was while he went on alone, Scott began climbing so swiftly that he seemed almost to be levitating, his hands and feet barely touching the stone. Jesus, I thought, that guy can move! It really did look as though he were dancing toward the sky with no thought to the consequences or even the possibility of falling. In a moment he had disappeared over the top. I heard him shout, "Bruce!" and then "Rope!" and while I didn't understand the first, I got the warning of the second as the uncoiling line whistled down from above, the end landing near my feet. "Tie into your harness and double-check your knot before you start up," Scott called out, "then take your time."

I swallowed hard. I didn't have to do this. It wasn't in my nature to put myself at risk this way. Still, there was the rope. Scott continued to encourage me. "You're going to do it," he said. "Just get started and it's going to happen."

I attached the rope to my harness and climbed a few feet up the rock and then a few feet more. So far so good. Scott kept the slack out of the line but left it loose enough so that my upward movement was mine alone. The cracks and nooks where I could put my hands and feet seemed better to one side, so I worked my way that direction without realizing that I was moving onto a face of the summit block away from the slope we had climbed. When I glanced down, I saw only empty space. My knees began to shake. Scott urged me to keep climbing. "I've got you," he told me, his voice reassuring. "Test every hold before you put your weight on it and don't forget to breathe."

I climbed higher, wondering how I had let myself get into this mess. "Lean out from the rock," Scott said. "Keep your weight over your feet. Did you breathe yet?"

Careful not to look down, I moved slowly from one hold to the next. I stalled out a couple of times, but then I felt above for the next good grips until there were no more holds to find. "You're almost up!" Scott said. With a grunt I pulled myself onto the top of Mount Olympus and, kneeling on the summit, remembered at last to breathe. My shirt was wet with sweat and I could feel my heart pounding, but the fear was below me now.

"Pretty much fun, eh?" Scott said, a huge smile on his face.

Well, that last bit of climbing had been scary beyond belief and much more than I had intended to do, but in discovering that it could be done, I felt a tremendous sense of achievement and a flood of confidence. It was silly in a way, putting two days of hard physical effort into nothing more than reaching the top of a tall rock in the middle of nowhere. It seemed foolhardy to have put myself on a cliff where a slip would have been painful if the rope had stopped my fall and fatal if it hadn't. But Scott was right. It had been pretty much fun, indeed. More than fun. It had been a self-imposed encounter with danger, an ascent through it and a rising above it. The power of the moment was exhilarating, an almost physical thing that left me acutely alert and aware.

We sat beside one another for a long time looking out over the mountains of the Olympic Peninsula. Further off we could see Rainier, Baker, Glacier Peak, and Mount Adams, the procession of snowy volcanoes that seemed to float detached above the dark forests of the Cascade Range. Somewhere in the distance Jeannie and Carol were at their jobs, working hard to pay the bills and keep the engines of commerce running. So were many others, and certainly most people our age, but for the moment Scott and I were far above all of that, too.

I'd experienced a similar surge of lightness and release when I had been hiking the Appalachian Trail, slipping along in the seams of society and feeling as though I had found the secret to getting away with something really good. I had known during my long journey that I would eventually reach the end of the trail and would have to figure out what I would do next, and I knew that Scott and I would soon descend from Olympus and return to Seattle to figure out ways to make a dime. But that would be then. At the moment we were on mountain time, and there was no reason not to stretch that moment for as long as it would last.

We drank from our water bottles and felt the warmth of the sun. I was both surprised and grateful that Scott made no mention of my struggles to climb the rock face. He was genuinely pleased that I was with him, and it seemed not to matter to him how I had reached the top.

Scott belayed me as I started down by letting out the rope a little at a time. My descent was slow while I searched with my toes and fingers for holds that I hoped would be secure, and when I finally reached the base of the summit block I shouted up to let him know I was back on somewhat solid ground. Without the protection of the rope he down-climbed the face so quickly that he was standing beside me almost before I'd had time to untie the knot from my harness.

With the line coiled again and stowed, we continued toward camp. Scott led the way, showing me how to plunge rapidly down steep snowfields with a goose-step cadence. "Keep your nose out over your toes," he said. "Lean way forward so your heels don't slip out from under you, and then we just go!"

Coming toward us was a party of four climbers. We stopped to exchange greetings. "You climb to summit by the hard route?" one of them asked.

"I guess so," Scott replied, apparently having given no thought to degrees of difficulty.

"Well, isn't there a tough section toward the top?" the climber wanted to know.

"Can't say that we noticed."

There was a moment's silence. "There isn't a tough spot or you guys are just that good?"

"We're just that good," Scott said with a mischievous smile in my direction, and then we were on our way once more, plunging down the snow slope with our noses over our toes.

We reached the tent at dusk, cooked and ate a quick supper, and then zipped ourselves into our bags, too tired to play chess. The next morning we had breakfast and plenty of caffeine as we broke camp.

"I'm going to use the trip back as a training hike," Scott told me as he swung his pack onto his shoulders, "but I'll wait for you in the parking lot." He turned and strode down the trail.

Wait for me? I felt a jolt of competitive anger. You're going to the parking lot and *wait* for me? Look, pal, I thought, I may not be much of a climber and it may have taken all the willpower I could muster to get up Olympus, but when it comes to hiking, you're on my turf, now. Had I not just walked from Maine to Georgia? Did I not have legs of such length that they could have been designed for little else than devouring great distances of terrain and trail? Wait for *me?* You might get to climb the Himalayas long before I do, but I'll be damned if I will let you or anybody else beat me to a trail-head a mere sixteen miles away.

Scott was almost out of sight by the time I got my pack on, but I caught up with him and we hiked as fast as we could all the way to the car. We visited as we rushed along, but never about the fact that we were moving so quickly or that we weren't stopping to rest or even have a sip of water, or that we were within a step or two of one another the entire way.

We didn't say anything about it when we reached the parking lot at the same moment and threw our packs into the trunk of the Dart, or as we drove toward Seattle laughing and shouting and pounding on the dashboard while Joni Mitchell sang us toward home, or when a motorcycle passed us on the narrow highway and the two young women on board, each in jeans and a flannel shirt, got a good look at Scott as they flew by. A few minutes later we passed them idling by the side of the road, and a moment after that they passed us again. This time the girl on the back held open her unbuttoned shirt and flashed her breasts, then waved over her shoulder as the motorcycle sped out of sight ahead of us, her shirttail flapping in the wind.

"Hey, did you see that?" Scott shouted. "They like you, Bruce!"

I told him I doubted that I was the one who was the object of their interest. "And my name's not Bruce," I added.

"Oh, I'm thinking you might be a Bruce, all right," Scott said, and turned his attention back to the music and the motion and the road.

Well, maybe I was and maybe I wasn't. What I did know was that something between us had been decided on the way up Olympus and as we had hiked through the forest to the parking lot. A bond had formed with some understanding of where our strengths lay and perhaps a sense of our weaknesses, too. We had learned a little about what we could expect of one another, and I, at least, sensed that the world where I roamed had become suddenly larger and much more interesting. Yes, there was an element of testosterone-fueled machismo to it all. Some might argue we were engaged in nothing more than male head butting, chest thumping, and pit scratching, and I wouldn't disagree. But whatever it was, it had settled what needed to be settled between Scott Fischer and me so that the next time he offered me the end of a rope, I wouldn't hesitate to tie it around my waist and see where we might go.

As for where he had already been, I was eager to discover what had triggered Scott's launch out of the flatlands of New Jersey and turned his world vertical. For that I was going to need to dig through videotapes of the television programs of his youth, looking in particular for a grainy film that many of Scott's friends would mention to me, the show about climbing that had set Scott's life in motion.

CHAPTER 2

Thirty Days to Survival

Rules are for fools.
—Paul Petzoldt, founder of the National Outdoor Leadership School

IN THE WINTER of 1969, aspiring documentary filmmaker Michael Wadleigh read a story in *Life* magazine about Paul Petzoldt, an aging mountaineer who had started some sort of outdoor leadership program that sent teenagers into the Wyoming backcountry with the hope that they would make themselves better by doing good. Petzoldt was a colorful enough character to have been considered for the cover of the magazine, but had been bumped to make room for the scary visage of cult leader and mass murderer Charles Manson, who had recently made himself famous by doing evil.

The article described Petzoldt as a modern-day wilderness guru who had been "known to kill an elk with a pocketknife, walk a tightrope, and disguise himself as a Sikh potentate during an anti-Western street riot in Calcutta. He has played water polo and football, raised alfalfa, hopped freights, and been a chef, a fur trapper, a downhill and slalom ski champion, a traveling lecturer, a golfer, a used car salesman and a dude rancher." Raised on a farm in Idaho, he had set out as a teenager to experience America, picking up odd jobs, hitchhiking, jumping freights, climbing mountains, and winning hands playing poker. "I wasn't running away from anything, but toward something," the *Life* magazine article quoted him as saying. What he was running toward was adventure, especially if it was outdoors, it was rugged and, at least to Petzoldt's way of thinking, it was real.

That was enough for Wadleigh. The following summer he packed his cameras and spent a month in Wyoming filming Paul Petzoldt as he directed five teenagers through one of his National Outdoor Leadership School courses. Entitled "Thirty Days to Survival," the film about NOLS aired on January 10, 1970 on *Alcoa Presents*, a weekly television program sponsored by the Alcoa Aluminum Corporation. Among those who happened to tune in was fourteen-year-old Scott Fischer.

Considering all that was to come, the most remarkable thing about Scott's childhood up to that time may be that it was so reassuringly unremarkable. There had been little to differentiate it from the childhoods of millions of other middle-class American kids with parents trying to make successful lives for themselves and their children while America evolved from the conservatism of the Eisenhower era through the turbulent years of Kennedy, Johnson, and Nixon.

Gene and Shirley Fischer, Scott's parents, had grown up in Muskegon, a town on Michigan's Lower Peninsula just across Lake Michigan from Milwaukee. Gene's grandfather had come to America from Germany and his grandmother from Holland, while Shirley's parents had immigrated from Hungary. There was no tradition of higher education for either Gene or Shirley to follow. "After high school, I didn't want to go to college," Gene told me recently. "I drove a truck delivering pipe organs around the country, then I got a better paying job on an assembly line at a company called American Seating." The firm made old-fashioned school desks. "My job was taking an electric screwdriver that hung from a coiled wire top and attach the wooden tops," he said. "It took maybe seven screws." It was exactly the sort of mind-numbing labor that would cause a young man to reconsider his educational possibilities. Gene left the school desk factory after a month and enrolled at the University of Michigan to study languages and science. Shirley finished high school a year later and they were married.

By the time Gene graduated from college, he and Shirley had a daughter, Rhonda. Two more children followed. Scott was born in 1955, and Lisa several years later. Gene built a successful business career with an insurance company, then with Kimberly-Clark, and then thirty years with a Swiss company called Sandoz. He described his work as varied, his assignments changing frequently enough to maintain his interest and for him and Shirley to build a stable suburban life for their children.

Part of the fun the family shared was camping. "In Michigan you camped with your kids," Gene said. "It didn't cost much. You buy a tent and a little gear and you can go. We camped in Wisconsin, Michigan, and two or three times on Martha's Vineyard. Most of it was in campgrounds where you had showers, but we did some more rugged camping in the Catskills."

As Scott was about to enter high school, Gene's work took the family to Basking Ridge, New Jersey, a community close to the Sandoz corporate headquarters clustered in the Morristown area and within commuting distance of New York City. The Fischer family moved into a two-story house that soon became the place where Scott and his friends liked to hang out. After school the boys would tumble into the kitchen, cook a pot of the Kraft macaroni and cheese Shirley kept stocked in a cupboard, then head down to the basement family room to watch television, talk, and challenge one another to games of bumper pool. Sometimes they crossed the street to a city park to play soccer or platform tennis, a form of tennis played on a quarter-size court surrounded by netting. Scott's friends were in awe of his sister Rhonda, who was just enough older to pay them little attention. Scott's younger sister Lisa sometimes tagged along on their adventures. Not to put too much of a Ward and June Cleaver spin on life in the Fischer household, but Scott even had a friend named Beaver.

Scott liked school and developed an interest in theater, taking part in *The Crucible* and appearing on the stage at Ridge High School dressed as a Puritan. He was the quarterback of the freshman football team, went out for tennis, and played for a season in a local hockey league on a team called the Express, the jersey logo featuring a streamlined locomotive. The league had after-hour's access to an ice rink, and Scott's father would drive his son and several of his friends to and from the late-night practices.

It was very normal and all-American except that something was missing. There was an edge to Scott's take on life, a restless energy that wasn't fully satisfied by the usual activities of boys in their early teens. Growing into a handsome and strong young man, he was eager to see where his strengths might take him, but was finding little in the way of challenges other than school and camping with his family and spending time with friends. Even organized sports began to lose their appeal, the rules of the games and the boundaries of the playing fields too orderly and confining for him to take very seriously. There had to be something more.

Scott and his sisters had the good fortune to have parents who were together and supportive of their children, but while the template of a successful family deeply impressed itself upon him, Scott couldn't build up much enthusiasm for the career model his father had followed. "I was a corporate guy, trying to move ahead in the corporate world, taking care of a house and a family," Gene said. "I think Scott and lots of other people his age simply rebelled against that kind of life and the discipline that involved, or the constraints and repressions. This is always the story of children growing up. They react to the situation in which they find themselves with their parents and say they're going to do things differently."

The late 1960s presented teenagers with plenty of external situations to rebel against, too. The Vietnam War was heating up and playing out in America's living rooms each evening on the nightly news alongside stories of racial strife and political turmoil. The news broadcasts were followed by the disconnect of *The Smothers Brothers Comedy Hour, The Ed Sullivan Show, Candid Camera,* and *The Partridge Family. The Mod Squad* went up against the *Don Knotts Show. Bonanza* followed *The Wonderful World of Disney.* Surely that was plenty for any teenager who was paying attention to want to push at the boundaries of suburban familiarity and see what might be on the other side.

Scott and his dad didn't have a particular program in mind to watch on a January evening as they settled in front of the television in the family's basement recreation room. Clicking through the channels, they happened upon the documentary, "Thirty Days to Survival." The program opens with snowy, windswept vistas of the mountains of the Wind River Range in northwestern Wyoming, a landscape about as far removed as one could imagine from the settled neighborhoods of Basking Ridge, New Jersey. A group of teenagers with packs on their backs enters the scene.

"They are five days' march from civilization in America's most rugged wilderness," the narrator intones as the youngsters make their way through the mountains. "They are without food. There is nobody to help them. Paul Petzoldt has put them in this predicament." The narrator goes on to say that Petzoldt is a legendary American mountaineer who "believes that adventure is a part of growing up." He had challenged these young people to live in the backcountry for thirty days while he taught them how to camp, use a map and compass, cook their meals over an open fire, and practice leadership skills. Now he has sent them off by themselves and without food to travel on foot across seventy miles of rugged mountainous terrain to reach a rendezvous point where he has promised he will be waiting to meet them.

A moment later Petzoldt himself appears before the camera. Sixty-two years of age at the time of the filming, he exudes the presence of a physically powerful man at ease in his element, and his element of the moment is the high peaks and wide valleys of the Wind River Range. Over six feet tall and weighing 240 pounds, he is dressed in wool knickers, gray knee socks, and a red-and-black-checkered woolen shirt. His bushy eyebrows, perhaps his most prominent feature, seem blown back over the black beret he has pulled down at an angle on his head. His hair is going white and his face is ruddy, weathered, and lined. He speaks in a deep voice with the rhythms of Western ranchers and mountaineers and the bedrock convictions of a man who has thought through his stands on the issues and come to be convinced he is right no matter what anybody else might say.

"Out here it's nothing like New York City," Petzoldt tells the television audience as he looks toward the mountains. "It's nothing like a vacation in Atlantic City or Miami or something like that. It's an entirely different world. It's a world with a different set of values. A world where other things count." He goes on to explain that those other things, whatever they might be, become self-evident when one goes into the wilderness with a pack on his back and relies solely upon his own wisdom and wits.

The program that Petzoldt is building at the National Outdoor Leadership School (NOLS) requires students to carry all their camping gear for thirty days in the mountains. Their provisions are replenished every ten days, the food brought to remote drop-off points by pack horses. As they move about the mountains, the course participants are introduced to the skills of backcountry survival. "They have a powerful incentive to learn well," the narrator explains. "At the end of thirty days they are left alone, without food, five days march from the nearest ranch. They must find their own way out. They must survive as best they can."

"You don't do anything for them," Petzoldt adds. "You make them do everything for themselves."

Petzoldt knew a thing or two about self-reliance in the backcountry. In 1924 at age sixteen, he and a friend had been among the first to climb the Grand Teton, the great tooth of granite rising out of the prairie on the Wyoming-Idaho border. The boys had shown up in Jackson Hole at the foot of the Teton Range and found Billy Owen, a man who had summited the Grand twenty years earlier in what was probably the first successful climb of the mountain. He gave the lads a description of his route and they set off to scale the peak themselves. They carried a couple of quilts and some canned food and wore denim jeans, cowboy boots, and cotton shirts.

"We did everything wrong," Petzoldt said later. "If we had known what hypothermia meant, we would have frozen to death!" Despite inexperience that bordered on fatal ineptitude, they managed to get through a cold night high on the mountain and then scramble to the top. They were hailed as heroes when they returned to Jackson, and Petzoldt was soon making a little money leading eager amateur alpinists up the Grand. A photograph taken during one of his earliest guiding trips shows him holding a rope and an ice axe. He is wearing woolen clothing and leather boots much more suited to mountain travel than had been the cowboy boots and cotton of his first ascent.

Through the 1920s and 1930s, Petzoldt continued to guide clients on ascents in Grand Teton National Park. A feature of his outings became the teaching of outdoor skills, something he instituted as much for removing from himself the responsibility of having to do everything during a trip as it was for the edification of those paying to be led. In 1934 he climbed in the Alps and made a celebrated one-day over and back traverse of the Matterhorn. His exploits brought him to the attention of a circle of serious climbers in the United States, and in 1938 he was invited to Pakistan for the first American expedition to attempt then-unclimbed K2, the world's second highest mountain. Through sheer tenacity and application of his self-taught skills, Petzoldt managed to reach a point more than 26,000 feet up the mountain, just 2,000 feet short of the summit.

Out of that trip came the beginnings of what Petzoldt would call *expedition behavior*, the skills and leadership qualities required to lead or be a member of a team in the backcountry. He honed his understanding of it when he was assigned during World War II to help teach winter survival skills to soldiers of the army's 10th Mountain Division training in Colorado. After the war Petzoldt realized that mountain guiding, the thing he loved doing most, wasn't going to pay the bills, perhaps the thing he loved least. He tried his hand at farming, failed, and resigned himself to a decade of selling used cars. Then in 1962 he learned that a friend he had known since the 1940s was opening an Outward Bound branch in Colorado, and the next year Petzoldt found himself on the payroll as the school's chief instructor.

Outward Bound had been started in England during World War II as a way of giving young men the endurance and character to withstand the rigors of warfare. The methodology of Outward Bound put teenagers in a structured backcountry environment and pushed them to work through challenges at the edges of their abilities. Petzoldt saw value in that, but chaffed at what he perceived as too little emphasis on teaching participants the skills that would help them avoid crisis situations in the first place. He was also rebuffed when he suggested that Outward Bound open a school in his beloved Wyoming. In 1965 he and Outward Bound parted ways and Petzoldt settled in Lander, Wyoming, to launch a program he could run in the manner he believed would better fulfill the real needs of teenagers. He called it the National Outdoor Leadership School and he took an active hand in the instruction of the courses.

On the first day shown in "Thirty Days to Survival," Petzoldt is teaching students how to descend cliffs by rappelling down a rope. He begins by showing them the steps for tying three basic knots. "These are all you need to know for everything all the way to climbing K2 or Everest or anyplace else," he tells them. It's as simple as that, he suggests. Learn these skills and you can get to the top of the highest mountains in the world.

With the rappel rope secured to a harness around his waist, Petzoldt leans back over the lip of the cliff. He lets the rope slide through metal carabiners attached to his harness and walks backwards down the cliff, the soles of his boots flat against the rock. For such a large man, he moves with the easy grace of someone who has spent his life on less than level ground.

From the base of the cliff he monitors the students as they make their first rappels. He insists that they use a set of standard mountaineering verbal signals that he had helped devise decades earlier. "Tension!" "Climbing!" "Off rappel!" The students make beginner mistakes—holding the rope too tightly, failing to lean back far enough, bending their knees too much. Petzoldt is supportive, encouraging, and demanding. "Lean out from the cliff," he shouts. "Knees stiff!" When a student reaches the bottom, Petzoldt tells him, "For a first rappel that was very good. Excellent."

Turning to the camera, Petzoldt explains that "The philosophy I try to bring forward in this school is the fact that this is the time not to lecture. This is a vacation from lecture. People get told too much what to do. They don't get a chance to do things for themselves. They're preached to every day by their parents, at school and church, how they should think. Out here is a good opportunity for them to sit and relax and view everything they've heard their whole life and maybe get some ideas of their own. We hope that they're going to discover themselves. They're going to see other people in their more natural state. We hope they're going to get another view of people."

He also tells the audience that in the mountains there is adventure for young people. "This is a good way of giving it to them," he says. "Maybe it's even better than LSD or marijuana or hot rods." He stresses the fact that while the mountains hold the potential for adventure, there is also risk.

"I had to learn climbing by myself," Petzoldt continues. "I started by climbing the Grand Teton when I was sixteen. I was lucky to get back alive. But I came back contrite and with a great respect for the mountains. I sympathize with the kids who go off on their own. I know the dangers they face."

After four weeks of instructing them, camping with them, and getting to know them well, Petzoldt sends the students off on their own. They have their camping gear in their packs, but they are given no food. They are expected to live off the land for the five days it will take them to travel to a rendezvous point on the far side of the Wind River Range. Petzoldt has taught them how to fish for trout and which plants are safe to eat, but for most of them it will be five days of fasting, hiking, and working through complicated group dynamics. The teens followed by Michael Wadleigh's film crew become increasingly cranky as they move along. When they discover that not all the food has been removed from their packs, they debate whether to honor their pledge to live off the land or to take advantage of the nutritional windfall and satisfy their hunger. After much discussion one boy eats the food while the others go without.

Expansive, jovial, and embracing, Petzoldt is waiting to greet them as they come down from the mountains. He directs them to a big spread of food and encourages them to make sandwiches for themselves. "Now you know what civilization is," he tells them. "The only meaning of civilization, the only meaning of culture is how much you can control yourself and your own gentle instincts in relation to your own fellow men." For no apparent reason, a man playing a bagpipe roams about in the background of the scene.

At the end of the documentary, Petzoldt again turns to the camera. "Young people need adventure," he says. "This is a happy way to get it. They need to know their own strengths and weaknesses, and they never need to be afraid again."

In an overstuffed chair in the family room, one leg bent up against his chest and his arms wrapped around his knee, Scott Fischer sat transfixed as he watched the credits roll on the television screen. Petzoldt's message was exactly what he had been waiting his entire life to hear. "Scott and I were watching television together," his father told me recently. "I suspect we just stumbled across the program. We watched the whole show. Scott said, 'Boy, I think that would be fantastic. I would really like to go.'

"I told him, 'Go! Save your money and I'll help you.' And that's exactly what happened." They agreed that if Scott came up with half the $450 tuition for the course, his father would pay the rest. The next day Scott got himself a paper route.

By early June, Scott had completed his freshman year of high school and was headed west, setting out on his own for the very first time. Well, perhaps not that much alone, for he was soon joined that summer by 750 other teenagers getting on buses and trains and airplanes all over the country, drawn to the promise of adventure that watching "Thirty Days to Survival" had planted in their heads. When they got to Wyoming and the Wind River Range, nothing would ever be the same.

Michael Wadleigh moved on, too. A few weeks after filming "Thirty Days to Survival," he traveled to upstate New York to make the definitive documentary of a little music festival that came to be known as Woodstock. The man did like his countercultures, and as countercultures go, the gang at NOLS was going to prove to be every bit as interesting as the musicians and hippies of that better-known icon of the American scene.

CHAPTER 3

A Bunch of Bruces

FIRST BRUCE: *G'day Bruce!*
FOURTH BRUCE: *Bruce.*
SECOND BRUCE: *Hello Bruce.*
FOURTH BRUCE: *Bruce.*
THIRD BRUCE: *How are you, Bruce?*
FOURTH BRUCE: *G'day Bruce . . .*
FIRST BRUCE: *Is your name not Bruce?*
MICHAEL: *No, it's Michael.*
SECOND BRUCE: *That's going to cause a little confusion.*
THIRD BRUCE: *Mind if we call you "Bruce" to keep it clear?*
—"The Bruce Sketch," *Monty Python's Flying Circus*

(permission to come)

WALKING DOWN THE wide, dusty streets of Lander in the summer of 1970, Scott Fischer discovered he was but one of hundreds of teenagers who had been drawn to Wyoming by the promise of freedom and adventure offered by Paul Petzoldt and his National Outdoor Leadership School. Some came by bus and by plane. Some drove. And some hitchhiked across the sandy, rolling plains toward a cowboy town in the middle of nowhere, showing up with long hair and faded jeans, in cutoff shorts and T-shirts, carrying duffel bags, suitcases, and backpacks. Their heads were full of sixties' music and a view of the world heavily influenced by counterculture themes shaking the nation. Many were risk takers. All were searching for something they could not readily define, but if finding it meant that

29

they go to Wyoming, then to Wyoming they would go. "A lot of individuals showed up," Pookie Gipe told me recently. She had been a NOLS instructor for several years before the summer Scott arrived, and had seen the school in its earliest forms. "We were outcasts in a way, but in a great way."

The National Outdoor Leadership School was beginning its sixth summer. As an organization, it was going through its own adolescence, its years of wild and awkward growth. Petzoldt and his staff were experimenting with ways to make the program work, and if something was successful, it stayed. If not, they dropped it. One idea Petzoldt promoted was that NOLS courses be affordable for anyone who wanted to attend.

"Paul had this thing called *Pay back when able*," Pookie remembered. "He'd make you come up with fifty bucks, and you would pay the rest of your tuition when you could. So the individuals who came were truly adventurous people, but they were not all from the same world. They didn't come to NOLS because it was popular or because their parents had sent them. They were here because they had found this thing for themselves."

At the NOLS headquarters, Scott met his course leader and the other members of his patrol. There were three courses from which to choose. The Mountaineering Course focused on climbing and rappelling. Those who signed up for Wilderness Travel would learn how to live out of a backpack, find their way through the back-country, and handle a fly fishing rod. Scott was assigned to a patrol in the Adventurers' Course, a program designed for NOLS students ages thirteen to fifteen intent on sampling a bit of what the older participants were doing in both the Mountaineering and Wilderness Travel courses.

The staff member serving as the patrol leader was assisted by one or more instructors who would help teach backcountry skills for the coming month. Patrol leaders needed to be at least sixteen years old, though instructors could be younger. So could unpaid aides enlisted to help out with the courses.

Petzoldt put great faith in the abilities of young people to thrive in positions of leadership and felt that a good way to train them was to give them all the responsibility they could handle and then some. He also had no other choice. Due to the awareness raised by "Thirty Days to Survival," the number of young people signing up for NOLS courses threatened to overwhelm the school. Petzoldt and his staff offered positions of responsibility to anyone who showed promise.

Scott and his fellow patrol members named themselves the Jets. At the NOLS Lumberyard, an all-purpose storage building and staging area a few blocks from the center of downtown Lander, they were outfitted by Thelma Young who headed up the NOLS equipment program and had stitched together some of the tents and much of the clothing the groups would use while they were in the backcountry. Petzoldt had made bulk purchases at army surplus stores to bolster the school's stockpile of wool pants, sweaters, and boots. Thelma would cut the body off one sweater and stitched it to another to form a "double sweater" that came down to the wearer's knees, then use the leftover sleeves to make socks and neck gaiters. For foul weather wear, Petzoldt had drawn patterns for her to sew waterproof parkas. Students were asked to bring durable woolen clothing with them, though if she needed to, Thelma could equip them from the skin out. When the wool pants she issued were too long, she would snip off the extra length and sew drawstrings into the new cuffs. She used scraps of wool cut from old blankets to reinforce the seats of the pants that participants had carried from home. A floppy, wide-brimmed hat topped off the outfit.

In another part of the Lumberyard the Jets drew their portions of rice, pasta, oatmeal, cocoa powder, and other basic provisions they measured into plastic bags. They tied the necks of the bags with loose overhand knots, but were instructed not to pull the knots too snug since "panic knots" were difficult to loosen. They added blocks of cheese and several large tin cans to use as cook pots, and then they climbed into the backs of stock trucks where they stood watching the scenery bounce by during the drive to a trailhead somewhere in the Wind River Range.

With their patched wool pants, double sweaters, slouch hats, and heavy backpacks, there was no mistaking a NOLS patrol on the move, and the Jets did move, priding themselves on traveling farther and faster than they imagined other patrols were able to go. They practiced using a compass and a map. They learned the basics of climbing and rappelling, and they summited several peaks. They caught trout on fly lines and cooked their meals over open fires, and the adventure exceeded even their wildest dreams.

Thriving on it all, Scott was especially drawn to climbing. Scaling a vertical rock face proved a profoundly physical act that drew on every bit of his strength and agility to move about in a vertical plane. It was mental, too, as he focused his attention on the present moment, making him aware of the smallest nubs and cracks in the rock and discovering he could overcome obstacles by sheer force of will. Climbing allowed him to ascend into a world without boundaries where anything was possible and there was no restraint save for the law of gravity. It was immediate and intensely demanding, and there was no limit to what he might do if he were to work harder, practice more, and be bold.

Paul Petzoldt visited each patrol for a few days during their time the mountains, riding on horseback to teach some of the backcountry skills and reinforce the message that he trusted the students to make good decisions. "Rules are for fools," he told them, a line he repeated so often it became a mantra for those who heard it. "Rules are for fools because fools have no judgment." He wanted young people living on their own in open country to conduct themselves wisely so that they could avoid difficulties in the first place. He explained that emergencies would arise, but that they should train themselves to be calm when something unexpected happened, gather as much data as they could, and then make good choices that utilized all of their skills.

"When we learned about the mountains, we learned about judgment," Pookie Gipe recalled. "We didn't learn, in this situation you do this or that. Instead we learned a lot of what you don't do so you don't get in trouble."

Petzoldt's willingness to allow his programs to operate with young people relying on their judgment rather than on sets of rules is a philosophy of outdoor education that would be suspect in much of today's litigious culture. Concerns about liability were different in the 1960s and 1970s than they are now, and the visionary ideas upon which Petzoldt was building NOLS had not yet been vetted by more practical-minded risk managers. When he sent students without food to travel across the mountains for the final days of a NOLS course, Paul pulled no punches. Staff members didn't shadow the patrols. There were no checkpoints along the way, and no tightly woven safety net. Often for the first time in their lives, students had little choice but to determine among themselves how they would proceed. Petzoldt's desire to give young people the freedom to develop trust in their decision-making abilities encouraged fierce self-reliance.

"That whole freewheeling nature of NOLS fit Scott perfectly," Pookie told me. "He was too free-spirited for something that had more rules, that said you had to do it a certain way. Petzoldt put his judgment in you and trusted you to figure things out on your own, and Scott thought that was very cool."

At the conclusion of his course, Scott was invited to stay for the rest of the summer as an unpaid aide. He had stood out as a strong lad with boundless enthusiasm, a huge smile, and an eagerness to try everything his instructors could offer. Equally important, new students were arriving by the hundreds as Petzoldt scrambled to keep up with the rush.

Reloading his backpack and heading up a trail for more time in the Wyoming mountains was exactly what Scott wanted to do. He could continue to practice his new backcountry skills and explore more of the high country. He could push himself to excel in terrain that, unlike New Jersey, provided a challenge worthy of pushing back. Best of all, he could be around the other NOLS students, patrol leaders, and instructors who were already becoming deeply important to him.

"It was a time when people were searching for their tribes," Pookie observed. "At NOLS, Scott found people who saw the world a lot like he did." In their patched-up army surplus clothing, they were vagabonds of the high country, novice adventurers exploring the wilderness, teenagers connecting with one another and laying the foundations for friendships that would carry them through the years. They encouraged and validated one another, and invented the standards by which they would judge themselves.

Scott went home at summer's end much different from the person he had been several months earlier. The Wind River Range had been the site of a metamorphosis that had broadened his view of the world and focused his understanding of the means by which he would engage life. He wanted to be a climber. Everything else he had ever done paled by comparison to the simple act of scaling a cliff. He had begun to transform himself into a mountaineer, and he returned to school with the evangelic zeal of the recently converted, eager for his hometown friends to share his newfound passion.

"In high school Scott was real popular," Scott's buddy Jeff Long told me recently. "He was friendly with everybody and had a kindness about him. The girls liked him and he'd been the quarterback of the freshman team, but after NOLS he started putting all his energy into working nonstop at being a climber. That's how he defined himself. That's who he was." He and Scott studied books about Mount Everest, tracing routes on the panoramic photographs and dreaming of becoming a climbing team. "We decided we wouldn't go to college because we would be mountain climbers going all over the world."

Another New Jersey friend was Greg Martin, a teammate with Jeff Long on the Basking Ridge soccer team. "When I was a high school sophomore I weighed a hundred and two pounds," Greg recalled. "After I got to know Scott coming back from those NOLS courses, I got built up big time. Scott was having me do non-stop pull-ups and a hundred push-ups every morning and every night, no matter where I was." It wasn't just physical strength that Scott was promoting, it was also the attitude of taking responsibility for their decisions in life. "I was probably a bit wilder than him, but he got me going in a better direction."

That better direction had climbing as its core. Jeff, Greg, and their friend Beaver began joining Scott for weekend trips to the Schwangunks near New Paltz, New York. Overlooking woodlands and villages, the Schwangunks are a band of sedimentary cliffs rising several hundred feet above the floor of the Hudson River Valley. The area had been a center for rock climbing since the 1930s, though climbing was still an obscure enough sport when the boys started going there that the cliffs were seldom crowded.

They would leave Basking Ridge at dawn. Greg had learned to prepare meals while working at a restaurant, and would bring bags of sandwiches for everyone. "Scott liked tuna fish sandwiches with cheese on them microwaved," Greg remembered. "I would have a nice hot one ready for him when he came to pick me up."

Sometimes just Scott and one or two of the others made the trip to the 'Gunks, but often the car was jammed with friends eager to spend the weekend together. "We had a favorite camping spot around on the back side of the mountain," Jeff Long remembered. "We'd climb all day Saturday, camp out, climb on Sunday and drive back that night."

They started out by bouldering—practicing climbing moves near the ground. With a rope, carabiners, and some nylon sling they could go higher. Scott would hike around to the top of the ridge, tie the rope to a tree or through one of the eyebolts he found set in the rock, and toss down the free end. One by one each of his friends could tie the rope to a harness around his waist and be belayed from above as he worked his way from one hold to another, knowing that a slip would result in a fall of only a few feet rather than all the way back to the ground.

"After a climb we walked down to the Carriage Road at the base of the cliffs and we were ready to start up another route," Jeff grinned. "If you were good, you could do quite a few routes in a day."

Each autumn when he returned from Wyoming after another summer working for NOLS, Scott would teach his buddies the latest climbing techniques he had mastered. He introduced them to tight, thin climbing shoes that were much better for gripping the rock than the stiff hiking boots they had been wearing. When he learned how to lead climb—using hardware to establish intermediate anchors while going up a route rather than always being belayed from above—he taught that to his friends, as well.

"I learned so much from Scott about camping and knots and how to set up a tarp twenty different ways," Jeff told me. "He really took the time to teach us. In the Schwangunks we'd eat mac and cheese because that's what he'd eaten at NOLS. Scott was really big with hot drinks, so we'd have lots of cocoa. When we climbed, we snacked on cheese and granola and trail food. Scott would tell us stories about NOLS and encouraged us to get out to Wyoming real soon." As they broke camp each Sunday, Scott insisted that they leave the site in better condition than they had found it, just as if it were a Wind Rivers camp that a NOLS patrol had used.

The boys sometimes saw Henry Barber and John Stannard climbing at the Schwangunks. "Barber at the time was considered to be one of the best climbers in the world," Jeff explained. "We knew he'd made a name for himself everywhere—up in New Hampshire and New York, out in Yosemite." Barber wore a trademark white canvas painter's hat and moved about on vertical rock with tremendous grace. "We'd watch how well he climbed and we knew we had a ways to go."

When he was sixteen, Scott used money from odd jobs to buy an old red plumber's truck with toolboxes on the sides of the bed. With the help of his friends he added a plywood roof to transform the back into a makeshift camper just big enough to store his camping gear and roll out a sleeping bag. Gene Fischer, who was adept at mechanical projects, took great delight in overhauling the engine with his son, who was not. Scott named the vehicle the Truck and used it to drive to the 'Gunks for weekends and to Wyoming in the summer.

Scott would remain extremely loyal to his New Jersey friends. He convinced Jeff and several others to enroll in NOLS courses, and even those who weren't interested in climbing felt themselves always included in Scott's inner circle. Through the years he got together with them whenever he was near their homes, and they weren't surprised to open their mailboxes and find letters Scott had posted from the mountain ranges of the world. In the weeks following his death, nearly all of them had the similar poignant experience of receiving postcards Scott had mailed to them from Everest Base Camp before setting out on his last climb.

For those who were going to rope up with him for his biggest expeditions, though, Scott was finding his people in the mountains of Wyoming, and they were finding him. They had come to NOLS by a variety of routes. Randy Cerf, for instance, decided at the age of twelve that it was time to say farewell to Washington, D.C., run away to the wilderness of Idaho, and live off the land. He left his house at six o'clock one morning, knowing his family wouldn't miss him until evening. He managed to buy a bus ticket and as the Greyhound headed west, he wrote a letter to his parents to inform them of his plans. To calm any fears he imagined they might have, he scribbled down a list of the equipment he was carrying with him. It included a sling shot and a snare wire for catching the animals he expected he would soon be cooking over his little campfire in the Idaho wilds.

"While I was writing, a woman in the bus seat behind me was reading over my shoulder," Randy told me. "She called the police!" Authorities picked him up at the next stop and returned him to his parents, though that was not quite the end of it. Human interest coverage of the exploits of the young runaway appeared in several newspapers. A reader forwarded one of the articles to Paul Petzoldt in Wyoming, thinking the story would amuse the man who had just launched the National Outdoor Leadership School.

"Paul wrote me a letter in April of 1966 and said, 'Well, we've got this program out here, and you're not old enough yet, but hey! Come on out!' So I went to Wyoming for the summer and enrolled in courses one right after another. I was there for three months and it was great."

Ingrid Hamann was a Basking Ridge girl who knew Scott and his friends as interesting younger boys who were always heading off to do some sort of weekend climbing thing. With persuasive enthusiasm Scott described NOLS and urged Ingrid to make it out to Wyoming where, at the age of sixteen, he would be working that summer as a fully certified NOLS instructor. "You're gonna spend a month in the mountains," Scott told her. "You'll love it!"

With some misgivings she signed up for a course. For thirty-five days of backpacking and climbing in the Wind River Range, she and the others in her patrol saw almost no one. As she was pitching her tent one afternoon, her instructors told her that they'd run into Scott Fischer camping nearby. She hiked over to visit. "He was with other NOLS instructors, and he was so comfortable being there. They had caught some fish and were fixing really good meals over a campfire. They were having so much fun and really loving what they were doing. This was his life, being in the mountains," she concluded. "This was who he really was."

Ingrid realized she was changing, too, in ways familiar to many NOLS students. "I went through a huge transition from 'What am I doing here?' to 'I don't ever want to leave.'" When her course ended, all she wanted to do was take a hot shower, eat some fresh food, and get back into the mountains.

Steve Goryl, another of Scott's peers, had been drawn to NOLS by "Thirty Days to Survival." He arrived in Lander with a Beatles haircut and bell-bottom jeans, and was soon thriving as a student on his first NOLS course. The skills he learned laid the groundwork for what he soon realized would be his career as an outdoor leader. He also knew from seeing the television program that his course would end with a long, foodless hike, but he was nonetheless startled when his instructors took away the last of his patrol's provisions, pointed out an "x" on a map as the destination of the survival hike, and sent the students on their way in groups of four.

"We were all trying to be the leader," Steve reminisced. "We had one fishing rod, but we couldn't catch any fish. We got into an area where our map was too smudged to read and we went in a big circle."

As the days of their survival hike wore on, they tried to eat their toothpaste and the contents of their spice kit. Snow fell the night they decided not to pitch their shelter. "Probably one of the lowest points I remember was the day before we were done, we came to a horse packer camp," Steve told me. "I picked through their trash and found a little bottle with a quarter inch of pancake syrup on the bottom. I smashed the bottle to get at it, and the four of us divided it."

When they finally reached their destination, other patrols were coming in from all directions. "In the television program there had been lots of food at the end of the hike, but what they had for us was four hundred chocolate-covered donuts and lots of jugs of milk," Steve laughed. "Then they loaded us into cattle trucks and we're standing up bouncing along the road. Suddenly people are projectile vomiting chocolate-covered donuts everywhere."

They were smiling again by the time the trucks rolled into Lander, but after a month without showers and their encounter with the donuts, they appeared to be very much worse for the wear. "You could see the locals looking at us in these vomit-covered trucks and saying of Petzoldt, *What does that man do to those children?*"

Goryl and the other students celebrated the conclusion of their course with a party in the basement of Lander's Fremont Hotel. "There was a piano player and cake fights," Steve told me. "That's how my NOLS course ended, and the next morning I was ready to go again."

Michael Allison enrolled in a NOLS course in 1973. His father had passed away from a lingering illness, and after finishing college at the University of Tennessee, Michael had moved home to help his mother. A year of being the dutiful son left him eager for any kind of adventure. Outward Bound appealed to him, but then he saw an advertisement for NOLS in *The Whole Earth Catalog* and decided to give Wyoming a try.

"It was just what I needed," he told me recently. "NOLS was incredible for me. I went from complete unhappiness to such astounding freedom and friendship that I thought I was in heaven." He moved to Wyoming and was soon instructing as much of a full-time NOLS schedule as the calendar would allow—a climbing course in the spring, two summer courses, an autumn semester course, and one or two winter courses. Between NOLS courses he would work as a carpenter or embark on adventures of his own.

"I liked instructing for NOLS, but the real attraction was the peer group," Michael remembered. "The NOLS community was a riot to be around. Free spirit, free lifestyle, the opportunity to roam the world and hang out with people who had your same interests. It was remarkable."

Wesley Krause had grown up in Fort Collins, Colorado, where he began camping as a Boy Scout. He hoped he might find something more adventurous by signing up for one of the first NOLS courses offered in the desert Southwest. At the end of the month his instructors invited him to rendezvous with them in the Tetons to do some climbing. They were called away to help with a mountain rescue, though, and Wes detoured to Lander where he presented himself at the NOLS Lumberyard with the hope of finding work. Paul Petzoldt was building a log home, and Wes soon found himself in the woods near Driggs, Idaho, helping fell trees and running logs through a jury-rigged sawmill.

"My hair was kind of long at the time," Wes told me. "A couple of local fellows drove out to our logging camp and made it clear that they didn't like hippies in their mountains." To emphasize the point, one of them challenged Wes to an arm-wrestling contest.

"This guy was the arm-wrestling champion of the Tetonia, or whatever, and I beat him easily," Wes recalled. "That settled that. But then the news got back to town that there was this big hippie arm wrestler living out in the woods, and I had to do all these other arm-wrestling matches, too."

In Lander, the National Outdoor Leadership School already had a recognized arm wrestler in Scott Fischer, who delighted in taking on all comers in a friendly match or two, and was almost always victorious. Word spread around the NOLS community about these two guys, and many looked forward to their eventual confrontation.

"When we first met, Scott was out of high shcool and had been around NOLS quite awhile. It was like two bull moose pawing around and claiming the territory," Wes told me. "I'd been hearing about Scott and he'd been hearing about me, and we had to arm-wrestle each other so much that we about ruined our arms." What could have been a meeting of opposites was, in fact, the beginning of a deep friendship forged in arm-wrestling contests and pull-up challenges and plenty of time together on mountain routes as they came to realize they were much better suited to be climbing partners rather than rivals.

Wes didn't stay around Lander long. NOLS was establishing a Northwest School based in the Cascade Mountains of Washington state, and he jumped at the opportunity to be involved in its founding. Much of his work as a NOLS instructor would take place on the glaciated volcanoes of the Northwest, but like Scott, he was always eager to go climbing with his friends. He had a green Chevy pickup that he used to pull an old wood-paneled Winter Weiss camping trailer that he had refurbished to give himself a place to live. It had a good gas oven for baking bread and preparing meals, and it often served as a mobile headquarters for NOLS veterans launching off on climbing adventures when they weren't instructing courses. "People would pitch tents around the trailer wherever we were skiing and climbing," Wes said. "We'd use it for eating, lounging, and getting warmed up."

A less mobile hangout for the Lander-based NOLS instructors was a camp some of them established near the waterfalls and rock slides a few miles out of town in Sinks Canyon. The site was out of view up a trail, and they could adjourn to it as a private hangout for getting away from town and being together.

The British comedy group Monty Python had a sketch at the time in which all of the characters are named Bruce. Scott and his buddies began mimicking the routine, and on a whim started using the name to address one another. Before long it had become a password to shout up the trail when they were approaching the Sinks' Canyon camp. While they were instructing NOLS courses in the backcountry, they would yell "Bruuuuuuce!" down the valleys and from the mountaintops and then listen for the return shout of "Bruuuuuuce!" from any other Bruces within earshot.

The Bruce thing probably would have disappeared along with other fads of summer, but during instructor meetings in Lander, the frequency of Bruce references became tiresome to some of the NOLS administrators. They tried to put a stop to it, but if it irritated the elders, it was even more cool to be a Bruce. The name gained longevity and an air of notoriety, and decades later at NOLS reunions, someone shouting "Bruce!" in a crowded room was sure to see a lot of heads pop up and turn with anticipation.

As with the mountaineering skills and climbing shoes, Scott brought the name *Bruce* back to New Jersey and used it to christen his friends there, too. It was more than a nickname. For Scott it was a recognition and an encouragement, shorthand to identify those who were open to the adventures of the moment and the possibilities of the future. Anyone had the potential of becoming a Bruce, and Scott delighted in seeing people rise to the occasion.

Among the Bruces, Scott found like-minded young people who were to become loyal friends and climbing companions through the years to come. They adventured together, completed remarkable climbs, and suffered spectacular falls and a few fallings-out. Energetic affairs emerged among the Bruces of opposite sexes, and more than a few of them discovered on their belay ropes the people they would marry. The world of the Bruces was a meritocracy of alpine achievement and youthful excess at a time when many were looking for their places to belong. Paul Petzoldt had dared these individuals to push their limits, and they had embraced the challenge. He had entrusted them with as much responsibility as they could handle and then a little more, and they became accustomed to operating on their own in open country according to standards that they were setting themselves.

Smart, capable, and driven, many of the Bruces would channel their energies into becoming physicians, attorneys, teachers, scientists, and business executives. Scott, though, received such validation at NOLS for his skill in the backcountry that as he neared his high school graduation, he saw no need for college. He had long known that he was going to be a climber, and his higher education would be just that—an education that would literally take him higher and higher—and the campus would be the mountain ranges of the world.

CHAPTER 4

Off Belay

Thou shalt go for it. I say.

—Scott Fischer, age nineteen

IN THE LIVING room of a comfortable home in Lake Bluff, Illinois, two young women read again the brochure describing the upcoming 1974 summer courses offered by the National Outdoor Leadership School and tried to decide what to do. Alta Price was completing the second year of an accelerated curriculum at Northwestern University to become a physician. Her younger sister, Jeannie, a freshman at Northwestern, also planned to enroll in medical school, a choice influenced by their father, who was a doctor himself. Alta was looking forward to a summer away from studying. The opportunities advertised in the NOLS brochure seemed perfect for what she wanted to do. She had shown the brochure to Jeannie and suggested it might be fun if both of them went to Wyoming.

It wasn't the first time the Price girls had embarked on an adventure together. Several years earlier Alta had become interested in learning how to fly an airplane, had joined the Stick and Rudder Flying Club at the local airport, and had begun taking lessons. She encouraged her sister to join her, but Jeannie, then fifteen years old, was shy and couldn't bring herself to approach flight instructors Peewee and Jim to ask if they would teach her, too. Alta broke the impasse by scheduling a lesson, then telling Jeannie that if she wasn't going to show up, she would have to telephone the instructors and tell them herself. It was easier for Jeannie to go to the airport for the lesson than it would have been for her to make the call.

Seated in the cockpit of a light plane, Jeannie soon found herself at ease in a world very much to her liking. She felt confident in the aircraft and enjoyed being surrounded by the gauges and switches, by the checklists and rituals of aviation, and by the camaraderie of the instructors and the other students. Most of all she loved spooling up the engine, pushing the throttle forward to maximum power, then pulling back on the controls as the plane roared down the runway and lifted into the air. Until she touched down again, the aircraft was under her command, going where she willed it as the sky opened wide and the earth rolled beneath her far below.

Jeannie had her pilot's license before she graduated from high school and was steadily filling her log book with hours in the sky. Flying also became a shared interest of the rest of the Price family. Alta became a licensed pilot and so did their sister Veda. Before long the girls' parents had completed pilot training, too, and the flight instructors came to call the family the High Prices.

Jeannie and Alta told their parents about their interest in spending a month at the National Outdoor Leadership School. Dr. Price agreed to help pay their transportation and tuition costs and as their part of the deal, the girls promised to paint the family's house at the end of the summer. They sent their applications to Lander, both of them asking to be placed in a NOLS Wilderness Course that emphasized backcountry travel and survival skills. Space was limited, though, and only Alta got her wish. Jeannie was bumped to an empty spot on the roster of a NOLS Mountaineering Course.

Arriving in Lander, Jeannie met the other four members of her patrol and went with them to the NOLS Lumberyard to pack the clothing, equipment, and provisions they would need for their month in the mountains. They climbed aboard a stock truck for the drive to the trailhead, then hiked into the Wind River Range. The leader of Jeannie's Mountaineering Course was Jim Hamilton, a veteran staffer. An instructor assigned to her patrol was Scott Fischer, a young man beginning his fifth summer working for NOLS.

In the early years of NOLS, the instructors' interests could determine the course content. If an instructor liked fly fishing, participants spent their days on riverbanks casting lures onto the water. If those in charge of a group would rather backpack long distances, that's what the participants ended up doing. Jim liked fishing and was also good at going up rock. Climbing held far more appeal for Scott than catching trout or racking up miles of cross-country travel, and Jeannie and the other students soon found themselves learning the skills of climbing and rappelling and then following their leaders up one mountain after another.

In the evenings they pitched their tents, cooked their meals, and sometimes visited around a campfire. Scott told Jeannie and the others that he had just graduated from high school. He was wearing gold metal-framed glasses with round lenses, and the students commented that he looked like the singer John Denver. He explained that he was planning to continue working for NOLS in the summer and in the winter might attend college in Colorado. Scott was also up front about the fact that he was still sweet on a girlfriend from his New Jersey high school. That was enough for Jeannie to decide that the beginning buzz of something between her and Scott wasn't going to go anywhere.

"We both agreed that made any serious relationship between us unlikely," Jeannie told me recently. "It certainly was not going to happen on my part." Even so, she asked Scott how NOLS felt about instructors socializing with students. "He said something about how instructors were told that they were absolutely not supposed to be carving notches on their ice axes while on the courses."

But there was that buzz. Scott was the handsome mountaineer, the self-styled alpine renegade just out of high school and finally on his own. Jeannie was the sparkling Midwest girl with a great laugh who had been playing by the rules all her life. She was studying to be a doctor and could pilot an airplane across the sky. Where he had a shy smile and could stumble over his words trying to explain himself, she was effusive and quick witted and could, if she wanted, talk circles around him. They each had the ability to dazzle the other with what the other did not have, and when Scott invited Jeannie to stay in Wyoming after their NOLS course and spend some time with him, she changed her travel schedule.

As Scott drove the Truck around Lander, Jeannie sat next to him.

When he climbed in Sinks Canyon with Swiss alpinists who were visiting NOLS, she came along and watched. When Scott and friend Jim Hamilton did a typical NOLS instructor days' off activity of hiking back into the Wind River Range, Jeannie hoisted her backpack and stuck with them all the way to a spectacular place of granite and ice called the Cirque of the Towers where they climbed a peak called War Bonnet. Scott signed the summit register notebook as *Scott*, explaining to her that one day everybody would know exactly who *that* Scott was and that he would never again have to write more than his first name.

Scott also told Jeannie more about his interest in mountains and his determination to keep having adventures. He admitted that despite his earlier claims of wanting to go to college, he didn't intend for that to get in the way of his dreams. "He told me that he had this idea of being the best climber he could," Jeannie recalled, "and climbing harder and harder mountains until one day he just didn't come back."

As mission statements go, that's a very clear life plan for a teenager, and for many young people, beginning to figure out life is a big part of what the first year out of high school is all about. The curriculum of higher education offered Jeannie a glide path from undergraduate school to a medical program, an internship, and a residency. She could simply navigate that blueprint long enough, and a career as a physician would unfold before her.

Scott, however, was already discovering that if he wanted to be a full-time mountaineer, he might need to invent the whole thing as he went along, hammering a lifestyle out of very little of substance, yet with his youthful certainty that he could scale anything came Scott's absolute assurance that he would succeed as a climber. Summer was an easy call as he instructed NOLS courses in the Wind Rivers. Through June, July, and August, he could talk about autumn possibilities all he wanted, but there was really no need to worry about putting plans into motion until September rolled around and the busy season at NOLS came to a close. With little likelihood of income from NOLS until the following spring, Scott was about to begin the real work of inventing his life, and he was determined to do it without the advantage of a belay.

Jeannie and Alta fulfilled their agreement with their father by painting the Price house at the end of the summer, discovering that the skills they had learned at NOLS had immediate benefits. "The tricky part of the project was reaching the third floor over the concrete porch," Jeannie told me, "but we set up a belay system and tied ourselves in with climbing harnesses. Worked slick."

Scott hitchhiked to New Jersey at the end of the summer to surprise his mother on her birthday and to wear a tuxedo at his sister Rhonda's wedding. He spent time with his high school friends and helped send off those enrolled at university campuses. He felt increasingly restless as they departed, and when his parents pressed him on his immediate plans, he told that he didn't want to attend college.

"We of course pushed him to go," Scott's father remembered, "but he wasn't interested." Gene went so far as to accompany his son to a community college near their home in hopes that Scott would sign up for a couple of courses to get him started, but there were lots of others ahead of him patiently waiting to register.

Scott waited for a few minutes, too, then turned to his dad. "This is too much for me," he said. "I'm not going to stand in this line." He headed for the door and pushed outside into the open air.

"And that," Gene told me, "was Scott's college career."

The open air outside the registration building soon became the open road as Scott thumbed his way across the continent, conversing with the strangers who gave him rides and watching through the windshields of their vehicles as the great, varied landscape of America flowed toward him. He went all the way to British Columbia where his high school girlfriend was visiting relatives. He stayed a few weeks, did some canoeing and fishing on Vancouver Island, then stepped back to the edge of the highway and caught rides to Lander. The pull of the mountains and of friends planning to winter over in Wyoming was more than he had been able to resist, and Scott was convinced he could get something going to keep his mountaineering hopes alive. Even if he couldn't, he would rather be ranging across the West than stuck somewhere without vertical relief.

Jeannie was restless, too. At Northwestern University for her second year, she was coming to realize that her aptitude for studying medicine might not be all that she had hoped and that her interest in becoming a physician was waning. She began receiving letters from Scott as he traveled around the country, and late at night when the long-distance rates were low he would call her as he fed coins into the roadside pay telephones of what he called the booniebooths. He told her about his travels, about what he was reading, and about his always-optimistic plans. "One old guy that picked me up was penniless so I helped him out," he reported. "He gave me a cowboy hat, but *I do not* look like John Denver." He mailed Jeannie a copy of a book that encouraged Buddhist meditation and introspection. He explained that the Swiss mountaineers she had met with him in Sinks Canyon were still in Wyoming, and that he had been climbing with them in the Winds. "Did a lot of smiling and saying *yep, yep,*" he added. "You see they speak only German and I don't."

Sometimes he shared his frustration with trying to figure out a way to make money but without giving up time he would rather spend climbing. He was reminded, too, that going up mountains can also involve crashing back down. A scar from an operation performed several years earlier to repair the hip he had fractured during a fall had herniated, and a Lander physician warned Scott that further surgery would be necessary to repair the injury.

"So upon hearing this I say *Well goddamn Fischer, you got to CLIMB. Just GOT to,*" he wrote to Jeannie, referring to himself in the third person almost as if he were watching himself to see what might develop. "I'm going to Yosemite. Jim is going with me and we will have a great time, I'm sure of it. *Thou shalt go for it,* I say." He was off again, going for it, the craving to be in motion overcoming what to many would be the far more pressing needs of tending to his employment and medical affairs.

Several weeks later he was sitting under a Sequoia tree, shading himself from the California sunshine beaming into Yosemite Valley. He was drinking wine, eating cheese, chatting with tourists stopping to visit with the climbers lounging at the base of the huge granite walls, and scribbling a postcard to Jeannie. "Yosemite is just as great as I expected," he said of his first trip to that Mecca of rock climbing, then exuberantly described the technical aspects of ascents he had been doing on the massive granite faces. He referred to a rope length as a *pitch* and used a standard measurement of climbing difficulty that described pitches above 5.0 as more than scrambling, 5.6 as respectable, and anything greater as quite good for young climbers. "You wouldn't believe the rock," he said. "We did 5.6 and 5.7 climbs. Not too impressive but these climbs are like ten to fourteen pitches high."

Scott returned to Lander with no fresh ideas about how to make a living. "Still have the leg bummer but might just leave it," he told Jeannie of his herniated hip scar. He drove The Truck to New Jersey for Thanksgiving and was examined by the Fischer's family physician who told him that surgery wouldn't need to happen right away. "Which is decent," Scott reported. "I'm waiting and doing special exercises. So basically except for a couple bumps I'm healthy."

His economic health, however, was dire. The autumn's wanderings had eaten up his summer's earnings, and his financial future looked bleak. "Driving here and all my travels did in my money but good," he explained, "so plans are vague. It looks like I can work on a boat off Venezuela, but then again maybe not. I want to be out West. Monday I find out for sure about the boat. I'll write NOLS about work but if all else fails I'll have to work here, and I *don't* want to work here."

The Swiss climbers had invited Scott to join them in the Alps, and he decided that if he could put some money aside, he might be able to make that trip the following year. For the moment, though, he needed to earn some cash to cover his current expenses, so he took a job at a local restaurant where his friend Greg Martin was a cook. "The boat job still might come through," he told Jeannie.

"It's a seismograph boat to check for oil. They are in harbor for a month so I got this other job in the meantime. It's a high class joint, and Greg and I have a blast."

The Truck was stuck in the driveway of Scott's parents' home, too decrepit to pass the New Jersey auto inspection standards required for relicensing, and Scott used the vehicle as his personal refuge. "Just sitting," Scott said of his Truck times. "Buddha would say everything will work out, but I agree there are a few holes in that whole philosophy."

Sitting on a flat wallet in a broken down pickup on very flat ground in front of his childhood home, Scott was a long way from where he hoped to be. He wanted to climb, *needed* to climb, but the route to the summits was no longer clear. Although he had contacted NOLS about teaching winter courses and he still held out hope for the Venezuelan boat job, he was coming to realize that no news probably actually did mean no news. His plans were as stalled as the Truck.

Scott lasted until after Christmas, then hitchhiked to Lander, telephoning Jeannie from boonie-booths along the way. She had a lot to share with him including the fact that she was dropping out of college at the end of the winter quarter. She knew she would eventually get a college degree, but for the moment she thought it exorbitant for her family to pay tuition when she had no idea what she wanted to study, just that it wasn't going to be medicine.

"I have so many varied thoughts," Scott replied, "but the question I ask is what would you do? I think that a person should have some sort of goal—be it far in the distance, or short range. Listen, I'm just saying *think*. No judgment passed. Sounds weird coming from me, yes?"

Overjoyed to be back in Wyoming, Scott thumbed his way to the oil fields outside of Casper only to discover the petroleum company he'd heard had work wasn't adding employees after all. With his money gone, Scott hired on at a uranium mine near Jeffrey City, an hour out of Lander. It was last-ditch employment, the kind of job that in the summer he and his friends would never have considered. *If all else fails*, went the dark humor, *you can always work in the uranium mine.* All else did seem to be failing, and Scott found himself punching a time card and working as a motor man in the mine running ore trains. "Why do I do this? What good toward my goal?" he asked, then answered the question himself. "Lots of money enabling me to climb lots. Plain, simple, very short- range, but that's it." He concluded, "I'll endure."

And he did endure, at least for a while, but a mountaineer dreaming of the high and windy places can be underground only so long. Burrowing deeper into the earth was taking Scott in the opposite direction from his natural inclination to ascend. He lasted five weeks in the mine, then bolted for the surface and hit the road again, heading this time for Zion National Park with his friend Randy Cerf.

Compared to the dark depths of the uranium mine, Zion was paradise for Scott, especially in the sunny warmth of spring in the desert. The park featured astounding sandstone towers and sheer walls rising hundreds, even thousands, of feet above valley floors. Systems of cracks in the cliffs offered climbers routes that, in the early 1970s, were just beginning to be exploited. He and Randy started big, setting off to scale an enormous face on a sandstone spire called Jacob in the Three Patriarchs, among Zion's best known features. "There is only you and the wall," Scott said of his attraction climbing a face so huge. "It was really far out. After a while you have no choice but to climb. All you want is the top."

They attacked the wall for three days, jamming their hands into the cracks and then arching their fingers to lock their hands in place. They twisted their feet inside the fissures to gain purchase, and fitted the edges of their flexible climbing shoes against the smallest of ledges. They protected themselves by wedging pieces of hardware into the cracks and then clipping their rope to those temporary anchors so that if one of climber slipped, the other could hold the rope and stop the fall. Chalk on their fingers helped them grip the sandstone, and when their hands bled they wrapped their scraped knuckles with white athletic tape and kept going.

Hour after hour the sun beat down as they concentrated on each move, each piece of protection, each foot of upward progress. The magnificent vistas of Zion spread below them, and at night they would unroll their sleeping bags on ledges and sleep under stars ablaze in the clear desert sky. "We did a new route by accident," Randy remembered. "We started up an existing route but then went a different way and it was pretty hard. We ran out of water and got very, very, very thirsty." In the guidebooks to Zion climbing routes, "Afternoon Stroll" is credited as first climbed and named by Randy Cerf and Scott Fischer in April of 1975 and rated at 5.9, a respectable degree of difficulty. It was Scott's first recorded first ascent.

From Zion, the lads motored to Yosemite to climb some more, then came back to Utah for a job with students rafting down the Colorado and Green Rivers. "I floated rivers and taught climbing on the canyon walls," Scott told Jeannie. "Got paid two hundred dollars, too. Was the greatest time, and now we are going to finish the quota of rivers needed to get our boatman's license. Pretty neat."

Pretty neat, indeed. As he and Randy drove back to Wyoming, Scott had his new boatman's license and some fresh currency in his pocket. The mug shot on the license showed him very tanned, his neck and shoulders heavily muscled, his smile that of a young man who had figured out, at least for a few weeks, how to earn a living while having the greatest time.

As he waited out the final weeks until NOLS launched its summer courses, Scott worked as a bartender at Lander's Noble Bar. Gene Fischer took advantage of Scott being in one place to come to Lander for a visit. Scott took his father backpacking in the Wind River Range, an adventure Gene enjoyed very much. He liked carrying a pack, and his long stride allowed him to keep pace with his son. Their time together gave them opportunities to talk about what Scott had been doing in recent months and where he was headed. As best he could, Scott tried to explain his need to climb, to be in motion, and to embark on one adventure after another.

"If that's something that you do and you're into that, it's wonderful," Gene told me of their conversations. He saw his own life as having been shaped differently. He delighted in being outdoors and had liked embarking on family camping trips with his wife and children, but had taken a more traditional approach to building a career and supporting those around him. "I always had a job," he said, "and worked for a company from eight to five."

The NOLS summer season finally rolled around and Scott could sort gear and write provision lists as he prepared for the first of several thirty-day NOLS courses that constituted his own attempts at gainful employment. He and Jeannie agreed that she would come out to meet him after the last of that summer's courses. She rode the train two days to reach Lander only to discover that NOLS had changed Scott's schedule and he was still in the backcountry. She also learned that Scott's New Jersey girlfriend had been in town just before he had gone out on his NOLS course.

Well, Jeannie thought, whatever. She made herself at home in the basement apartment Scott was sharing with four other NOLS instructors and resisted the impulse to clean up the piles of climbing gear and dirty laundry. She noticed that there were two photographs on the wall that she had taken the previous summer and had mailed to Scott. The pictures were precariously close to a dart board with the holes from errant dart tosses not only all around it, but also in the ceiling above.

Greg Martin and several of Scott's other high school friends drove in from New Jersey and unrolled their sleeping bags in the apartment, too. Jeannie had heard about them for nearly a year, but had no idea that they were coming to Lander or what Scott might have said to them about her. "So," they asked, "what are *you* doing here?"

What she was doing was what they were all doing—waiting for Scott. Greg used his culinary skills to bake cookies and cook pots of pasta and sauce. They played many rounds of darts, even figuring out how to land darts in the ceiling. When Scott finally tumbled through the door, he was delighted to find everyone there. Buoyed by the infusion of Scott's energy, the party that had been simmering along in his absence kicked up to a full boil as everyone ate and drank and stacked the record player with Grateful Dead albums and Pure Prairie League.

Scott suggested they climb the Grand Teton. "You're in Wyoming," he told his friends. "We gotta climb the Grand!" Soon they were on their way, hoping to make it to the top in two days. The New Jersey boys had climbed with Scott in the Schwangunks and Jeannie had learned how to climb during her NOLS course, so all of them could rope up and manage the technical challenges. Jeannie also knew from the previous summer that as she got up high she would suffer from the nausea and headaches of mild altitude sickness. Scott stayed with her as her symptoms developed, encouraging her and insisting she would succeed. When they reached the top Scott signed in with only his first name. They commemorated the climb when they returned to town by buying T-shirts with the legend, I GOT HIGH ON THE GRAND.

Summer was drawing to a close. Jeannie headed east to enroll at the University of Wisconsin in Madison with a renewed sense of what she intended to study. Alta had shown her newspaper clippings describing several women who were flying for commercial airline companies. "You could do this," Alta told her sister. "You could be a professional pilot." It had never occurred to Jeannie that flying might become her career, but once she started to think about it, it felt absolutely right. She could major in meteorology. Added to the pilot training she had completed and the hours she was logging in small planes, she hoped her degree would someday help open the door to the cockpit of a jetliner.

Jeannie also realized that other than the thirty-day NOLS course she had taken with him as the instructor, she and Scott had been together only for the week following that program and for the eight or nine days she had just spent with him in Lander and on the Grand. It hadn't been much time, and yet there had been all of those phone calls and all those letters and cards, and that had to mean something, didn't it?

"Greg gave you a good buildup," Scott told her of the stories about her circulating in the Fischer household after his friends had returned to New Jersey. When Scott's mother had asked what Jeannie was like, Greg had replied that she was the nicest girl he had ever met.

"You Jeannie Price are no longer secret," Scott continued. He told her that if she could put up with knowing his high school girlfriend might still be in the picture, he thought it only fair that the other girl should be ok with Jeannie, too, though he didn't indicate that he had asked her opinion on the matter.

For the immediate future, sorting out the women in his life was a puzzle Scott was willing to put on the back burner. His first year out of high school was coming to an end, and he was about to inaugurate the second by flying to Europe to climb in the Alps. He felt he had remained true to his vision of being a climber, even though he still had little idea how to turn that into a viable pursuit. He had scraped together enough money for a barebones trip overseas, but before leaving for Switzerland he spent a few of his scarce dollars on a tabletop book of mountain photographs and sent it to Jeannie.

"This book would look great in your apartment," he wrote. "I plan to climb the Eiger, Matterhorn, Mt. Blanc. Just have to see. And listen babe I'll bring you a rock from the summits in the Alps. Deal? Deal. You can follow my climbs in this book and when I get to Madison we'll look at it and I'll say ah yes I did that, that and that and that, etc etc. . . ."

At least that was the deal. Ah yes.

CHAPTER 5

Follow the Rainbow

That's impressive, coming from this New Jersey family and after a couple of NOLS courses hitchhiking to Asia. I like those harebrained stories better than the later stories about the Everest expeditions.
—Brent Bishop, climbing partner and Everest mountaineer

IN THE EVENINGS in the high places with the camp stove roaring and the stew bubbling in the cook pot, Scott would sometimes tell a little about hitchhiking and traveling by train and bus across Europe and Asia to get his first look at the great, snowy peaks of the Himalayan Range.

"Didn't get all the way up any of them," he would say, "but we made a pretty good try," and then he would break into the stuttering *k-k-k-k* of the Bob Seger song and sing to himself, "I'm going to Katmandu! That's what I'm gonna do! K-k-k-k-k-k Katmandu. . . ."

He had been nineteen years old at the time and had stayed on the road for five months. It was a trip Scott claimed he had dreamed up with a guy named Rainbow while working in a Wyoming uranium mine. I knew that the boys had reached Nepal, but beyond that, what had happened on Scott's first journey to Kathmandu had always been a mystery. If I wanted to learn more, I was going to have to find Rainbow.

Scott's friends from his days at the National Outdoor Leadership School told me that Rainbow was a fellow named Bruce Cartwright who lived in Lander, the Wyoming town that had always been home to NOLS. When I telephoned from Seattle, his wife, Barbara, answered. Bruce was on a night shift as a nurse at the hospital in Riverton, thirty miles up the road from Lander. I explained who I was and that I was hoping that Bruce would have the time and the interest to visit with me about his youthful and far-flung adventures with Scott Fischer.

"I'm so glad you called," Barbara said. "Every couple of years Bruce tells that story. Last year we were on a cross-country drive with the kids and he told the story the whole time."

I phoned back later and spoke to Bruce himself. He was under the impression that I wanted to hear his story over the telephone. "No, no," I told him. "The way we do this is that I'll show up at your front door with a six-pack of beer. We'll start talking and when we need more beer, I'll go get it." Bruce seemed greatly relieved. We settled on a convenient time, and a couple of weeks later I found myself driving to Wyoming.

Lander today has the wide streets of a frontier town laid out when there was still plenty of space for laying out a place the right way. The skyline of Main Street is dominated by a gray Lander Mills grain elevator with a red and white Purina Chows checkerboard trademark painted high on its side. Main Street is a mix of shops, upscale restaurants, mini-marts, and liquor stores. A block off Main is the new headquarters building of the National Outdoor Leadership School, a three-story environmentally advanced structure that speaks to the current success of the organization. I saw people on the sidewalks wearing Western hats and clothing suitable for riding the range, fleece jackets designed for the backcountry, or both. At first glance the town appeared to represent an exact confluence of cowboys and climbers.

I parked in front of the Lumberyard, the building that had served since Scott's early Wyoming days as the storehouse and staging area for NOLS courses. I assumed it had been spruced up over the years. There were rooms filled with gear and maps. A large space was set up with tables for packaging the trail food that could be drawn from plastic buckets and bins. Vintage photographs of NOLS instructors lined the hallway, each picture an assemblage of healthy, glowing groups of young people posed in tiers behind a sign indicating the summer of their service. As I looked at the pictures I was startled to see Scott Fischer looking back.

I called Bruce Cartwright to let him know I had arrived in Lander and he invited me to dinner at his home on the edge of town. That evening he met me at the door, a tall, youthful man of about fifty, his age belied by a full head of sandy hair that showed no hint of gray. The meal included venison and elk that Bruce and his son George had shot during a hunting trip. George was being a good-natured teenager. His sister, Marie, two years older and much more serene, seemed resigned to the fact that she was still living under the same roof as her brother. We blessed the meal and talked about Barbara's long-distance running and the competitive skiing of the children. Instead of beer I had brought wine to go along with dinner, and after the table was cleared, Bruce and I refilled our glasses.

"I was from Detroit and knew early on that I had both a certain level of adventure-seeking behavior and a strong desire not to live the rest of my life in Detroit," he began. His stepfather thought it would be good for him to travel for a few months and had helped him fund a trip overseas. "I was seventeen years old and alone in Europe with a backpack for the summer." He had gotten along pretty well as he figured out how to make his way from place to place, how to talk to strangers, and how to size up situations on the road.

The next summer he set off again for Europe, this time with the offer of a job at a veneer plant in Germany. On his way there he met several girls who were touring Europe in a minibus. The idea of driving with them through Turkey and Iran seemed much more inviting than a summer at a wood products factory, so he rode with the girls to the Pakistani coast of the Arabian Sea. "I wanted to keep going to India, but I was out of money," Bruce told me. "I also had a major case of giardia, so I flew home from Karachi."

Back in Detroit he was at loose ends, wondering what to do next. Then he saw the movie *Jeremiah Johnson* about a mountain man in the Rockies. "I had been thinking about going to Sweden, but after that movie I decided to hitch my way out West and check that out," Bruce explained. A series of rides brought him to Yellowstone where he met a backpacker on his way to Grand Teton National Park. Bruce tagged along to Lake Solitude tucked in a cirque of cliffs near the base of the Grand Teton. "I had a great revelation that it just doesn't get better than this," Bruce told me, his eyes lighting up. "I realized I could live here."

Through family friends, Bruce had a letter of introduction addressed to the owner of a dude ranch near the Tetons. Bruce wanted the job badly enough that he had a barber in town cut off his long hair. "I kept a goatee so I wasn't quite fitting in, but I thought I might get by," Bruce told me. "At the time it was as much as I could give."

It wasn't enough, at least not for gainful employment on a dude ranch, so Bruce got back on the road and stuck out his thumb in hopes of returning to Yellowstone and perhaps finding work there. "These hippies picked me up in a purple VW bus," Bruce continued. "They told me they were on their way to a Rainbow Festival on South Pass under Freak Mountain not far from Lander and invited me to come along."

The VW bus chugged over Togwotee Pass and down the highway toward Lander, picking up more hitchhikers until the engine threw a rod and the bus coasted to a stop near Crow Heart. The hippies flagged down someone to tow the VW into town. "The other hitchhikers stayed in their seats," Bruce said, "but I figured the country looked real nice there so I got out and waited for another ride."

A few minutes later Paul Petzoldt slowed his car, pulled onto the shoulder of the road, and offered Bruce a ride. "By the time we got to Lander, Paul had convinced me to take a NOLS course and offered me a job," Bruce said. "He also told me I could go ahead and attend the Rainbow Festival first, which I did." When word of his Festival detour got around NOLS headquarters, Bruce's Technicolor nickname was assured.

After completing his NOLS course, Rainbow went to the Woodstock music festival in upstate New York, then returned to Wyoming and found a job for the winter. The following summer he enrolled in the NOLS instructor training course and, one night at the Noble

Bar in Lander, met Scott Fischer. Scott had just graduated from high school and was hoping that when his summer's work with NOLS ended he could find enough employment and stay in the Rockies, but by the following February that had come to mean a job in a mine. "In those days you could always go up on South Pass and get a job at US Steel or you could go out to the uranium mines," Bruce told me. He had also gotten work at the mine. "I was a skip tender at the bottom of the shafts, shipping the ore to the top. Scott was a motor man running the trains."

As they sat around after their shifts drinking beer, Bruce told Scott about hitchhiking around Europe and riding with the girls into the Middle East. They agreed that after they had instructed NOLS courses through the upcoming summer they would get themselves to Europe, retrace Bruce's route into Pakistan, and then keep on cruising to Kathmandu. And as long as they were going that far, they might as well climb a Himalayan peak.

Summer arrived. Bruce and Scott put in another season as NOLS instructors, though they saw little of one another. "I came out of the mountains in September and found a note from Scott that told me to meet him in Andermatt, Switzerland." A Swiss guide named Karl Kempf had worked in Wyoming for NOLS that summer, trading the cozy huts and European guiding traditions of the Alps for the wide-open challenges of the Wind River Range, and Scott had followed him back to Switzerland.

Bruce made his way to Andermatt and came upon Scott at a sidewalk café. "Bruuuuce!" Scott shouted when he saw Rainbow. He jumped up to give him a huge hug, then told him he had pitched a tent on a mountainside above town and had been climbing the local rock. He was eager for Bruce to spend a few days with him knocking around the Swiss villages and mountains, but mostly he was ready to get on the way to the Himalayas.

They walked to the edge of Andermatt and started trolling the traffic for rides. The cars whizzed by. Scott and Bruce soon realized that nobody in a little European motor vehicle was going to stop for two tall, broad-shouldered, shaggy-haired Americans wearing cowboy hats and hauling big backpacks strapped with ice axes. Splitting up seemed the only sensible solution. Bruce told Scott about the city square in Kavala, a coastal town in Greece he had visited the previous summer, and suggested it would be a manageable place to rendezvous. The two would travel separately and the first one three would wait for the other to arrive. If the wait seemed too long, the backup plan would be to move on to Istanbul and try to connect there. Before they could fine-tune the plan, a car stopped and the driver told the boys he had room for only one of them. "See you in Greece!" Rainbow shouted to Scott, and folded himself into the backseat of the car.

"I had an epic of hard hitchhiking after that," Bruce told me. "Somewhere in Yugoslavia on the main highway going to Belgrade an Italian truck driver dropped me off and I waited all day without another ride. The buses wouldn't even stop to let me on. I went into a truck stop to get something to eat, figuring then I'd go sleep in a cabbage patch across the road." Two Englishmen driving a beaten up Morris Bentley economy car pulled into the truck stop parking lot and Bruce asked if they would give him a ride. No, they said, their car was already loaded down. Rainbow persisted and at last they decided not only to let him come with them, they put him behind the wheel.

Bruce steered the Bentley through Belgrade, skirted Kosovo, and entered a Macedonian landscape that reminded him of the countryside around Lander. He hoped he was making up lost time and would get to Kavala soon, when a leaf spring under the Bentley broke and the weight of the car banged down on the rear axle.

"The English guys were ready to abandon the Bentley, but hey, I told them, the car still runs! I got them to help me lever it up and put some rocks between the axle and the body of the car, and we managed to drive it to a garage in Sophie. I took the bus from there."

Bruce waited three days in Kavala for Scott to appear. "I was killing time, slapping mosquitoes at night in a motel room full of bugs," Bruce told me. "I finally got a ride out of Kavala with a Greek officer who drove me almost to the Turkish border, then I took a train the rest of the way to Istanbul.

Scott and Bruce caught up with each other at the Pudding Shop, one of many famous travelers' havens dotting the globe where travelers can find one another, get the latest information from other wanderers, and make plans for where to go next and how to get there. "Bruuuce!" Scott shouted when he saw his traveling companion appear. He explained that he had been in Kavala a few days earlier, hadn't seen Bruce anywhere, so had headed for Turkey.

Scott also told about his own travels in the days since they had last seen one another. Soon after Bruce had motored away, Scott had been picked up by a well-to-do American couple. "They invited me to come with them on this cruise ship going along the Adriatic coast," Scott said. "So I went. They have a house in Mexico. They've got one in Italy, too."

"I'm out struggling through Yugoslavia and thinking about sleeping in a cabbage patch and you're on a cruise ship?"

"Yeah," Scott said. "Double portions of shrimp, Scott? Well, yeah! Still hungry, Scott? Yeah! Want to meet our daughter, Scott? Well, hell yeah!" On his first foreign trip, Scott was already discovering the joy of dropping into a scene, smiling his shy grin, infusing the situation with his energy, and having things turn out better than all right.

Scott and Bruce studied notices on the Pudding Shop bulletin board left by drivers looking for riders to share costs to go deeper into Asia. A few travelers sat at the tables with their knapsacks and maps, either going or coming but, at least for the moment, just staying. "There were definitely a lot of people out there on the hashish trail," Bruce told me.

The lads sized up their options and decided to make their way east from Istanbul by bus. "We were cruising with the Turks," Bruce told me as he stood up, stretched his arms overhead, and suggested I refill the wine glasses while he got a map. The place names of his narrative were beginning to blur together, and we needed the clarity both of visual aids and of more wine. Bruce returned with a globe the size of a basketball. He spun it and traced the route the bus had taken him and Scott into Iran and then Afghanistan. The names of the cities rolled off Bruce's tongue as if the trip had been thirty days ago rather than thirty years. His fingers caressed the globe, retracing the journey.

"And then we were cruising with the Afghans," Bruce said. In the cities where they had layovers, they would pitch their tent in the protective privacy of motel courtyards and cook meals over their backpacking stove, an Optimus 111-B that would burn anything from white gas to kerosene. They drew on their NOLS backgrounds to camp well and to stay healthy, and they used their growing confidence to have as much fun as possible.

"The thing about traveling with Scott was that he had no fear, not an ounce," Bruce told me. "I was a fairly cocky young man myself, but when I was with Fischer that further emboldened me." They would talk with anyone who interested them, often going out of their way to engage people. "We were not afraid to expose ourselves to the local populace," Bruce said.

At a motel in Kabul they struck up a conversation with a man from the Afghan travel ministry. He invited Scott and Bruce to come with him to a Buzkashi competition, and although they knew nothing about where they were going, they jumped at the chance to see something new.

The travel ministry official led them to the stadium's ticket window where an agent told him that Scott and Bruce would have to use a special entrance for Westerners. For a five-dollar fee, they could sit in grandstands shaded from the sun; however, the boys saw no reason to segregate themselves from the Afghanis. "All right, then," the man told them, "when I say go, just go and don't stop." He shoved money into the ticket agent's hand as the crowd swept them through the gate and into the stadium.

"There we were, two blond-haired boys from America sitting in this sea of thousands of Afghanis," Bruce told me. "Everybody around us who could speak any English was talking with us, telling us what was going on down on the field." What was going on was the Afghani national sport. Teams of players on horseback maneuvered to get control of a headless goat carcass and carry it to a scoring area. The action was fast, wide-open, and reminded Bruce of home.

"The Afghanis were spirited like Wyoming people," he said. "Respectful, too."

He and Scott also made a side trip in an overcrowded taxi to Bamyan to see giant statues of Buddha carved into cliffs honeycombed with caves. I told Bruce that his description of the statues sounded familiar. He got out a *National Geographic* magazine with photos of the statues and pointed to the caves where he and Scott had scrambled past the Buddha's heads. Then I remembered that a few years ago when the Taliban still ran Afghanistan, they had deemed the statues an affront to Islam and had destroyed them with explosives and artillery fire.

Walking through the streets of Bamyan, the two Americans had passed a group of children. "They were jabbering away at us," Bruce told me, "and then one tossed a rock in our direction. It seemed like a friendly sort of deal, but we made the mistake of tossing a rock back. Well, these dudes threw rocks for a living."

"We can't throw near as good as these guys," Scott had shouted to Bruce, "but I think we can outrun the little tykes!"

"And he could run," Bruce told me. "You know how Scott was. We were exercising all the time. Running. Doing push-ups in the courtyard. He was always finding something to climb and we arm-wrestled all across Asia. Walking over a bridge, he'd see a good post for us to put our elbows on and say, 'Time for a match?'"

From reading books about climbing in the Himalayas, Scott knew that the window of stable autumn weather over the mountain range would be closing in a few weeks and that winter storms would end any chance they might have to get up high. They caught a bus out of Kabul and sat in the front seat as the driver took them over the Khyber Pass and through the mountains of the Hindu Kush, then rolled across Pakistan to the city of Lahore.

Finding nowhere cheap to stay, they slept on a porch stoop, holding their ice axes across their chests for protection and hoping that the next day their travel karma would improve. In the morning they went to a square where taxis were loading. They picked one that they hoped would get them at least to the edge of town, and they threw their packs on the vehicle's roof rack. As they were about to jam themselves into the crowded car, a man approached and introduced himself. "I am Henry Harrison," he said. "Where is it you wish to go?"

"We're headed for Delhi," Bruce told him.

"Oh, I can take you there," the man replied. He explained that he drove a truck for the British embassy in Delhi and offered to let them ride with him. They could stow their packs in the large wooden crate on the back of his truck. The taxi drivers saw what was happening and yelled at William, warning him not to steal their business. Startled, he nodded to them and apologized to Scott and Bruce. "Sorry," he said, "I can't take you after all."

"Well just a second now, William Harrison," Scott told him. "You wait here and we'll be right with you." He and Bruce grabbed their packs off the taxi and, ignoring the shouts of the drivers, headed toward the truck. They weren't about to miss a ride that would take them all they way to Delhi.

"We had a great trip," Bruce told me. By evening they had covered half the distance to Delhi and William Harrison got himself a motel room for the night. He offered to let the boys sleep in the crate on the back of the truck, locking them in so they would be safe. "We were hoping he would let us out in the morning," Bruce told me, "and sure enough, he was right there."

William dropped them at a campground between Old Delhi and New Delhi. "It was cheap and had a wall all the way around it," Bruce told me. "We could cruise Old Delhi for culture and fun while all the business things we needed to do were in Connaught Place in New Delhi." They kept their food inside of their tent to protect it from the rats running around the campground and from the feral cats running around after the rats. They bought some Persian carpets and shipped them home, one of several profit-making schemes they had cooked up, though the carpets never reached their destination. Near their campsite was a store that offered hot milk. "They would sell you a cup of milk with a chunk of fat floating on it," Bruce told me. "They would sprinkle some sugar on it and that was our treat at night."

"Delhi is a beautiful, beautiful city," Scott wrote in a postcard to

Jeannie Price. "There is so much history here; everywhere you look there is a building, mosque, minaret, palace, something worth seeing."

From Delhi they took a train 600 miles to the city of Patna in northeastern India. The toilet in their passenger coach was nothing more than a seat over a hole that opened onto the tracks. Scott had become preoccupied with watching the railroad ties flash past and had leaned forward a little too far. His glasses slipped out of his shirt pocket and dropped through the hole. He had a backup pair, but his good lenses were gone.

"Scott had moments like that," Bruce told me. "On the bus going across Iran I found his passport lying underneath the seat. I said, 'Scott, I'll just hang on to this for you.'"

Bruce shook his head and smiled. "And finding his way around cities, Scott would be lost all the time. I wish I had traveled with him later on when he was a successful guide. It would have been interesting to see how he had matured. But at least back then he was out there cruising, having a good time, and he just didn't pay attention to where he was."

It was, after all, Scott's first trip out of North America. It takes awhile to learn how to travel well, and Scott was immersing himself in on-the-road training. "I can say there were times when I was Scott's guide. I had experience with traveling abroad and showed him how to get around," Bruce told me. "Sometimes Scott was a real knot head."

In Patna, the boys realized that even with only 250 miles to Kathmandu, continuing overland would be a slow trip by train, ferry, and bus across the many headwaters of the Ganges River. They would have preferred to travel by land since it would allow them to see more of the countryside, but time was no longer with them, so they caught a plane to the Nepalese capital.

For a decade Kathmandu had been a destination of young Westerners, many of them hitching rides and taking buses and trains as Scott and Bruce had done. Some were on self-directed quests for spiritual enlightenment. Others were looking for alternatives to what they perceived as the decadent culture of the West.

Many were chasing cheap and easily available drugs, and quite a few had no idea at all what they were doing. While plenty of them were toting backpacks, only a few were also carrying ice axes.

Scott and Bruce had no real plan either, other than to climb a Himalayan mountain with a summit more than 20,000 feet above sea level, an elevation they chose because it would be higher than any peak in North America. On a postcard featuring a photograph of Mount Everest, Scott wrote to Jeannie, "Hey, what do you think? Should I try to climb it? Maybe I'll wait. Going to spend next month up high. It's really great. I am pretty excited. Plans of climbing. Hope so. Will grab a rock for you."

In a mountaineering shop they looked at the maps that were then available for the Himalayas but showed little other than roads, villages, and basic outlines of the mountains. One of those outlines was a peak called Langtang Larung with a trailhead a day's bus ride from Kathmandu. "Well, let's see, twenty-three thousand, seven hundred feet, that's doable by a couple of boys like us," Scott told Bruce. "We ought to be able to do that." There was the small matter that Langtang Larung had never been climbed.

They rented crampons and then visited other stores in Kathmandu's Thamel district to outfit themselves for their two-man Langtang expedition, figuring on a trip of six or seven days. They bought rice at a street stand and loaded up on cheese. They purchased summer sausages at a shop that specialized in making meat products from water buffalo. "We put together a nice ration," Bruce remembered. "We planned on eating in the villages on the way up to Langtang to conserve our food."

Scott and Bruce caught a bus out of town, and eight hours later were dropped off in the village of Dhunche. They swung their packs onto their shoulders and hiked a dozen miles through rhododendron and pine forests. They gained nearly a mile in elevation along the way and were astounded by the size of the terrain through which they were passing. Resting in a village clinging to the mountainside, they could look down 4,000 feet to a river and then 4,000 feet up to the other side of the valley to a neighboring village. "You could hear a rooster crow over there, but the people on this side might never have been over there to meet the people on that side," Bruce told me. "It was just amazing."

Following the faint lines on their map, they continued to hike up the precipitous valley of the Langtang River. Near the village of Ghoratabela they got their first view of Langtang Larung. "We were just cruising along the trail and came around a turn in the valley and suddenly up ahead there's this really huge peak with a snow plume screaming off the summit."

"Whoa!" Scott said. "Bruce, I'm just kind of thinking that might be Langtang."

They couldn't possibly climb a mountain rising so far above them, at least not without a lot more planning and preparation. They hadn't brought a rope or the hardware to protect themselves if they were to cross glaciers and climb ice. They didn't have much in the way of warm clothing, and they'd not gotten a permit from the Nepalese Ministry of Tourism, something required of anyone wishing to scale a peak the size of Langtang Larung. It was early November, too, and the weather was becoming marginal. Storms were likely to settle in at any time. "We were pushing the matrix of even thinking about going up," Bruce told me.

And yet they had come all this way. They had traveled around the world from that Wyoming uranium mine to this bend in the trail in Nepal with Langtang Larung straight ahead. Sure it was big. Jesus, it was big! But it was just a mountain, wasn't it? Hadn't they climbed mountains before? Weren't they supposed to be mountaineers? NOLS instructors? What the hell, they thought, as long as they were already so close they might as well keep going until Langtang itself decided they could go no farther. They studied the mountain, looking for a workable route.

"Langtang has this long ridge coming down from the summit," Bruce told me. "We figured our best plan was to climb several thousand feet up these flutes of snow we could see, then get on the ridge and run it to the top. No problem." There appeared to be a cirque—the upper end of a valley—far down at the base of the ridge. "We thought we would go up into that cirque and then see if we could get something going from there."

Scott and Bruce stayed in Ghoratabela for a couple of days to rest and eat plenty of Nepalese food, then hiked onto the slopes of Langtang itself. "We weren't on snow yet, but we were way up in yak country," Bruce said. The yak herders were gone, driving their animals from the meadows where they had been grazing down to lower elevations before winter settled in, and Scott and Bruce moved into one of the stone huts of the yak herders. "We borrowed small amounts of the wood they had stored to get our fires going, then burned yak turds like the herders do," Bruce said. "We were very conservative with their wood because obviously it's all got to be hauled up there. We left them some money."

Throughout their travels they had been careful to drink only bottled water or to purify their water by boiling it or treating it with iodine tablets. Now that they were above the villages they began drinking straight from the streams as they would in the Wind River Range back in Wyoming. Scott soon came down with diarrhea. "He had a schmeet attack," Bruce told me. "The quick trots. He became Scott Trotsky." They stayed two days in the relative comfort of the yak hut waiting for Scott to recover, but as Scott's health improved, Bruce's declined, and he quick-trotted his way down to Ghoratabela to see if he could scrounge some antibiotics.

While Bruce was gone, Scott decided he was ready to have a go at Langtang. He loaded his pack with gear and food for a night out, then left the yak hut and climbed until dark, tenting on the snow. The following morning he climbed high enough to look into the cirque. Above him he could see a route he was almost certain he could follow thousands of vertical feet up the steep snow to the sky-line ridge. He knew that the ridge would lead to the summit, but he also knew that he had gone as far as he could without the support of a mountaineering team, a lot more equipment, and a good deal more time. He took a last long look at the tremendous mass of mountain still above him, then turned around and descended.

Bruce was at the hut to greet him. He had found trekkers in Ghoratabela with medicine to spare, and was feeling better. Scott regaled him with his account of his climb on Langtang Larung and Bruce got caught up in Scott's enthusiasm.

"The next day I busted up Langtang as far as I could get, too, probably about as far as where Scott had camped," Bruce told me. The air was thinner there than any place Bruce had been before. "It was exhausting. I just wanted to sit down and take a nap." Instead he returned to the hut in the yak meadows. December had arrived and the weather was deteriorating. The boys knew they had pushed this adventure about as far as their skills, planning, and finances would allow. It was time to head for home.

"Nepal was great," Scott wrote to Jeannie as he and Bruce were getting ready to leave Kathmandu. "Can't even describe the mountains. They're so huge. Elevation gain of 5, 6 thousand feet was fairly common trekking for one day!! That is the place Jean. They are really the granddaddy of them all."

Back in Delhi, Bruce checked their plane tickets in his passport pouch. The departure date was still a month away, but Scott was fine with that. "Every day was an adventure," Bruce explained. "You got up in the morning with Scott, you were going to do something. You just didn't know what."

As they walked one evening around Old Delhi, they passed a pavilion tent. A man by the doorway saw them and asked, "You want to come in? You want to eat?" Scott and Bruce went closer and asked the man what was happening inside. "It's a wedding," the man said. "You want to come to the wedding?"

"Sure," Scott told him. "We're not doing anything." Ducking into the pavilion, they found themselves in the midst of a Hindu wedding feast. They settled into chairs at a table, smiled and cheerfully chatted with the wedding guests, then dug into a big spread of Indian food.

"Scott and I were having a great time," Bruce told me. "While we were there some other Westerners looked into the pavilion and the man invited them in, too, but they said no. It looked as though they were afraid of the man's motives. People are always trying to get something out of you, but Scott and I were open to whatever was happening."

When they checked in with William Harrison at the British Embassy, he invited them to come to his home to share Christmas with him and his eight children. "It was another one of those amazing cultural experiences," Bruce remembered. "William cooked a chicken. He used mashed potatoes to make a head for it. I wore my cowboy hat and sang 'Ghost Riders in the Sky.' It was a pretty good Christmas."

It had been a pretty good evening for Bruce and me, too. As I drank the last of my wine, he told me about their return to Wyoming after the trip to Nepal. Scott got back into leading NOLS courses, but Bruce had broken a bone in his wrist while skiing and no longer had the range of motion to do much rock climbing. Instead of teaching outdoor courses he found a job on a government survey crew. One thing led to another, and for many years he had been living the sweet life in Lander with his wife and children.

I thanked Bruce for sharing his story, and he saw me to the door. "Sometimes I really miss him," he said, looking past me toward the night sky. "Scott never sat around saying he was bored. He lived more in his forty years than ninety-nine percent of people live in eighty."

We shook hands and it was pretty clear to me that while the path he had chosen had been much different that of Scott Fischer, Rainbow had also done a fine job of filling his years on the planet with more good living than most.

CHAPTER 6

The Fallingest Man in Climbing

The reason Scott is famous is because he died on Everest and not during any of the twelve fatal falls that he survived.

—Randy Cerf, NOLS instructor and climbing partner

LONG BEFORE PUBLISHING his book *The Perfect Storm*, a youthful Sebastian Junger enrolled in a course at the National Outdoor Leadership School. His instructor was Scott Fischer. "Every so often, if we were camped near some cliffs, I would look up to see Scott far above me, unroped, climbing some offset crack," Junger wrote in an article for *Outside Magazine* after Scott's death. "He climbed slowly and deliberately and with tremendous strength. He climbed in a way that almost made you feel sorry for the rock. He climbed as if he couldn't fall."

Climbers fall, and in his early years as a climber, Scott fell a lot. He was the Flying Fischer. He was the Fallingest Man in Climbing. While any fame may be better than remaining unknown, if Scott were serious about sticking around long enough to become the mountaineer he wanted to be, he would need to negotiate a better treaty with gravity than the fragile truce he seemed to believe he had forged.

The first of Scott's serious falls occurred during a National Outdoor Leadership School course when, as a fifteen-year-old assistant instructor, he was assigned to help a more seasoned instructor teach the basics of descending a cliff by rappelling down a rope. The students watched as the instructor set the anchor by wedging a piece of mountaineering hardware called a nut into a crack near the lip of the cliff, then securing the rappel rope to it with a loop of nylon sling and a carabiner. He handed the rope to Scott and asked him to demonstrate how the rappel should be done. Scott clipped the rope to his seat harness and began paying out the line as he backed over the cliff.

A golden rule for climbers is to trust an anchor only if they check it themselves, which Scott had failed to do. Under the strain of his weight on the rappel rope, the nut shifted in the crack, popped loose, and sent him into a freefall. Somersaulting through the air, he smashed his face against the rock and then by sheer chance landed on an isolated pile of snow that somehow absorbed enough of the impact to prevent him from being killed. He was knocked unconscious and had broken his pelvis. Scott's sister Lisa, a student on the course, rushed to her brother's side and waited with him while a helicopter evacuation was arranged. "He was a mess," she remembered, "all bloody and dirty. It was really scary."

Gene and Shirley Fischer came to Lander to be with their son and were in his hospital room as he became aware of his surroundings. "Boy," he told them, "that was a bummer." When he was well enough to travel, he flew back to New Jersey to recover at his parents' home.

Scott would have other opportunities in the next few years to recuperate on the Fischer family couch. During a NOLS course in the Wind River Range he had fallen more than a hundred feet into a crevasse on the Dinwoody, a glacier in the Wind River Range, and dislocated his shoulder. He wrenched the shoulder again while climbing in Colorado. In Zion and Sinks Canyon and the Schwangunks, he took many falls that were stopped by belay ropes—falls that sometimes left him bruised, scraped, and sprained. A thirty-foot tumble against granite in Yosemite knocked him senseless before he bounced off a tree and struck the ground. Rescuers carried him in a litter to safety.

Nothing, though, suggests Scott's proclivity for falling, and his unusual success in surviving that most dubious of activities, than his launch off a frozen waterfall called Bridal Veil.

Returning from his trip to Nepal with Rainbow, Scott had instructed NOLS winter mountaineering courses in Wyoming. He and several other instructors pooled their resources as the 1977 winter season was coming to a close and hired climber Jeff Lowe to put on an ice-climbing seminar for them in Utah's Provo Canyon. Well known for his rock-climbing ability, Lowe was also a recognized expert in the emerging sport of ice climbing—using crampons strapped to one's boots and an ice axe in each hand to climb frozen waterfalls, couloirs, and other frosty features that suggested a route to someplace higher. At intervals during an ascent, a climber could screw a threaded metal tube into the ice, then use a carabiner to clip his rope into the eye at the exposed end of the screw. That would anchor the line so that in the event of a fall, a belayer managing the rope could stop the climber's plunge before he dropped too far.

Jeff Lowe was also involved with a climbing equipment company working on a new generation of ice tools. Among the innovations was the Lowe Hummingbird. Where earlier climbers had used standard ice axes for gaining purchase on vertical ice, the Hummingbird was a smaller axe that, instead of a pick, featured a sharpened, hollow metal tube with a diameter the size of a dime. When swung against the ice, the tubular bill of the Hummingbird felt to many climbers more secure than the chisel-shaped picks of traditional ice axes.

The NOLS instructors were eager to pick up some pointers on ice climbing from Jeff Lowe and to get their hands on the Hummingbirds to see how they performed. Add the fact that the seminar would be an excuse for a heck of a good party, and none of the Bruces could see a downside to a trip to Provo Canyon. Wes Krause parked his travel trailer on the road near the base of Bridal Veil Falls as the unofficial seminar headquarters. Soon Scott showed up, as did Michael Allison, Randy Cerf, and a small crowd of other climbers, and the adventure was on.

Bridal Veil in the summer cascades hundreds of feet down the canyon wall. In the winter it becomes an elegant pillar of ice glistening in the sunlight and featuring all manner of giant icicles, frosty pillars, and frozen curtains. "At that time, amazingly enough, it had never been climbed," Wes told me. "It was big—seven pitches if you were going to climb it. For the 1970s, that was a really big piece of ice."

The morning after Jeff Lowe's seminar, Scott, Randy Cerf, and Wes set off to make the first ascent of Bridal Veil Falls. Because it was so high they would need to do it in stages, each pitch about a hundred feet high. They planned to take turns leading the pitches. The leader had the most difficult job and arguably the most enjoyable, for it would be up to him to figure out the route and use ice screws to anchor the rope along the way. The second climber would belay the lead climber by being ready to secure the rope if the leader fell. When the leader reached the literal end of his rope, he would find a place to stand, anchor himself to ice or rock, and belay the second climber while he came up. The third climber would retrieve the ice screws as he ascended.

Randy led the first pitch and came to a small ledge about a hundred feet up where he used a carabiner to secure his waist harness to an ice screw, then belayed Wes as he climbed. The ledge was barely wide enough for two people, to say nothing of three, so Wes left Randy anchored there to belay him as he began leading the second pitch. The idea was that when Wes was another hundred feet higher, he would anchor himself in and Randy could then belay Scott from the base of the falls to the top of the first pitch. From there, Wes would belay each of them as they ascended the second pitch, and they would continue the process of switching leads for five more pitches to the top of the falls.

"It wasn't vertical, but nearly," Wes remembered. "Having a belay rope was definitely advantageous."

Waiting his turn while Wes climbed the first pitch, Scott became impatient and began climbing without the security of the rope. Not that wise, Wes thought when he saw his friend moving up the ice, but not that bad either.

Scott climbed quickly with a standard ice axe in each hand. By maintaining three-point contact with the ice—two feet and one hand or two hands and one foot—he felt secure enough to move his free foot upward and kick in the pointed front blades of the crampon, or to reach overhead and get a fresh bite with an ice axe. It was Spider-Man motion, whacking at the waterfall with the axes and kicking the crampons into the ice as he climbed. Ten feet. Twenty-five feet. Fifty. A hundred. And then he was crowded on the ledge with Randy and Wes.

"Wes led the second pitch," Scott told Jeannie a few days after the climb. "Randy hadn't started up and I took off solo again." While he had been on the belay ledge, he and Randy had discussed whether he should go higher without being tied to the rope. "We decided that I *couldn't* fall, because it would be a tough one to live through if I did."

Still without the protection of a rope, Scott swung one of his tools hard against the ice and was startled to feel the tool twist in his hand as the point snapped off. He took a good look at it, realizing that without a functional axe in each hand and with no belay rope attached to his harness, he was stranded on a pillar of ice at the height of a ten-story building. He couldn't move up, down, or sideways. All he could do was wait for help.

Belayed by Wes, Randy climbed up to Scott and handed him the team's spare ice tool, a Lowe Hummingbird. In hindsight, Scott realized that with an unfamiliar tool he should have taken the opportunity to descend carefully to the ledge, wait for Randy to finish climbing the pitch, and then tie himself to the rope for his turn at that section of the route. Instead, he continued his unprotected ascent toward Wes.

"I hadn't climbed much with a Hummingbird," he said later. "They are a good tool but take a lot of practice." He swung the Hummingbird against the ice and embedded the tube, put his weight on the handle, and was astonished to feel the tool pop free. The next thing he knew he was airborne.

"All of a sudden he falls," Wes told me. "Whish! Out of sight!"

Randy made a grab for Scott as he flashed past him but couldn't hang on, and Scott was gone, careening down the ice and disappearing from view. "I couldn't go down to him right away," Randy recalled. "Wes was a hundred feet above me. We each had to rappel, and it took awhile."

"We got to the bottom of the ice climb and Scott wasn't there!" Wes said. "We looked, and way on down he's lying in the rocks. The way the ice had formed at the bottom of the falls had made a sort of a smooth scoop. Scott had come skidding down this thing and been launched off and landed below the waterfall. It was unbelievable."

"It was a long way to fall, and I thought Scott was probably dead," Randy told me. "When climbers do those horrendous falls, if they hit the ground squarely, they're dead. But if they hit at an angle that breaks their fall, then they've got a chance. Scott had reached the bottom of that waterfall at a high rate of speed and then slowed as the ice angled out until he launched off the ramp and out into the rocks."

Scott was conscious, and though he was bruised and his chest hurt, he seemed to have escaped serious injury. Randy and Wes helped him hobble to the road and then drove to a hospital emergency room in Provo. That's when they noticed the hole in one of the heavy fabric gaiters that Scott was wearing around his ankles to keep snow and ice out of his boots.

"We thought, what is the deal with that?" Wes told me. He and Randy took off the gaiter and saw that the hole continued through the side of Scott's boot. They unlaced the boot and when they slipped it off, they saw that there was a hole through his sock, too. When they got his sock off, they realized that the hole went all the way through the back of his ankle and out the other side.

"While he was falling he had flailed around trying to jam his ice tools into the waterfall to stop himself," Wes told me, "and he had punched the tube of that Lowe Hummingbird right through his boot and between his Achilles tendon and his ankle bone. While he's in mid-air! He didn't even know he had done it."

Scott had taken an in-flight core sample of his own flesh. "What came out of the tube of that Hummingbird looked like one of those little Slim Jim sausages," Randy added. "He'd hit nothing but meat. It was miraculous."

Word of Scott's fall got around quickly, and the next day all the good ice climbers within driving distance were turning up for a chance at completing the first ascent of Bridal Veil Falls. "There were three different two-person-on-a-rope teams," Wes told me, "and zoooop! We all went up. It was pretty fun."

What was not so much fun for Scott was the reaction of his family when they learned of his accident. "Apparently my folks and my sister Rhonda think I am hell-bent on killing myself and want to know how I can lead the life I do," he wrote in a letter to Jeannie. "Now, that was very disconcerting to me. I really don't think about that sort of stuff too often, perhaps never. Until it was put right to me. Rhonda said when the doctor called from Utah everybody just broke down and cried. That's a bummer for me to hear because, again, that is something I have never thought of (I mean here the reaction that people who are dear to me have to my accidents or may have to my death). Of course *now* this is very much on my mind. I have little or NO fear of death, but care very much about my loved ones and their feelings and lives."

After a few weeks resting in Lander, he made his way to Zion National Park in search of springtime warmth and vertical sandstone on which to address again his need to climb. "The weather has been just perfect, with shirts off during the day," he wrote from Zion just over a month after his Bridal Veil Falls accident. "Was so psyched when I got here. Did a couple real good pitches, then just blew my ankle out." He kept himself away from the heights for another week in hopes that he would heal quickly, but then he insisted on climbing, took a forty-foot leader fall when he was being belayed from below, and hurt his ankle yet again. "I would like to be able to say I'm learning from experience," he told Jeannie, "but it doesn't look that way, does it?"

He resigned himself to hanging around his campsite and watching others play on the cliffs. Among them was Stacy Allison, a young woman who had come to Zion from her home in Oregon with her friend Evelyn Lees. "I'd never spent time around climbers and didn't know what they were," Stacy told me recently. "Scott had put an ice axe through his foot. He couldn't climb, couldn't do anything. He said, that's all right, I'll just teach you girls how to climb. He took us to the bottom of a cliff and told us what to do."

Scott gave them suggestions as they made their first tentative moves on the rock face. He helped them figure out where to put their hands and how to lean out from the rock so that their weight was over their feet. He encouraged them to link moves together so that even as beginners their climbing had rhythm and flow.

"Scott was so generous with his time and knowledge," Stacy told me. "He wanted to help out, wanted us to climb and have a good time. It was as if he felt that he had lived in that world and now he wanted us to get up some climbs so we could be part of it, too. That's what it was all about."

Others had also noticed that about Scott. Len Pagliaro, with whom Scott led several NOLS courses, recalled that "Scott had evolved his teaching of climbing to a remarkable degree, starting out with everybody climbing barefoot on the slabs, doing follow-the-leader. For Scott it wasn't about ropes, it wasn't about knots, it wasn't about hardware, it was about climbing, and he had a wonderful ability to teach that."

While Scott was willing to take tremendous risks himself, he could be harsh with those for whom he had accepted responsibility, especially if they put themselves in dangerous situations. "A year or two later in Zion, Scott did a short new route of one or two pitches," Stacy explained. "Evelyn and I went to do it after he was done. Scott had a reputation of going for it and not always being very careful. On this route there's a huge runout of maybe thirty feet—a stretch of the route that has no protection—and it was pretty hard, but Ev and I did it and got to the top." Had they fallen, they could have been badly injured.

The next time they saw Scott they proudly told him what they had climbed. He wanted to know who had led the difficult, exposed pitch. Stacy told him that she had, and that she'd not used any hardware to secure the belay rope on the runout.

"He got so angry," Stacy told me. "He was livid that I had done this runout lead and not protected it. He laid into me. I almost cried. He was so harsh and pissed off that I would do a runout with the possibility of getting hurt."

"You don't *ever* do that!" Scott had told her.

"It was real interesting how he had worked that out with himself," Stacy remembered. "It was okay for him to take risks, but it wasn't okay for me because he had coached us when we first started climbing and he felt a responsibility for our safety."

Notwithstanding his cautions to others, Scott continued to stretch the limits of what he could do. "That first spring in Zion, Scott was very bold," said Randy Aton, a Zion climber who had found Scott in the same campground where Stacy Allison had encountered him. "I met Scott not long after he took that Bridal Veil fall. When he flexed his foot, you could see the innards of his ankle kind of moving in and out." Even so, Scott had felt fit enough to climb. With Randy Aton handling the belay, Scott led the way up a difficult crack, took a twenty-foot fall, and when he hit the end of the rope pulled Randy off the ground. Dangling from the ends of the rope, they hung in the air looking at one another.

"Nice catch," Scott said.

"That was my introduction to climbing with Scott Fischer," Randy told me, "and I wondered who the hell is this guy and do I really want to climb with him?"

Wes Krause, Randy Cerf, and Michael Allison arrived in Zion, too, and they climbed together for a month, beginning a tradition of the Bruces migrating to the desert Southwest each spring after the NOLS winter courses concluded and before the summer programs began. Sometimes they returned for another month in the autumn, leasing a house in Rockville near the entrance to Zion National Park.

"We'd get up in the morning and jog over to some tennis courts," Randy Aton recalled. "We'd play a set of tennis, jog back and have breakfast, and then go climbing." Speaking of the falls that can be an element of rock climbing, Randy added, "Scott in those days probably had more air time than a lot of airline pilots."

"Scott was strong and he would go for it," Randy Cerf told me. "There's a climb in Zion called Fisher Crack. It involves a long, vertical off-width crack, probably 5.10 difficulty. We didn't have a lot of modern gear and no protection that would fit in that crack. About eighty feet up there's a foothold where you could stand and finally clip your rope into an anchor bolt." In other words, the route required someone to lead eighty feet of difficult rock climbing without the protection of a belay, relying fully on wedging his hands and feet into a wide crack in the vertical wall. Once he had reached the foothold, the lead climber could attach himself to an anchor and then belay his companions as they came up, but for the lead climber, a fall on that pitch would smash him right into ground.

"I wouldn't lead it," Randy Cerf said. "Wes wouldn't lead it. Michael Allison wouldn't lead it. We could all *second* it without difficulty, but we weren't going to lead it. It wasn't beyond our ability, but whoever led it was unroped for eighty vertical feet, and the only one willing to do that was Scott. He went scurrying right up."

Scott was pushing the envelope as far as any of them had ever seen it pushed and taking chances none of them were quite willing to take, but doing it in a way that made it possible for them to push farther, too. It wasn't just waiting while Scott went first on the toughest routes so that he could anchor the rope and belay them up. The very act of doing what others could not conceive of doing brought it into the realm of the possible.

Yet gravity never sleeps. The pull of the Earth is patient and omnipresent. If Scott had continued to play on the razor's edge of what gravity would and would not allow, the forces of nature were eventually going to win. He would make a mistake on an unprotected runout, or would lunge for a hold that really was just out of his grasp or would again be too bold high on a frozen waterfall, and gravity would gather him in. One day his ability to bounce would come slamming down against a hot desert floor or a snowy boulder field that afforded no second chances.

What he ran into first, though, was another force of nature in the guise of a longtime NOLS instructor and Outward Bound veteran Don Peterson. Don had been hired by NOLS to teach an advanced climbing course for NOLS instructors. To Scott and his young peers, Peterson seemed like an elder statesman.

"Don was a very bright, interesting character," Randy Aton remembered. "He wore glasses that were sort of skewed on his face and he had a big vocabulary. He may have had a Ph.D. in philosophy." Others remembered that the academic degree was in engineering, or maybe there wasn't a degree at all but rather enough mystique surrounding Peterson that no one could pierce the veil and figure him out. What they did know for sure was that Don had climbed in Yosemite a decade earlier with some of the biggest names of the era and had teamed up with legendary climber Royal Robbins for an eight-day first ascent of a route on Half Dome called Tis-sa-ack.

The Bruces also discovered that Don Peterson was a highly competitive athlete determined to win at everything from bicycle racing to mountaineering. He had developed ferociously demanding fitness regimens for himself, and had been known to work out so hard that by the end of a session he would throw up in the john or pass out in the shower. On top of all that, he quickly proved himself to be as graceful a climber as any of the NOLS instructors had ever seen.

"Don would brook no fools," Randy Cerf told me. "If he thought you were doing something inappropriate, he would not be diplomatic about sharing that with you in any sense. If he didn't think your climbing style was cool, he would tell you."

Peterson had a lot to tell Scott Fischer. What was cool for Don was climbing with control. "He was one of the first guys who talked about climbing quietly," Randy Aton said. "When you put your foot down on a hold, put it there to stay. Don't flap your foot until it sticks. He was good with that."

Scott's willingness to extend himself until there was no margin for error did not fit well with Peterson's view of climbing, and Scott's habit of lunging for almost impossible holds offended Don's sense of artistry on the rock. And while Don was the kind of guy who could rub just about anyone the wrong way with his judgmental attitude, by the end of the course he and Scott had developed enough mutual respect for one another that they agreed to an end-of-summer climbing trip in the Alps. Scott was in good shape, but Don challenged him to be even stronger, and in the weeks leading up to their departure for Europe, Scott ran long distances every day and worked out so hard that he managed to make himself nauseous, too.

The fitness routine seemed wasted, though, as foul weather followed them to the climbing center of Chamonix in the French Alps. Three weeks into their stay the weather finally improved, and the two completed a long, difficult climb on the North Face of the Grandes Jorasses and another on Mount Blanc.

"I really think I am getting good," Scott wrote in a letter to Jeannie, but he was ready to come home. "Climbing with Don is weird because he thinks he is SO good. Which is true, but I'll definitely be ready for this apprenticeship type setup to end." By the time they came back from Europe, Scott had bought into Don's approach of climbing quietly with grace and strength. Scott's new mantra was "Perfect Control," and he hoped it would take him to the next level.

Perhaps what would continue to move him ahead, though, was not Perfect Control while climbing up, but rather the positive reinforcement he received by living through the experience every time he fell. Hadn't he plunged 100 feet into a glacial crevasse and 150 down a rappel cliff? When he had peeled off climbs dozens of times in Zion and Yosemite and Sinks Canyon, hadn't the nuts and hexes and other protection he had set up kept him safe? And who except Scott Fischer had ever rocketed down a frozen waterfall, flown off the base, and lived through *that* with little injury other than punching an ice tool almost harmlessly through his ankle?

Sure it hurt like hell to fall, or rather to land after a fall, and no, Scott didn't want to fall very often, if ever. It was embarrassing when his friends heard about the latest terminal velocity descent, and it caused his family to worry if they learned about it, which they always did. But why not take ever bigger risks on cliffs and mountains of increasing danger when the price of failure was apparently so insignificant? What are the boundaries? Where is the dark line that, once crossed, would never let him return? Scott seemed increasingly convinced that if he put his mind to it and approached things with Perfect Control, he just might discover that there were no limits at all.

CHAPTER 7

The Alaska Factor

The thing about Scott was he had these incredible sur-
vival instincts. Of course, he had to because he kept get-
ting himself into these survival situations. But seriously,
when it came time to start fighting for his life, which he
seemed to do pretty often, he could do a good job of it.
—Michael Allison, climbing partner and Mountain Madness cofounder

WET SNOW WAS falling on the muddy streets of Talkeetna, Alaska, as
the Scrabble hustlers walked into town. A village appended to an
airstrip near Denali National Park, Talkeetna has long been a
jumping-off point for mountaineers being ferried in to climb on and
around Mount McKinley. For two days I had been waiting with
Scott Fischer, Jeannie Price, and several Mountain Madness friends
for the weather to improve so that we could fly to the glaciers, and
we had spent plenty of hours at the Fairview Inn, a brightly lit and
well-worn bar crowded with restless climbers rapidly running short
on ways to kill time. Being stormbound in a tent on a mountain was
one thing. That's part of the game. Stuck in town was something
else again, and it didn't help when Jeannie came back from the airfield where she had been studying the latest meteorological print-
outs and announced it would be at least another day before the
overcast broke and the small planes chartered by the mountaineering teams could depart. We groaned at the news and ordered more
beer.

It was my first trip to Alaska. I'd known Scott for a little more than a year, and in addition to our climb of Mount Olympus, I had been with him on Mount Rainier and was spending a few hours a week typing Mountain Madness mailing lists and trip promotions. One of the descriptions in the 1982 brochure was for a nine-day stay in the Ruth Amphitheater at the base of Mount McKinley, and Scott had urged me to come along. "We'll have so much fun," he insisted. "Murray the Fisherman's coming, and Jeannie and Michael Allison. We can ski and climb and hang out and you'll see what Alaska's all about." He was adamant and his enthusiasm was infectious. "Come on, you've got to do this. It's Alaska!"

Most of what I knew at the time about the forty-ninth state had come from reading—*The Call of the Wild, The Cremation of Sam McGee, The Shooting of Dan McGrew.* That may be why I was not surprised when the doors of the Fairview opened and in stumbled a man and a woman right out of those Jack London novels and Robert Service poems, dog dirty and loaded for bear. They were wearing old goose-down jackets and patched woolen pants, and their hand-knit stocking hats were pulled down close to their eyes. The man had a game board under his arm, and as he stroked his tangled beard and scanned the room he asked, "Scrabble anybody?"

"Bruce, you can play Scrabble, can't you?" Scott pushed me forward and extolled my virtues as a wordsmith, apparently figuring that the ability to type a trip brochure must somehow translate into being a Scrabble expert, too. Still, there was little else to do at the Fairview other than drink more beer, so I sat down with the newcomers at a wooden table in the middle room. The man opened the board, the woman shook a brown corduroy bag full of Scrabble letters, and we got started.

I drew seven tiles from the bag and arranged them on a wooden rack in front of me. For the first few rounds of the game there were promising places on the board for me to put my tiles, and I was more than holding my own. Curious climbers leaned in to watch. I found another easy line of spaces to lay down a high-scoring word. "Come on!" Scott shouted. "Let's beat these guys!" More climbers gathered around.

The man leaned back in his chair and stroked his beard as he studied the board. "Want to make it interesting?" he asked, turning to Scott. "A little side bet on your friend?"

"Well, sure!" Scott said, pulling a couple of dollars from his pocket and slapping them on the table. "This is easy money!"

The bearded man nodded and matched Scott's wager with cash of his own. Other climbers stepped forward to lay bills on the table, too, betting on me to win even though I wasn't convinced that any of them knew the intricacies of Scrabble. The bar began taking on the feel of a Scrabble frontier showdown with the climbers calling out encouragement and waving fistfuls of dollars, and the game rolled on. I was hoping this was all still just good fun, but as the pile of money on the table grew, the game became more serious. With each new word placed on the board, the crowd around us roared. I took off my fleece vest and rolled up my sleeves. Another score, another shout of approval, more money put at risk, and the board filled with words. I played, followed by the woman, and then the man, and as I concentrated on my letters to will them into words, our scores stayed about even. Climbers doubled down on their bets, the man with the beard accepting all wagers.

Then, with the bag of tiles nearly empty, I suddenly realized that the woman had begun playing not to win, but rather to set up the man with openings for him to hit the triple word squares along the outer margins of the board. They were quietly working together to defeat me, two against one. What they were doing was so subtle I would never be able to explain it to the climbers, but I had a very bad feeling I was about to be taken down by Alaska Scrabble hustlers and there wasn't a damn thing I could do about it.

The woman paved the way for the man to lay out a long word for a multiple score, and the climbers groaned. I did the best I could with my turn, but then she set him up again with a clear avenue straight into another triple score square. He slapped down the letters for a huge tally and the climbers howled with dismay. The game ended with a last setup by her and another enormous gain by him, and I was toast. The woman scooped the tiles into the bag while he pocketed the wagers. He tucked the game board under his arm, then with the faintest of smiles nodded in our direction, gave his beard a final tug, and followed her into the cold Alaska rain.

A hundred years earlier and Robert Service might have ended the Scrabble game with guns blazing, a woman screaming, and two wordsmiths lying stiff and stark. We had managed to finish our contest with only the loss of money, but I was quickly discovering that going remote in Alaska is always a gamble. It's the Alaska Factor, the realization that things in the forty-ninth state are bigger than they appear and often much stranger than one could have ever imagined. For Scott and his climbing companions, the stakes were much higher than those laid down for a board game, especially when it was their lives that they were putting on the line.

Scott had made his first trip to Alaska three years earlier with Wes Krause, the two of them driving up the Alaska-Canadian Highway to instruct a 1979 NOLS course on Mount McKinley. They'd set up Wes's truck so that one of them could sleep in the back while the other was at the wheel, and had made the trip from Seattle to Anchorage in three days. Scott's back was aching when they arrived. The accumulated injuries from nearly a decade of falling might have had something to do with it, or it could simply have been that he and Wes had just motored almost nonstop for 2,300 miles, much of it on unpaved roads.

"Oh man, Bruce," Wes said as they looked through the windshield at the glaciated peaks glowing in the distance, "they grow 'em big up here!" They were a month early for the NOLS course and hoped to climb at least one other mountain before taking on McKinley. What they had in mind was Mount Sanford in the Wrangell-St. Elias Range. With a 16,000-foot elevation, it is higher than anything in the lower forty-eight states.

"It looks perfect!" Scott shouted to Wes as they neared the town of Glenallen and got a good look at Sanford in the distance. It was a broad mountain, the snowfields and glaciers gleaming in the low angle of the sun. They also could see Mount Drum. A smaller replica of its neighbor, it appeared to be fairly close to Sanford. "And let's climb that one, too!"

They thumbed through a Glenallen telephone book, called a

bush pilot, and explained their newly formulated plan—get flown in and dropped off at the base of Sanford and climb it, hike over to Mount Drum and climb it, then get picked up.

The pilot told them he thought their idea was crazy but for $140 each he would ferry them to and from the mountains. His aircraft was a Super Cub, a tiny plane with room only for himself, one passenger, and some cargo. Scott and Wes emptied their packs so that the pilot could push their camping gear, provisions, ropes, and climbing hardware into the corners of the plane's cabin. He motioned for Wes to climb aboard for the first flight, and Wes reached up to hoist himself onto a wing strut. "No! Don't step there!" the pilot warned. "It'll break!"

"I'd never flown in anything like that," Wes told me recently, "and I thought, whoa, this seems just totally out there."

An hour later the pilot was back to get Scott and the rest of the food and gear. The aircraft again lifted heavily into the sky and turned toward Mount Sanford. The mountain seemed to lift with the plane, the shining whiteness filling the horizon as Scott studied the ridges and steep faces from his seat behind the pilot. With each passing minute Mount Drum grew larger and more defined, too. Scott gazed down at the tundra separating the peaks and thought it looked like a golf course, green and smooth, and he was sure that hiking from one mountain to the other would be easy.

The pilot banked the plane and circled down, a cabin by the side of the Sanford River at the epicenter of his turns. Scott looked for an airstrip and saw none. When they were at treetop level, the pilot righted the plane and brought it in to land on the shoreline of the river. The reconnection of earth and machine sent a jolt through Scott's seat, and he thought the plane might explode. The pilot cut the engine and let the aircraft roll to a stop not far from where Wes was sitting next to his pack and duffel bags. Scott tumbled to the ground and pulled his gear out of the cockpit. He and the pilot went over the plan which was, in its entirety, that in twenty-three days the plane would pick up Wes and Scott near Mount Drum.

"Have fun," the pilot told them as he climbed back into the cockpit, "and watch out for the bears." He got the propeller spinning, hit the throttle, and the plane was soon a black dot against the huge blue sky. Then even the sound of it was gone.

The log cabin next to the Sanford River had been left in a shambles by bears scrounging for food, but seemed just right as Scott and Wes sorted their gear. With the food, clothing, and equipment they would need for camping and climbing, their packs for their days on the Mount Sanford weighed close to a hundred pounds, and Scott felt a sharp pain shoot through his back when he swung the load onto his shoulders. He ignored it as much as he could and followed Wes to their first challenge, a crossing of the Sanford River. It was wide, five or six feet deep in the middle, and moving with a strong current. Scott and Wes had waterproofed their gear by stowing the contents of their packs in plastic bags. They waded into the cold current and when he reached water deep enough to give him buoyancy, Wes allowed the river carry him, pushing off toward the opposite shore whenever his feet touch the streambed. Soon he had bounced his way across and stood dripping on dry land. Scott either didn't get the bounce technique or refused to use it, perhaps figuring that he could just apply more brute force to the problem and slog his way through.

"Scott, you've gotta bounce, man!" Wes shouted from the shore. "Bounce your way over here!" Scott battled the current, his head under water more than above. "Well, bye-bye, Bruce," Wes yelled. "I'll be right here."

Scott finally emerged from the river and hiked up the riverbank to rejoin Wes as he was wringing out his socks. "Jesus, it can't get any worse than that, can it?"

That's when they discovered the tussocks. What had appeared from the air to be almost a groomed lawn was, in fact, a soggy tundra punctuated by thick tufts of vegetation. If they stepped squarely on a mass of plants, it might hold their weight. Step to one side or the other and they could plunge into muck up to their knees. "Three days of terrible hiking with hundred-pound packs and a lot of back bummers," Scott said later. "Not for mortal man."

They camped just shy of Mount Sanford's glaciers and looked up at the 10,000 feet of climbing that lay between them and the summit.

"We had a choice of going up Death Ridge or Life Spur," Scott recalled. "We sort of thought this Life Spur would be a cruise, so we went for it." It's always wise to choose Life over Death.

The mountains of Alaska are so far north that the summer sky never fully darkens. Scott and Wes climbed literally around the clock—forty-one hours in their attempt to summit Sanford, with only a four-hour bivouac to grab some sleep. Deep snow made forward progress arduous and the climbing exceedingly dangerous, even from Scott's point of view. "The whole way it was terrible," he said. "Such an exposed climb on a knife-edge ridge with literally thousands of feet either way, and a corniced ridge yet. Jesus! I have never been so afraid of dying." The mountain was much bigger than they had expected, and with thousands of vertical feet still between themselves and the summit they realized that conditions were not going to improve and that they were becoming too exhausted to go on. They descended to their camp, rested for several of days, then returned to the cabin.

It was good to be off the glaciers and back on green vegetation. They caught fish from the river. They sat in the sunshine and watched caribou grazing on the tundra. Along the riverbank they saw the footprints of huge bears. "My God, I don't want to run into a griz," Scott told Wes, "but two of us with ice axes? Hey, we can take on any bear. I just don't think it would be a problem." It wasn't much of a strategy, but at least he was giving some thought to the possibilities.

As for longer range plans, Scott composed a letter to Jeannie. She had been living most recently in Salt Lake City while earning her ratings as a flight instructor and a pilot of multi-engine aircraft. "I think about you most of the time," he wrote. "We'll pull it together this fall somehow. I want to hang out, listen to music, fix the car, buy a stereo, just sort of do all sorts of domestic stuff, stuff it seems like I never get to do. I want to have a place to call home. It has been such as long time since I had one. Can't we have a home?"

In the middle of the Alaska wilderness in the midst of an outrageous adventure, Scott was imagining putting down roots, a vision as fully counter to his current experience as any line of thinking could be. Perhaps that's part of the Alaska Factor, too, that the place is so huge and empty it causes one to think about the securities of home. In his poem *The Shooting of Dan McGrew*, Robert Service wrote about "a fireside far from the cares that are, four walls and a roof above . . ." Add a good stereo to that, put some new shocks on the car and install a decent muffler, and you might really have something.

Scott also told Jeannie that after watching the pilot ferry him in from Glenallen, he wanted to learn how to fly so that he could add being a bush pilot to his list of skills. "I hope you think it's a good idea," he wrote. "It would bring our two different worlds a little closer together." He suggested that at summer's end she teach him what he needed to know to get behind the controls of an airplane.

"Quite a rambling letter you are getting here," he closed. "So what are we going to do?"

What he was going to do in the near future was not in question. The attempt on Mount Sanford had eaten up most of their time, and in seven days the pilot would come for them at the base of Mount Drum. He and Wes replenished their packs with the provisions they had cached at the Sanford cabin and set off to cross the sixteen miles of tundra and tussock to another dilapidated cabin. What had looked like an easy cruise again turned into a multiday journey toward a mountain much farther and higher than it had appeared. When they finally got to the cabin, they realized they had time only for one sustained effort to reach the Mount Drum summit and return.

The weather turned nasty as they roped themselves together and started up one of Mount Drum's glaciers, but they climbed on, counting on their enthusiasm and the endless daylight to keep them going. "It was total whiteout the whole time, snow and wind," Scott reported later. "We went for twenty hours, never knowing where we were on the mountain, paranoid of our tracks filling in, total white. Once again outrageous trail breaking. We didn't have near the energy we needed." Their effort to climb Mount Sanford had drained them much more than they wanted to admit.

With the clock running down and their strength running out,

they turned around well short of the summit and discovered that their footprints had disappeared under the new snow. They could only guess at the route. They crossed several snow bridges over glacial crevasses, then came to a frozen span they weren't certain they had used during their ascent.

"Bruce, is this the right way?" Wes asked. "Do you remember a bridge looking like that?"

The crevasse in front of them was a good sixty feet across, and the snow bridge didn't seem as wide as the ones Wes recalled traversing earlier in the day. It did take them in the direction they wanted to go, though, and so he eased out onto it, the rope stretching from his harness to the one around Scott's waist.

Wes had almost reached the far side of the crevasse when the bridge disintegrated beneath him and dropped him into the abyss. He fell the length of the rope between himself and Scott, crashing against the icy wall of the crevasse and then slowly sliding farther down. "Come on!" he shouted, hoping Scott was still on the surface and figuring out a way to hold him. "Come on! *Come on!*" Then everything stopped.

The force of Wes's weight hitting the end of the rope had yanked Scott off his feet and dragged him toward the crevasse. He had twisted around and jammed his ice axe into the snow, stopping himself close to what was left of the snow bridge. With Wes's weight hanging from the rope, Scott didn't dare move. Adjusting his position in even the tiniest way might cause the axe to fly out of the snow, and that would send him and Wes pinballing deep into the glacier. He held on, muscles flexed, hands gripping the axe, and waited.

Dangling in midair, Wes managed to get some webbing out of his pack and tied loops of it to the rope with knots that enabled him to put a foot in each loop and then slide the loops up the rope one at a time, allowing him to ascend. The rope had cut into the lip of the crevasse. Wes chopped at the overhanging snow with his ice axe, burrowing a passageway as he hoisted himself up the rope.

They lost track of time, aware only that a great deal of it had passed before Wes heaved himself onto the surface of the glacier.

"Goddamn, man," Scott said when Wes's weight finally eased off the rope, "what took you so long?" Scott's arms were cramped from the strain of hanging on to the ice axe, and his back felt as though it were on fire. "Goddamn it!"

They flexed their sore limbs and tightened their crampons, then went around the end of the glacier that had nearly swallowed them. Finding their way again, they hurried down the glacier and back onto a ridge that would lead them to the cabin. That really had to be the worst of it, they thought. Surely Alaska had nothing more to throw at them, at least not on that day. And they would have been right had Wes not glimpsed a movement in the brush several hundred yards ahead. He pulled out his binoculars, adjusted the focus knob, and got a good look at a big sow grizzly. "Oh fuck," he said as he watched the bear feeding on blueberries. "Bruce, that is a rather substantial animal."

Scott borrowed the binoculars and took a look. "Well," he said after a long moment, "kinda big, but still no problem."

"Man, the arm of that bear is longer than my arm with my ice axe attached to it!" Wes whispered. "That's a big fuckin' bear!"

Scott was still of the opinion that the two of them together could handle the situation, but Wes was eager to avoid a confrontation. "It might be more of a battle than we want to get into," he cautioned.

They altered their route, dropping off the ridge and descending into a shallow valley to put distance between themselves and the bear, but just when they thought they were in the clear, the bear appeared on top of the ridge, much closer to them than before. Scott and Wes yelled and waved their arms, hoping to get the bear's attention so that they could scare it away. They got the bear's attention all right, and it responded by lumbering toward them.

"She's thinking we look better than those blueberries!" Wes yelled. He pointed to a glacial moraine not far away. If they could reach the top of that steep pile of rubble, he figured they would have the high ground and might be able to put up more of a fight. He dropped his pack and started running and assumed that Scott was running, too. When he didn't hear footsteps behind him, he looked back and saw Scott kneeling beside his pack trying to loosen the accessory straps to free his ice axe.

"Bruce!" Wes yelled to Scott. "Run!"

Scott glanced up, saw the bear closing in, and abandoned the ice axe plan. He sprinted after Wes and they scrambled up fifty or sixty feet of loose rock to the top of the moraine. The bear was still charging, passing their abandoned packs without a hint of interest.

"Grab a rock," Wes shouted, "because World War Three's about to start!" They picked up the biggest rocks they could hoist, which can be pretty big when a couple of fellows are being hotly pursued by an enormous sow grizzly, and stood poised to hurl them down at the bear. The grizzly stopped at the base of the ridge, rose on her hind legs and roared, then settled back onto all fours and rushed off in the direction she had come.

Scott and Wes stood a moment longer with the rocks over their heads and then dropped the stones as they watched her go. "What the hell did we do to deserve *that*?" Wes said.

"Maybe she was sending us a message," Scott said.

"Yeah, well, I think we kind of got it, then."

They were almost out of food when they reached the Mount Drum cabin, and so tired they could hardly move. In a cupboard they found a jar of donut mix that the bears had overlooked, and relaxed by making donuts over a fire they built in the stove. The next morning they heard a plane approaching and watched as the Super Cub came in to land.

"Have a good time?" the pilot asked as Wes and Scott stowed their gear in the airplane cabin.

"Can't complain," they told him. Nope. Not going to, either.

A few hours later they were back in Wes's truck, heading for Anchorage. They pulled to the side of the road for a last look at Sanford and Drum.

"Big ones," Wes said as he gazed across the tundra. "Really big mountains. We should get back in there someday and climb them."

"Come on," Scott said. "They can't be *that* big, can they?"

The Alaska Factor. Things are bigger than they appear. At least that's what I kept hearing. The sky was clearing on the morning after the Scrabble game, and it seemed as though I might soon get to find out for myself. We carried our duffels and backpacks to the Talkeetna airfield, hoping that the planes would soon fly. Some of the climbers who had been with us at the Fairview Inn were already there for flights to the Kahiltna Glacier to begin their ascents of McKinley. I imagined from their glances in my direction that they were sore at me for losing their Scrabble wagers.

"Hell, people lose money in bars all the time," Murray the Fisherman told me as he dropped his duffels near one of the aircraft. If there was an exception to the Alaska Factor, it was Scott's friend Jeff Murray, a massive man with a wild beard and a curly mane of reddish brown hair who was every bit as big as he appeared. His grin was highlighted by a silver cap jacketing one of his upper incisors. "Got that when I was eight and chipped my tooth," he told me with a big smile. "Supposed to be temporary, but I kinda liked it."

As we watched the pilots preparing the planes, Murray told me some of his story. He was raised in Minnesota and as a teenager had taken part in canoe expeditions through a YMCA camp that featured journeys of several months' duration on rivers above the Arctic Circle. After high school he had enrolled at Mankato State University where he played a season of football. The summer following his freshman year he had gone north again to see what Alaska was all about. He crossed the state and traveled down the Aleutian Islands to Kodiak, the harbor that shelters much of the Alaska fishing fleet. Needing money, he'd gotten a job gutting salmon in the hold of a fish processing boat for a few dollars an hour. It was terrible, sweaty work, and he was always happy for the break in the routine whenever a fishing boat tied up next to the cannery to unload its catch.

"The guys on the boats were having a great time," Murray said. "When I learned that they were making thousands of dollars for a few days' work, I could understand why." He asked how he could get a job like that and was told that nobody hired greenhorns. If he wanted to fish, he would have to volunteer. "I figured that even if I didn't get paid, it couldn't be worse than the cannery. At least I'd get fed and would see the ocean."

A double-rigged shrimp boat from Texas was moored at the dock. Painted orange with black trim, it was part of what the fishermen were calling the pumpkin fleet. Murray approached the captain, an imposing man wearing cowboy boots, a muscle shirt, and a ten gallon cowboy hat, and told him he wanted to volunteer. "A big boy like you wants to go for nothing?" the captain asked. "Get on board!"

"That's when the nightmare started," Murray told me. He had paddled a canoe into the Yukon, but he had never been on a large boat. When it hit the first swells beyond Kodiak harbor, the stern beneath him rose and then dropped. Murray fell, smacking his face against the deck.

"Bloody nose, fat lip," he said, shaking his head. "Then I got seasick. We ran fifty hours out into the Bering Sea, filled up with a quarter million pounds of shrimp in twenty hours, and then drove fifty hours back to Kodiak, me puking all the way. It was pure torture. I figured if I ever made it ashore I'd never fish again."

With the catch off-loaded, the captain handed Murray a thousand dollars. "He told me that nobody works as hard as I had for nothing," Murray laughed. "Then he said he was firing his nephew and that I could have the job at a half share, which turned out to be a lot money." He had been Murray the Fisherman ever since. "If you're just some college sophomore who doesn't show up for classes in the fall, nobody really cares," he continued, "but if you were supposed to be a lineman on the football team, they kind of come looking." Apparently nobody from the Mankato State athletic department thought to look for their defensive tackle on a pumpkin-colored boat tossing about in the middle of the Bering Sea.

Murray's friendship with Scott had begun a few years later when Scott decided to give commercial fishing a try. After their attempts to climb Mounts Sanford and Drum, Scott and Wes had helped Michael Allison lead a NOLS course on McKinley, Scott's first time to stand on the summit of North America's highest mountain. Scott had set off then on his usual migrations, climbing that autumn in

Zion, leading NOLS winter courses in Wyoming, and making his way to the various cities where Jeannie continued to pile up hours in her pilot's log book flying a variety of aircraft including cargo planes and Learjets. By the spring of 1980 Scott was nearly broke again and eager to earn some real money.

Scott's sister Lisa had migrated to Seattle from New Jersey to attend college and was funding her own adventures with seasonal work as a cook on Alaskan fishing boats and as a fish processor in the canneries. Scott hitched to Seattle and caught a ride north on a fishing boat called the Pisces. He was seasick much of the way as the boat coasted past British Columbia, west across Glacier Bay, and down the Aleutians to the harbor at Sand Point where Scott's hopes collided with reality when he learned the fishermen were on strike and no boats were going out.

"It sounds like jobs do happen, it's just life in the meantime that is a bummer," he wrote to Jeannie. "The weather is some of the shittiest I've ever seen, and believe me I've seen some shitty weather. Nobody is fishing so there is no job turnover and that is how I would get a job. Just waiting for someone to quit or get fired."

Determined to outlast the strike, he found a six-foot-square windowless shack next to the Sand Point skeet shooting range and made it his home, tucking himself into his sleeping bag at night and listening to the rain on the low roof. "I'm into the experience, but having a really hard time," his letter continued. "This is all such a whole new world for me. That in itself is neat, but it's lonely. I will get a job so I can just be Mountain Madness Bruce, won't I?"

Scott looked for work during the day and in the evenings would nurse a beer at a bar in town. He found himself in an arm-wrestling contest one night with the best arm wrestler of Sand Point and came out victorious. The captain of the Pisces happened to see the competition shaping up, bet fifty dollars on each of Scott's arms, and came away with some nice winnings. There was no trickle-down effect, though. "Needless to say," Scott told Jeannie, "I'm broke, broke, broke."

Jeannie responded by sending him money, but Scott returned the check. "I know how hard you're pulling for me and trying to help me out," he told her, "and I thank you for all the love and support you give me. I just decided it is time to stand on my own two feet and prove I'm not a bum, though I sometimes wonder."

The strike ended a week later and the boats prepared to set out for the fishing grounds, but Scott still had no luck getting on board. When he landed a carpentry job in Sand Point for six dollars an hour, his spirits soared. As long as he stayed at the shack and was careful with his earnings, he could keep things going awhile longer.

The salmon season came and went, and deck hands on the Pisces each made $35,000 from some spectacular fishing runs. Then with summer waning, Scott finally got the break he had been waiting for. There was an opening on the Pisces and the captain invited him to work the crab fishing season. Scott put down his hammer and climbed aboard. The deck boss was Murray the Fisherman, who had enough years of fishing under his belt to be a seasoned and sought-after crew member. Scott would have to heed custom and make his greenhorn voyage as a volunteer.

The Pisces carried large crab pots that the crew dropped into the ocean, each cage tethered to a float. The boat would return a few days later to haul in the pots and the bounty the crew hoped to find inside, up to 2,000 pounds of Alaska king crab in each pot. Dressed in heavy raingear to shield him from frigid waves washing over the deck, Scott struggled to grasp what was happening and where he should fit in. Much of the time he was helping Murray swing the heavy pots aboard and dump the crab into a hold. The captain assured him he would catch on, but Scott was not convinced. The accumulation of stress, long hours of work, and seasickness left him exhausted.

"Scott used muscle rather than leverage to move those big crab traps around the deck," Murray told me. "We tortured him with work, and when we weren't working I was always beating him at arm-wrestling."

"Okay, Murray," Scott would say after another arm-wrestling defeat, "let's do a toe-raise contest." They would stand with their toes on a ledge and then raise and lower themselves with their calf muscles, sometimes while holding another fisherman piggy-back.

Murray won those competitions, too, and Scott would devise more tests of physical strength that he would eventually lose.

"Our muscles would be so sore we could barely walk some days because of those contests," Murray told me, "but he kept trying to beat me and I just never let him."

Scott survived his first fishing trip and then stuck with the boat for two more months. He made a little money, but the Pisces didn't hit the jackpots that had blessed the boat on its earlier voyages.

"I think this is dangerous, dangerous work," Scott told Jeannie as the crab season came to a close. "I don't think I want to fish next summer. Maybe I will if we decide we need the money, but I'll just see."

Commercial fishing in Alaska is among the most dangerous careers a person can pursue. Scott was a mountaineer, not an angler, and fishing never came naturally to him. He did return to Alaska now and then to fish, usually on boats captained by Jeff Murray, but he eventually left its hazards behind. I've not found any statistics documenting the danger quotient of being a professional mountain climber, though if I were to mix the imagery of the career decisions Scott was making back in those early years, I might argue that he was simply jumping off the fishing boat and into the crevasse.

As we waited with our duffels at the Talkeetna airport, Murray and I and the other climbers watched the pilots of two bright red planes remove the seats from the four-passenger cabins to clear space for cargo. They instructed us to stash our packs and bags inside the aircraft, then they threaded the seat belts from the floor mounts up through the duffels. While the rest of the Mountain Madness team was getting aboard one plane, Murray, Scott, and I scrambled aboard the other, sat on top of our bags, and strapped ourselves in.

The pilot went through his preflight checklist, then as he warmed up the engine he told us that he sometimes carried sled dogs in the cabin. "They stay down when I take off, but during a flight they'll get restless and start moving around." He explained that he dealt with that by putting the plane into a dive and then pulling out hard, the centrifugal force flattening the dogs onto the floor. "Quiets 'em right down."

Scott tapped me on the shoulder. "Don't appear restless or start moving around," he said with a grin.

We were embarking on a Mountain Madness adventure, and I was smiling, too. The plane lifted off and the pilot cranked a lever to extend skis beyond the wheels, transforming the dry-land aircraft into one that could put down on snow. He turned the nose toward Mount McKinley and gained a little elevation, but not much. I looked down on the channels of the Susitna River braiding through low forests and wetlands. The vegetation became sparse and then disappeared as we glided into the Ruth Gorge and flew just above the glacier, close enough for us to peer into the pale blue crevasses cracking at right angles across the ice. Sheer faces of granite towering far above us moved slowly past as the plane followed the gradual turns of the gorge.

Thirty-five miles after we had entered the gorge we passed between Mount Dickey on the left and the molar-shaped mass of Moose's Tooth on the right and glided into the glacial bowl of the Ruth Amphitheater. The skis touched the snow and as the aircraft lost momentum, the pilot swung the tail around to position the plane for takeoff. We had come less than an hour's flying time from Talkeetna, and had gone back several million years in geological time.

The second plane dropped in beside us. We were just below a rib of rock rising out of the glacier and topped by a small octagonal shelter constructed in 1966 by bush pilot Don Sheldon. When Denali National Park absorbed the Ruth Amphitheater, the hut had remained a private in-holding available for lease by the likes of us. We unloaded our gear and provisions and, as the planes flew away, moved up the ridge.

The pilots flew farther into the amphitheater before turning back toward the gorge, becoming smaller but seeming not to have gone very far. The circle of mountains that formed the amphitheater served not so much to enclose, but rather to expand the sense of space simply by suggesting that there was so much of it. There was nothing to measure anything against, nothing of known size other than the hut, and the hut was significant only in being tiny.

We pitched our tents in the drifts and piled up walls of snow to block the wind. The hut was just big enough to serve as a gathering place for preparing meals and socializing, and each evening we crowded inside to cook pots of soup and pasta and stew, read books, and drink steaming mugs of cocoa laced with Yukon Jack. One night Murray told about climbing in South America with Scott. It had been the first Mountain Madness trip to Aconcagua, the continent's highest peak, and Scott had convinced Murray he needed to come along.

"Bruce, I told you I'd never climbed anything higher than the ladder of my boat," Murray said, "but it sounded like fun."

They had flown to Argentina with several other friends and had gotten close to the mountain. "None of us could speak Spanish," Murray continued. "We're in this town trying to figure out how to get permits and buy some pot and get to the climb, and we went to a restaurant for dinner." Murray told us he saw a plate loaded with steak heading for another table and gestured to the waiter that he would have the same.

"Hey, that's not the way you do it in foreign countries," Scott had told him. "Come on, you order like this." Scott had studied at the menu as if he could decipher the language. "Look, this Poncho," he said, pointing at one of the listed items. "That's what I'm going to have. No, make that a Super Poncho!" The waiter scribbled on his pad and a few minutes later came back with Murray's platter of steak and Scott's Super Poncho.

"It was the biggest fuckin' hot dog on a bun you've ever seen," Murray laughed. "Bruce is being this big international traveler, and he manages to order himself a hot dog! We just about split a gut laughing over that one."

Murray had followed Scott halfway up Aconcagua, discovering he was no more adept at mountaineering than Scott had been at working on a crab boat. Dizziness and general sailor-out-of-water malaise were doing him in, so Scott tucked him into a tent and went on with the others toward the summit, scooping up Murray a couple of days later during their descent. While he spoke of the Aconcagua trip as one of the better adventures he'd ever had, Murray felt no need to go to the high country again. "It was torture," he said. "I have no idea why anybody would want to climb mountains."

Scott stepped out of the hut to pee, and I asked Jeannie what had happened with his dream of becoming an Alaska bush pilot. "He'd seen all these airplanes in Alaska flying around, and here I'm a pilot, so he thought he should learn to fly, too," she told me. "He thought it would be something to fall back on, flying people into the mountains."

At the end of his first summer in Alaska, Scott had caught up with Jeannie in upstate New York where she was spending time with her parents and teaching flying. She took him to a local airport for his inaugural flying lesson and explained that before every flight he would need to get weather information, do a walk-around to inspect the airplane for safety, then see that the engine had enough oil and that the tires were properly inflated, and that was just the beginning of the checklist. He also had to learn aeronautical terminology and get a feel for talking over the radio with air traffic controllers.

"He did that for a couple of days, but he hated it," Jeannie laughed. "He just wanted to open the door and fly away like driving a car. We finally agreed he would never teach me to climb and I would never teach him to fly."

A few months after the flying lessons, Jeannie had come to visit Scott outside of Gillette, Wyoming, where he and some other NOLS instructors had winter jobs with a petroleum survey company. "We had a nice time, as nice as can be had in a grungy trailer in freezing Gillette in the middle of winter,'" she recalled. "We did a little partying, just the two of us, and Scott asked me to marry him. I said yes. He liked the sound of it so he asked me again. Then I tried it and asked him to marry me and he said yes. When all was said and done, he had asked me five times and I had asked him three times. So we pretty much decided that was what we were going to do."

They were married on Valentine's Day 1981. Many of the Bruces were there and Scott was as happy as he had ever been. The groomsmen wore dark glasses and presented themselves as the Blues Bruces. "We'd been together for all those years and we wanted to make it more permanent," Jeannie remembered, "but we knew we were so different from one another that we also agreed it might not work."

Our time in the Ruth Amphitheater settled into a wonderful simplicity. We had plenty to eat, lots to drink, fuel for our stoves, and endless space in which to roam. When we put on our cross-country skis, a destination I would think might be thirty minutes away would take us two or three hours to reach. McKinley looked plenty big too, so much so that if it were actually larger than it appeared, it had to be huge.

Nine days after we had had arrived in the Ruth, the planes returned to take us back to Talkeetna. I was disappointed to discover that the Fairview Inn was nearly deserted. I'd been building myself up for a rematch with the Scrabble hustlers, only this time I would have my wits about me and keep a more wary eye on the board. I'd come to understand a bit about the Alaska Factor. After being so close to McKinley I felt I was bigger than I might appear, too, and I planned to use that to my advantage. I was also going to have Murray the Fisherman on one side of me and Scott the Climber on the other. If the Scrabble hustlers were spoiling for fight, it was going be torture for them. It was going to be World War III.

But the street through Talkeetna remained empty. The Scrabble hustlers were nowhere to be found. The cowards.

CHAPTER 8

Mountain Madness

His motto for Mountain Madness was "Make it happen." Later, we would jokingly change the motto to "How the hell did it happen?" Scott thought that if he surrounded himself with the right people, things would come together. And they usually did.

—Ed Viesturs, climbing partner and Himalayan mountaineer

AT THE END of a logging road after an evening on the slopes of Mount Rainier, Scott Fischer is watching Dan McHale build a blaze the size of the biggest high school pep rally bonfire I'd ever seen. Snow covers the evergreen boughs surrounding us and a full load of stars shines overhead. The heat of the fire makes it difficult for us to get close enough to hold our weenie roasting sticks near the flames, but we've been waiting for hours for the logs to burn down, and a couple of hot dogs with ketchup and mustard would really hit the spot.

Dan's face is smeared with soot, and in the glow of the fire he bears a startling resemblance to Jack Nicholson in the movie *The Shining*. Wielding a heavy-duty garden rake with a six-foot handle extender, he beats down the fire and shapes the coals into a glowing bed four feet wide and a dozen feet long. The deep mound of embers glows in the night as though a lava-filled crack had opened on the forest floor.

"Time to do it," he says. A Seattle-based climber and builder of backpacks, Dan's not talking about eating hot dogs. He means it is time to walk through the fire. "When you know you can do it," he tells us, "you can do it."

Scott and I already know that Dan can do it. A *Life* magazine story on fire walking had mentioned that "Since 1978, 35,000 people have strolled, strutted and sprinted—one Seattle resident even made the trip on his hands—across 12-foot beds of glowing coals." That resident was Dan McHale. An article by Jon Krakauer, a young journalist writing for *Rolling Stone*, included an observation by McHale about the value of walking across the coals, noting that Dan believed if you put your mind to it, "you could survive a direct nuclear blast."

When I had asked him about that last comment, Dan admitted it might have been a little radical. Anyway, he added, he was nearing the end of his explorations of the element of fire. With his climbing pursuits he had dealt with both earth and wind. Walking barefoot on snow would add the element of water. I'd wondered, then, what was left. "Old age is going to be a real interesting one to explore," he had replied.

Dan's feet have been bare for more than an hour. Scott and I took off our shoes and socks, too, but only to humor Dan. There's no way the two of us are getting anywhere near the fire, but then Dan strolls across, leaving dark footprints in the glowing coals. He is nonchalant about it, walking with no more haste than if he had been on a sidewalk in downtown Seattle.

"Once you see somebody do it, then you know it can be done," Dan says. "That's all the preparation you need. Anything else is just a veneer layered on the surface."

I feel myself leaning forward. I've just seen somebody walk on fire, and suddenly Scott and I are tiptoeing across the coals, too. We're going much faster than the speed Dan had traveled, and I can feel a crunch underfoot as my naked soles press into the embers. I make it across with no sensation of heat, then suddenly feel blisters bubbling up. Sitting on a log I study my soles but find nothing. My feet are sooty but unharmed.

"Sometimes your mind can't believe what your body just did," Dan tells me. As if to prove the point, he tips himself into a handstand and goes across the coals balanced on his palms. "No heat," he says, pausing in the middle of the pit. "It's all just illusion."

That may be so, but it's a pretty damn impressive one. Perhaps not as impressive, though, as another dream both Dan and Scott were trying to realize, that of turning their interests in the outdoors into successful businesses. The Pacific Northwest seemed a good place to give it a try.

Scott and Jeannie had moved to Seattle in 1982. "We needed somewhere with airplanes and mountains," Jeannie recalled. "Denver, Seattle, Salt Lake, Anchorage—we were constantly talking about where we could find these two things." She'd been flying Learjets full of freight to build up the hours in her log book, and when she was offered a job by Seattle-based Alaska Airlines, she and Scott jumped at the opportunity.

They rented a little house in the Seattle suburb of Renton, then moved to a larger rental surrounded by farmland offering a view of Mount Rainier. When Jeannie's career as a pilot was sufficiently launched, they bought a place in West Seattle above the Fauntleroy ferry landing. From the back deck they could overlook Puget Sound and, if the day was clear, see the Olympic Mountains rising against the western sky. The finished basement became the office, store-rooms, and frequent crash pad for Mountain Madness, the adventure travel company Scott and several friends were forming with the intent of offering guided mountain trips anywhere in the world.

Seattle in the early 1980s was a long and laid-back way from the trendy town it was destined to become. The economy had begun recovering from the aerospace and timber industry downturns of the 1970s. The famous WILL THE LAST PERSON LEAVING SEATTLE PLEASE TURN OUT THE LIGHTS? billboard had been taken down, but Starbucks was still one modest shop in the middle of Pike Market that sold, of all things, unadorned black coffee. Bill Gates and Paul Allen were writing nascent computer code amidst empty pizza boxes and Coca-Cola cans. As if to punctuate the modest vision of the Puget Sound region, the eruption of Mount St. Helens had recently rendered the Pacific Northwest with one less snowy summit. But there were plenty more Cascade mountains where that one came from, and plenty of people eager to climb them.

The exploits of early climbers in the Cascades and Olympics were locally legendary, and organizations including the Seattle Mountaineers and Mountain Rescue brought together like-minded people to explore the backcountry. After World War II their numbers were increased by veterans of the army's 10th Mountain Division, fellows with an aptitude for alpine travel who had been organized to battle the Nazis in the mountains of Europe. They returned from the war with refined skiing and climbing skills, surplus army clothing and camping gear, and a brash confidence about what could be done on high.

Early American expeditions heading for the Himalayas practiced on the glaciers of Mount Rainier, sixty miles south of Seattle. At more than 14,000 feet, the mountain offered the closest approximation in the continental United States to conditions found in the mountains of Tibet and Nepal. The first American to climb Everest, Jim Whittaker, had grown up in West Seattle. He and his twin brother Lou suffered from hay fever as children and their mother had enrolled them in a Boy Scout troop with the hope that the fresh air they would breathe on camping trips might improve their health. By chance the troop's Scoutmaster was interested in rock climbing and, despite having lost an arm in World War II, he took the Whittakers into the Cascades and taught them the basics.

Seattle also had a longtime legacy of equipping and provisioning people going into the backcountry. The Alaska and Yukon gold rushes during the final years of the nineteenth century helped establish the city as a purveyor of outdoor gear as miners and camp followers passing through town purchased the clothing and supplies they would need in the gold fields. The tough wool and canvas outdoor clothing made by C. C. Filson had remained virtually unchanged through more than a century under the slogan MIGHT AS WELL HAVE THE BEST! Eddie Bauer had gotten his start in 1915 as a clerk in a Seattle sporting goods store, then in the 1930s developed his version of a vest filled with goose down and was on his way. The climber Ome Daiber invented Sno-Seal for waterproofing boots, and patented the Penguin, a sleeping bag that featured insulated sleeves and legs so that a camper could wander about camp without getting out of bed.

As a courtesy to friends who were having difficulty finding

equipment for climbing, Lloyd and Mary Anderson founded a co-operative in 1938 called Recreational Equipment, Inc. REI was busy enough by 1955 to hire Jim Whittaker as its first full-time employee, and by the early 1980s the company had grown into a Northwest institution selling camping and mountaineering gear through catalogs and at a big, rambling store on Seattle's Capitol Hill. Part of the building had once been an auto dealership. The wooden flooring had become impregnated with oil, solvents, boot dressing, ski wax, and nobody was sure what else, giving the place a distinctive and pungent aroma that, for nearly every outdoor-oriented Northwesterner of the time, came to be associated with the promise of adventure. Possessing an REI co-op membership card with a low number was a regional status symbol, an indication that the owner had been involved with mountain travel for many years.

Other equipment stores, too, served as gathering places for a populace eager to get more of the outdoors. On a summer evening soon after I had met Scott, we went to the North Face store in Seattle's University District. The staff had pushed back the display stands and rolled up the showroom tents to make space for us to sit on the floor. People in jeans and fleece jackets and vests wedged in around the slide projector table and all the way up to the screen set against a wall.

We were there to hear Ned Gillette speak about his recent circumnavigation of Mount Everest. An Olympic-caliber cross-country skier and a skilled alpinist, Gillette was creating a niche for himself by going around, rather than up, the world's great peaks. He had skied and climbed his way around Mount McKinley a couple of years earlier. Most recently he and a small team had made the first circumnavigation of Everest, and he was the latest of many adventurers to come through Seattle to present a program about his exploits.

Scott sat on the floor as he watched and listened, eager both to see the photos of Everest and to learn how Ned was making a living out of mountaineering. They shook hands at the end of the program. Scott believed Ned could lead to other connections that might help him realize his own dream of getting to Everest Base Camp and beyond. Such events may not happen often, but Seattle was one of the places where such magic could unfold.

By making backpacks, Dan McHale had found his own way to plug into Seattle's mountaineering impulses and its outfitting history. The packs he designed were heavy and nearly bulletproof, and Scott loved them. Weight didn't matter to him nearly as much as did durability and fit, and a McHale pack proved almost indestructible. He also liked the fact that what he carried on his back had been constructed by a friend in Seattle, and he would use McHale packs for almost all of his climbs.

Dan did his own marketing, selling the packs out of a tiny showroom in the building where they were sewn. His production line was too small and his customers too demanding for Dan to meet the commercial requirements of major stores like REI. McHale Packs appealed to a discriminating sliver of the outdoor market, but that's the way it was going to be and Dan was intent on making his business a success in his own way.

Scott was eager to get a business off the ground, too. Both the idea for a mountain guide service and the name Mountain Madness had been rolling around his mind for years. In the winter of 1976, NOLS instructor Len Pagliaro was in Lander, getting by between NOLS courses by working at the Lumberyard as a bus driver and mechanic. "In his usual fashion Scott said to me, 'What are you doing tomorrow?'" Len recalled. "He told me he had four guys from upstate New York who had hired him to take them up Wind River Peak, and he wanted me to help out."

The group set out the next morning with Len and Scott, ages eighteen and nineteen, in the lead. The clients were two men in their forties and their teenaged sons. "We ran into a NOLS course coming out as we were going in," Len told me, "and we ran into a NOLS course back there, and we ran into a NOLS course as we were hiking out, but we were the only ones who made it to the top of Wind River Peak." They had encountered a whiteout on the mountain, and as they came down from the summit had difficulty finding their tracks. "There were a few times when it was a little dicey and the clients were getting concerned, but it was fine," Len said. "It was a cruiser of a trip."

Scott organized a second and much more ambitious Mountain

Madness trip several years later, a climb of Mount McKinley. Fellow NOLS instructors Michael Allison and Paul Calver helped lead the expedition, and they succeeded in guiding several clients to the summit.

"I was always going to have a company called Mountain Madness," Scott told a magazine writer years later. "It's always been Mountain Madness because that's what I am, that's what we do." He had mentioned the name and the idea to Jeannie in 1974. Three years later Jeannie helped him design a Mountain Madness business card with an icon that was supposed to be the silhouette of a mountain with the moon rising over it. The Bruces delighted in pointing out that it more closely resembled an oil spill, or an Orca whale nosing a beach ball into the air.

By the time he moved to Seattle, Scott felt he was outgrowing NOLS and was ready to launch out on his own, enough so that he had bright yellow T-shirts printed with the mountain and moon icon. MOUNTAIN MADNESS was printed above the image and the line SCOTT FISCHER AND FRIENDS, RENTON WASHINGTON appeared below.

Wes Krause was another eager to begin breaking away from NOLS. He had been directing the school's Africa program from a base in Kenya. His contract with NOLS was coming to an end, and he was interested in organizing game-viewing safaris and climbs on Kilimanjaro and Mount Kenya for clients who would pay him directly rather than sending their checks to NOLS. "Scott and I talked about it and we said, let's work together and get our own company moving," Wes remembered.

It seemed natural to invite Michael Allison to join them, too. Michael was one of the early Bruces, and had plenty of experience leading trips in Alaska and instructing courses for NOLS. "Wes decided he would be the Africa branch of Mountain Madness," Michael told me recently. "Scott and I would team up to handle North America and the international travel side of the company. We each threw in $500, pretty much all of our life savings, and Mountain Madness was launched." That was 1982. One of their first acts was to replace the previous Mountain Madness emblem with one featuring a grinning Scott-like character sporting a climbing helmet, a mountain peak reflected in the lenses of his sunglasses. Several years passed before the founders got around to meeting with a lawyer to draw up papers for incorporation.

Mountain Madness would be something new, at least the way Scott, Wes, and Michael envisioned it—an adventure travel company that would take clients anywhere in the world, provide them with the logistical support they needed, and help them reach the top of whatever mountain they wanted to climb. It wouldn't be a skills school like NOLS, though there would be seminars to teach climbing and mountain travel, and the three founders were natural-born teachers, able to dispense plenty of knowledge along the way. Nor would it be a character development program like Outward Bound, though the three knew that an expedition would be fertile ground for growth. Mountain Madness was intended to offer the experience of mountaineering adventure. The joys and challenges of alpine travel had long been at the center of the lives of Scott, Wes, and Michael. Sharing that love of adventure with others seemed both obvious and logical. It would be fine if the company also made money, but Mountain Madness would allow the three to spend plenty of time in the mountains, something they felt compelled to do anyway.

The Mountain Madness business model had some precedent in the world of river running. Watercraft guide Richard Bangs had founded Sobek in the mid-1970s to take small groups on rafting trips down rivers far from home. The skills required for wilderness watercraft travel lay primarily with the guides steering the rafts. Clients were expected to share the paddling, but were mostly responsible for not falling overboard. Guides did most of the work in camp, too, as they set up the tents and prepared meals. So many supplies could be stowed on board a raft that menus often leaned toward the luxurious. Mountaineering, on the other hand, especially in remote locations and at high elevations, could be austere, demanding, and uncertain, presenting challenges to all who signed up.

The first Mountain Madness brochure offered climbs in South America, Alaska, Africa, and the Pacific Northwest, and an ice-climbing seminar near Ouray, Colorado. Scott filled undersubscribed trips by reducing fees and bartering services.

"A friend of mine who knew Scott took me to a seminar to learn how to ice climb," Dale Kruse told me of meeting Scott for the first time. A dentist living in Craig, Colorado, he found himself caught up in the energy of Mountain Madness and deeply appreciated Scott's optimism and encouragement. Dale had a four-wheel-drive pickup that could negotiate the narrow road to the frozen waterfalls outside of Ouray where the seminars took place, and Scott offered to waive Dale's course tuition in exchange for using the truck to haul gear and people up to the climbs.

"I spent the next seven or eight New Years there with Scott," Dale continued. "He would rent an apartment and the social thing was a big part of our time there. We did our own cooking and sorted climbing gear all night long, made lunches for the next day, and then went climbing. Scott got everybody involved, and it was a lot of fun."

Nowhere on the Mountain Madness brochure was there a mention of Mount Rainier, even though it is *the* mountain in the Northwest, the tallest of the volcanoes, and the most sought after by experienced climbers (who could ascend it on their own) and by novices (who needed guides and gear to get to the top). Rainier is so big that it creates its own weather patterns, sometimes fading into the mists for weeks at a time. When it reappears, it is a tremendous snowy presence rising above the dark forests.

The National Park Service had long controlled commercial access to the mountain by granting a single concession for a guide service to charge a fee to lead clients to the summit. Operated by Lou Whittaker, Rainier Mountaineering, Inc. was the only company to hold the concession. Most RMI clients went up the south side of Rainier, hiking from the Paradise Ranger Station at 6,000 feet to Camp Muir at 10,000 feet where they spent the night, then ascending the final 4,000 feet up glaciers to the top of the mountain.

Legally prohibited from guiding paying clients in the park, Scott did his share of bootlegging Rainier by guiding Mountain Madness clients to the summit via Camp Sherman and the Emmon's Glacier on the mountain's east side, a route not frequented by Rainier Mountaineering. It was a cat and mouse game with the Park Service rangers and others patrolling the heights of the peak. Len Pagliaro told me about helping Scott lead a group of Mountain Madness clients on a Rainier trip. "I remember sitting at Camp Sherman near some other climbers," Len said. "One of the Rainier Mountaineering guides came into camp, and when he saw us he said in a really loud voice so everyone could hear, 'So Scott, are you here with some of your *not clients* again?' Everybody knew what Scott was doing."

Many also knew that the Mountain Madness office in the Fischer-Price home was fast becoming the social center for Scott's ever-increasing circle of friends he met during backcountry journeys, while he was bicycling, and even as he ran errands around town. He made them all feel welcome in his mountaineers' world. NOLS instructors coming through Seattle could count on rolling out their sleeping bags on Scott's basement floor. When he flew down from Alaska, Murray the Fisherman would bring an ice cooler loaded with salmon and halibut for spontaneous backyard barbecues. Everyone was a potential Bruce, a possible Friend of Scott. It was in Scott's nature to connect with people, and if they happened to sign up for a Mountain Madness trip, that was fine, too.

Jeannie was woven into the Madness as an energetic partner in the fun radiating through the Fischer-Price house. At least she was engaged until it was time for her to go to work. She would disappear into the bedroom and return wearing her tailored Alaska Airlines pilot uniform, her hair pulled back and a look of serious professionalism on her face. The sorts of jokes that had sent her into gales of laughter an hour earlier now seemed to bounce off her, unacknowledged. She seemed to throw a switch and transform from Mountain Madness co-conspirator into seasoned airline professional. The conversion was similar to what I had seen with Scott who was always the life of the party in town and in camp, but absolutely serious and single minded once the climbing began.

Of the three cofounders, Scott soon found himself the only one in Seattle. Wes Krause was spending much of his time in Africa leading Mountain Madness climbs on Kilimanjaro and game-viewing safaris into the Ngorongoro Crater and the Serengeti. Half a world away from Seattle, though, Wes was more attuned to the needs of the program in Tanzania than the overall fiscal health of the parent company.

The realities of being co-owner of a tenuous start-up business soon became apparent to Michael Allison, too. "I was married and I needed to work, so I decided that Mountain Madness was fun and everything, but it wasn't going to support me." He turned over his share of the company to Scott and Wes, and moved to Atlanta to help his brother develop a more traditional company. "I told those guys I didn't want to be an owner, I just wanted to guide trips. So I led a lot of trips for free and was thrilled to do them." That left Scott, the most enthusiastic of the three but the least capable business-man, in the Mountain Madness office in Seattle where he would have the most responsibility for overseeing the company's day-to-day operations.

Across town, Dan McHale was building his backpacks. For many prospective customers they were overbuilt, but for the right person a McHale pack was the perfect match. Mountain Madness was shaping up that way, too. It could be an awkward, often jury-rigged experience, but for certain clients, the company adventures were more exciting than anything.

What Mountain Madness needed, in addition to someone with the savvy to manage the business side of the company, was to make itself known to more of those particular clients. Scott thirsted for good publicity for Mountain Madness, and that wasn't going to happen with sneaking around on Rainier and taking friends on trips for free. The Mountain Madness founders were simply going to have to become better known, at least prominent enough to draw crowds to the outfitting stores to see Mountain Madness slide shows and hear stories of alpine challenge and adventure.

Scott and Wes were all for that, of course. Soon they would em-bark on complicated climbs in East Africa and the Himalayas. Those who recognized the risk and difficulty understood that Scott and Wes were building resumes every bit as admirable as the Ned Gillettes of the world. Making Mountain Madness a success, though, was going to require even greater leaps of faith than walk-ing through fire.

CHAPTER 9

Kilimanjaro the Really Hard Way

I see the climb Scott and Wes Krause did on the Breach Icicle as a remarkable accomplishment. There were very few people in the world at that time who were attempting to climb ice at that standard. Also, because of the deteriorating conditions of the glacier and the ice on Kilimanjaro, it was an "end of an era" type accomplishment. These things position Scott as a young climber and adventurer of great status.

—Wally Berg, climbing partner and Everest mountaineer

KILIMANJARO RISES ABRUPTLY from the plains of Tanzania with little in the way of foothills and no surrounding range of lesser peaks. There is nothing to suggest the sudden appearance of the continent's highest mountain rising snowy and huge above the dusty brown swirl of the African veldt. Even so, from a mountaineers' point of view it rates hardly a mention. It comprises crumbling volcanic rock that is of almost no interest to rock climbers. Its summit is high, but steep trails reduce the challenge of reaching the top to endurance and the ability to acclimate to the thin air at 19,000 feet. Unless, that is, one sets out to ascend Kilimanjaro via the Breach Icicle, a route that had been completed only once before Scott Fischer and Wes Krause tried in 1984, and never since.

From a distance, Kibo—the main promontory of the Kilimanjaro massif—appears symmetrical and almost smooth. But approach closer, especially from the west, and it slowly reveals itself to be broken and ragged, the result of powerful volcanic forces that blew off a portion of the crater rim encircling the top of the mountain. That opening is the Western Breach. Beside and below it, the Breach Wall forms the enormous western face of Kilimanjaro. Two and a half miles across and lifting steeply from the convoluted lava-rock valleys of the Great Baranco and Little Baranco, the Breach Wall rises more than 4,000 feet to Kilimanjaro's summit. The upper half of the wall is encased in the huge expanse of the Diamond Glacier. The lower half is covered by the Balletto Icefield that was, when Scott and Wes first saw it, even larger than the glacier above. The icefield and the glacier are almost fully separated by a band of rotten volcanic rock, joined where the band is narrowest by the Breach Icicle, a frozen pillar rising nearly 300 feet.

As happens on almost every mountain, successful the first climbers seek the easiest way. The goal is simply to get up the thing and then get back down alive enough to tell the tale. Intentionally looking for added difficulty is far from the minds of those for whom reaching the top ahead of everyone else is achievement enough. In the case of Kilimanjaro, the first to set foot on the highest point was a German traveler named Hans Meyer, who made the trip in 1889 with Tyrolean mountain guide Ludwig Purtschelleer. A man of independent wealth, Meyer footed the bill for a Kilimanjaro expedition that included porters ferrying loads from lower camps to those higher up. Reaching the top, Meyer christened the mountain Keiser Wilhelm's Peak in honor of the emperor of the German Empire.

Over the next eighty years, mountaineers went up Kilimanjaro via nearly every conceivable route. The 1970s saw concentrated efforts by climbers to complete the most difficult ascents by scaling the glaciers draping the western side of the mountain. Their successes narrowed the remaining unclimbed lines until there was only one left—the Breach Wall Direct.

In theory, anyone attempting the Breach Wall would ascend the Balletto Icefield, climb the Breach Icicle, and then continue up the Diamond Glacier to the Kibo summit. The emphasis for many years was on the words *in theory* because, in addition to fusillades of ice and stone firing down the face, the Breach Icicle has about as much stability as a Christmas tree ornament. In places as thin as window glass, the icicle possesses a honeycomb consistency that can turn to dust under the blow of an ice-climbing tool, or disappear in a cloud of shards glinting in the light of the African sun. The existence of the Breach Wall Direct route was, then, only conjecture. Proving it could be done would involve such daring and risk that it seemed unimaginable anyone would try. Of course, that made it all the more attractive to climbers in search of the next impossible adventure.

In 1978, Americans Rob Taylor and Henry Barber climbed the Balletto Icefield to the base of the Breach Icicle. Barber was the same climber Scott Fischer and his buddies had respectfully watched years earlier climbing on the cliffs of the Schwangunks in New York state as he had made his way up routes the boys could only imagine climbing on their own. A portion of the icicle broke away as Rob Taylor began scaling it. He fell, fracturing his ankle. Taylor's book *The Breach: Kilimanjaro and the Conquest of Self* gives a harrowing account of his struggle to survive until rescuers, who had to travel for three days, could reach his remote location and evacuate him to a road.

Austrian climber Reinhold Messner happened to be on Kilimanjaro a few months after Taylor's accident. Recognized today as one of the most accomplished of all mountaineers, Messner was several years into a series of notable ascents. As a training exercise for an Everest attempt, Messner and his climbing partner Konrad Renzler had intended simply to dash up Kilimanjaro by one of the tourist trails, enjoy the thin air and distant views from the summit, then go back the way they had come.

Hearing of the recent failure of Taylor and Barber to complete Kilimanjaro's last unclimbed route, Messner and Renzler instead set off to give it a try. They positioned themselves at the foot of the Balletto Icefield and then ascended with tremendous speed, completing the climb in twelve hours, an effort energized by their eagerness to get off the Breach Icicle and out of harm's way. In his book *Free Spirit*, Messner remembered that "The risk had been incalculable. The technical difficulties of a face, I can estimate. But how to calculate avalanches of debris flying around our ears? How was I to estimate whether the piece of ice, on which my fingers were clamped, would bear my weight?" He went on to say he wanted no part of ever again climbing the Breach Wall Direct.

No one else did either, at least not for the next five years. But if Scott and Wes were going to climb with the big dogs, having the Breach Icicle on their resumes would be a pretty good way to go. At least that's how it seemed in January of 1983 as they were bouncing across Kenya in Wes's Land Rover on the road from Nairobi toward the Tanzanian border, eager to see what that Icicle was all about.

It was Scott's second trip to Africa. In 1978, the year Messner climbed the Breach Icicle, Scott and Wes had traveled to Kenya on their own dime to discover what there might be to do, especially if that meant going vertical and particularly if they could get a crack at Kilimanjaro. In Nairobi they met several members of the Mountain Club of Kenya who were preparing for the Kenya Triple Dash, a one-day combination road rally and rock-climbing competition consisting of a rock climb at each of three areas separated by distances of many miles. "Yeah, yeah, we'll do that," Scott told the club members arranging the race. "We're good to go!" There was the small matter of not having a motor vehicle, which can be a disadvantage when one is entering a car rally, but Scott and Wes were willing to deal with that little complication if and when it became an issue.

The day before the race they hitched a ride to Lukenya Hills, the site of the rally's first rock climb, a few miles south of Nairobi. Early the next morning they broke camp, completed the required climb, then approached another climber and explained their pedestrian situation. He was happy to let them ride along with him to the next climbing area, but he intended first to stop by his house and have lunch. "You want to join me?" he asked.

Food *and* a ride? That sounded fine.

At Ndeiya west of Nairobi they finished their second climb, then hitched fifty miles farther west to climb the basalt cliffs of Hell's Gate.

Throughout the day the boys quizzed the local mountaineers

about climbing Kilimanjaro, and were cautioned that the border between Kenya and Tanzania was closed due to political tensions. Scott and Wes also learned that there was a Kenyan Outward Bound base not far from Kilimanjaro. "Hey, it's a big border," Wes said. "Nobody's going to see us sneaking across to climb Kili."

They thumbed their way in that direction for several days, but rides were scarce until the driver of a beer delivery truck took them to Loitokitok, the village closest to the Outward Bound facility. Scott and Wes walked the rest of the way to the OB headquarters, where the staff told them that, yes, as if they hadn't already noticed, that was Kilimanjaro filling the southern skyline. They also explained that although crossing into Tanzania without permission was ill advised and perhaps quite dicey, it was physically possible to hike from Loitokitok to the mountain.

That was all Scott and Wes needed to hear. They put on their packs, walked south, and a few miles out of Loitokitok came to a road marking the border between Kenya and Tanzania. They jogged across the road and hurried into brush on the far side. Just when they thought they had made it over the border undetected, a man emerged from behind some trees and demanded to know their business.

"Oh, you know, just on our way to go climb Kilimanjaro," Scott told him.

"Do you have permission?"

"Yeah," Scott said, "sure we do."

"Let me see it."

"Well, it's not like we have anything in *writing*," Scott replied. "We just talked to this guy who said it was okay."

Six more men materialized suddenly. They weren't in uniform, but one was carrying a rifle. The men demanded that Scott and Wes open their packs and show what they were carrying. It wasn't much, just camping gear and food for the Kilimanjaro climb. The first man told Wes and Scott that they were trespassing in Tanzania, they had no paperwork to be in the country, and it would be very good if they went back the way they had come as quickly as possible.

Scott and Wes gathered up their gear and trudged dejectedly back into Kenya where they sat awhile in the shadows of some trees. "Let's try it again," Scott said. "I know we can get in there." They peered out from behind the trees toward the border and caught sight of the men on the Tanzanian side of the road looking back at them. The patrol showed no signs of going away anytime soon. Scott and Wes thought about ducking through the brush for a few miles and crossing the road somewhere else, but they finally resigned themselves to the fact that they were under surveillance and that at least for the moment, Tanzania just wasn't going to happen.

"We blew off Kili for that year," Wes told me later, "but we knew we had to get back over there sometime and climb that bloody mountain."

Wes was the first to return to Africa. In 1979 he was offered the directorship of the Kenya-based East Africa branch of the National Outdoor Leadership School. Teaching three-month courses for NOLS students, he learned much about the local flora and fauna, became fluent in Swahili, and explored the cultures of East Africa. He also continued to study Tanzania and investigated ways to enter the country legally. When Scott next came to visit in 1983, Wes felt that the pieces were falling into place so they could at least get to the base of Kilimanjaro. After that, the way they reached the top would be up to them.

Wes was eager to introduce Scott to the part of the world he now considered his home. They stayed with a Maasai family Wes had befriended, sleeping in a grass-roof hut made of sticks and mud. They shared meals of cow milk and blood and goat meat, and watched the Maasai boys tending the cattle.

Wes explained to Scott that when the boys reach puberty they dye their hair red, dress in colorful robes, build ornate headpieces of bird feathers, and attend rituals to become Maasai warriors. "A boy used to have to go out and kill a lion with a spear, but the shortage of lions and Maasai boys has kind of put an end to that." A boy must also allow himself to be circumcised, Wes said, and should he flinch during the application of the blade, he would be shunned from the heart of the tribe. He could have pointed out that other cultures have other ways for young men to prove themselves. They might, for instance, try climbing Kilimanjaro's Breach Icicle.

From Nairobi, the two set off in Wes's Land Rover to cross the hundred miles of Kenya to the Tanzanian border. The urban clutter of Nairobi did not extend far beyond the city limits, and in a few miles they were speeding along a crumbling blacktop in open country. Giraffes loped in slow motion past termite mounds ten feet high. Gazelles ricocheted off the shadows of eagles and vultures drifting overhead. The passing scene was a picture book come to life, full of vibrant colors and the rich smells of smoke and dust and wildlife spun up by dry winds and baked in the heat of the equatorial sun.

At the border village of Namanga, the pair let the Land Rover cool down while they sat in the shade of a tin-roof café and ate hard-fried eggs and chapatti bread, and drank cups of sweet tea. A Maasai woman walked through the shed where they were eating, her head shaved, bright beads and dangles hanging from her ears, a red-and-white-checkered cloth falling loosely from her shoulder.

Even though Wes had a permit and thought he understood the process, crossing the border for the first time still proved to be a hassle. Tanzanian officials questioned them at length on why they had a permit and what they intended to do while in Tanzania. Scott and Wes filled out currency declaration forms, which at the time didn't seem like a big deal. Meanwhile, Maasai streamed back and forth over the border, oblivious to proprieties of boundaries or the documentation of a national identity.

After they were waved through, Scott and Wes drove another hour to the city of Arusha where they were suddenly confronted with the realities of the money scene. Foreign currency was tightly controlled. Everytime the two paid for something, the amount was to be recorded on their currency declaration form. Before leaving Tanzania they would have to show any money not accounted for on the document. The adventurers also discovered that stepping into an Arusha alleyway to trade American dollars on the black market would yield a grocery sack full of Tanzanian bills worth ten times what they could get at a bank, but that produced no paperwork to show that they had handled their funds in a manner acceptable to the authorities.

Kilimanjaro was buried in clouds, but as Wes steered the Land Rover toward the mountain they could tell by the strained pitch of the vehicle's engine that they were climbing. The road lifted them from the hot plains of Maasai country into the misty forests of the Wachaaga tribe. At road's end they came to a park entry gate manned by uniformed Tanzanian officials. The officials knew enough English and Wes knew enough Swahili to understand that he and Scott would have to hire a guide and at least two porters to proceed any farther. The officials tallied up the costs of the park fees and payment for the support staff. The total was more than all the money Scott and Wes were carrying.

"Look," Wes told them, "we've come all this way to climb the mountain and here is how much money we've got, so we just have to figure out a way to make this work." The officials were unmoved, watching impassively as the would-be climbers felt their frustration rising.

A man overhearing the conversation motioned for Scott and Wes to follow him. "Come here," he said. Beyond earshot of those at the gate, he introduced himself as Francis Kishingo, a Chaaga tribe member who lived near the park and had led many people up Kilimanjaro. "You wish to climb the mountain?" he asked.

Yes, Wes said. They wanted to take the tourist route and camp in the summit crater for a couple of days to get used to breathing the thin air. Then they planned to descend partway down the far side of the mountain and climb the Western Breach Direct route, right up the Breach Icicle. He told Francis how much money they had, the problems they were encountering because of their currency declaration forms, and their eagerness to get started toward the top of Africa.

"The Breach Icicle?" Kishingo asked, alarmed. "You sure you want that?"

"Well, Francis, we looked at the map pretty hard and that really does seem like the best thing to do," Wes said.

Kishingo told them that five years earlier he had helped Reinhold Messner get into position to climb Kilimanjaro that way, and while Francis hadn't gone up the Breach Direct route himself, he knew about it. If they were really serious, he could help them. "Wait here," he said. It was a remarkable coincidence that they should find not only someone to help them with paperwork, but also a man who knew exactly where they were headed. "Pretty good Bruce karma," Scott whispered.

Francis talked with the gate officials and came back with a currency declaration form left behind by a previous Kilimanjaro visitor. Scott and Wes couldn't quite follow all the fine points of the arrangements Francis was working out, but before long they were inside the park and Francis assured them they had enough money to cover all their plans. That included hiring Kishingo to guide them and three porters to help carry their gear. The climbers would have preferred to go on their own and felt more than capable of finding their way and hauling their packs, but park regulations required them to hire local help and they knew from the start that they wanted Kishingo to be their guide.

Kishingo instructed the porters to take the mountaineering hardware, rope, and extra provisions halfway around the mountain and up to a hut beside Arrow Glacier near the Breach Wall. Then he accompanied Scott and Wes for the two-day ascent of the Marangu Trail that leads from the park gate at about 5,000 feet of elevation to the broad floor of the summit crater at 18,600 feet. They pitched their tents and for several days were the highest people on the continent of Africa. They strolled along the rocky rim of the crater to the very top of Kilimanjaro. They scrambled up the loose gravel of the cinder cone in the middle of the crater and looked down into the steaming throat of the volcano, their nostrils filling with sulfur. They walked past the glaciers draped across the northern half of the crater. Before they crawled into their tent they peered into a night sky so crowded with stars they had difficulty picking out familiar constellations. They both felt great to be mountaineers, happy to be together again, and exhilarated to be approaching a climb that would require every bit of their daring and skill. Even if they didn't succeed on the Breach Wall, they would be able to say they had camped on top of Africa. It was a very good time, indeed.

The landscape was hidden in cold morning fog as they broke their crater camp and followed Francis through the Western Breach and down the west side of the mountain. For several hours they descended the steep rock, barely able see their feet in front of them. The fog dampened sounds and there was hardly a breath of wind. "Kishingo, man, I don't know," Wes told their guide, "I think you've got us lost."

"No, no," Francis said, "I know exactly where we are going." Having no other choice, the two stuck close to him for the rest of the morning, and by some sort of internal reckoning, Kishingo brought them to the Arrow Glacier hut. True to his word, the porters had deposited the gear and food inside the circular metal shelter.

The sky cleared, giving Scott and Wes their first look up at the massive Breach Wall that makes up much of that side of Kilimanjaro. The lower half of the wall was covered with the Balletto Ice Field and the upper half was shrouded by the Diamond Glacier, the two expanses of white joined by the slender pillar of the Breach Icicle. Wes and Scott were stoked by what they saw, excited to get started but also aware that great difficulties lay ahead.

Francis retraced his steps to the summit crater and then hiked down the Marangu Trail to Kibo Hut at 15,000 feet on the east side of the mountain where he promised to meet the climbers after their climb. The two friends were completely alone on their side of Kilimanjaro. If they ran into trouble, no one could offer aid or know, at least for several days, that something had gone wrong. And there was plenty that could go wrong.

For starters, the long ascent to the lower edge of the Balletto Ice Field was on almost vertical volcanic rock so crumbly they could find few places to secure the hardware that would allow them to anchor their rope. They climbed with tremendous care, and by midday had reached the Balletto Ice Field. They put away the rope, strapped crampons onto their boots, and climbed the steep ice and snow to a bivouac site below the Icicle. In the golden light of late afternoon they rolled out their sleeping bags, collected water melting off the rocks, and brewed a pot of tea, all the while looking above them at the Icicle. "Whoa," Wes said to Scott, "this could be harder than we thought."

In the journal that Wes kept during the trip he recorded the details of the following day's climb:

July 21—Up at 4:55. Started coffee and early morning organization, and belayed Scott up from his bed for coffee and a quick breakfast. Packed and gone by about seven.

The rest of Balletto Icefield looked like a long, fairly steep traverse, and it was, with lots of climbing into and back out of runnels with pretty brittle ice in places. Scott's feet were a bit cold to start with, but a 10 minute stop-and-swing session cured him. Finally under the Icicle we could climb vertically instead of horizontally—a real relief. Scott reached a nice belay scoop about 20 meters up from the base of the Icicle on its right hand side, where he sunk in a tube (ice screw) and threw me a rope. Good to have a belay after lots of cruising without one. The climbing was no harder than what we had been doing, but there is always a bit of relief to know a fall doesn't mean the long ride.

Looking up, it became obvious that the really hard pitch on the Icicle would be the first one. It was meant to be mine, but I'd been away from serious ice climbing for over two years, and I was a bit leery of the steepness. I convinced Scott the pitch had his name on it.

The pitch started with a couple of overhanging moves, though Scott had no problem with them. "We've got it now," he shouted when he got above the first bit, but little did he know what really lay ahead—curtain ice so thin in places it was barely a sheet of glass. What few tubes were put in were thankfully good, but much too far apart.

The pitch moved out from a small stance about 40 ft. from the belay onto a sheet of overhanging ice some 40 ft. long and less than 5 in. thick. Full of large holes, the sheet ended abruptly, and standing precariously at the top, we could look down behind it and see that much of the sheet was totally free-standing.

Next came about 30 ft. of hard, unprotected rock climbing. It led back to the right onto a vertical ice ribbon so narrow it was safest to climb just on its edge, using an ice tool with the right hand and fist jams between the ice and rock with the left. With one bare hand banging on rock and the other on ice, Scott marked the route with a trail of blood.

The very last bit of rope I could squeeze from the belay stance put Scott on a nice rocky ledge nearly at the top of the famous Icicle, but his workout wasn't quite over. As he hauled the line to bring up his pack, the pack caught on overhanging ice and hung tight, refusing to move up or down. Scott gave the haul line slack and I opened fire on it with softball-sized rocks. A square hit finally freed it, and it continued its journey to the belay ledge.

My own ascent of the Icicle made me quiver a bit. Since the pitch had taken Scott an hour and a half to lead, it was obviously a hard one, most likely overhung. Not only was I a bit rusty on serious ice, but I also had to climb with a pack on my back. The top rope assurance was not only appreciated but also used in the long overhung section. I managed not to add any more blood stains to the route, passed Scott, and led right through to the much lower angle summit snowfield. An hour of third class cruising brought us to a small low-angle rock outcropping where we tanked up on snow melt and filled our bottles for future use. We stowed all gear and set out across what seemed an endless snowfield to Kilimanjaro's main summit, Uhuru.

They neared the top of Kilimanjaro at dusk, watching the sun glide down into the clouds, and as they came over the summit they saw the rise of a nearly full moon. Its light was strong enough for them to complete their climb without using headlamps, and they came down to Kibo Hut under what Wes called full moon power. There had been times when they were on the icicle that they had wondered if they would ever witness another sunset or moonrise, and now they were blessed with a double display. They hiked easily down toward Kibo Hut, feeling the relief and exhilaration of the accomplishment and the deepening of their already strong friendship.

"The hut was a welcome sight to us," Wes wrote in his journal, "and since we were a few hours late, Francis was glad to see us. We were extremely happy. The climb had been *great!*"

Look in the climbing books and you can find documentation of

Reinhold Messner's first ascent of the Breach Wall Direct, a feat he lists as among his finest. Finding mention of the second and only other ascent, the one made by Scott Fischer and Wes Krause, is almost impossible. And yet, they had done it, too. They had proven themselves able to climb with the best in the world.

Over the years many other climbers have looked at the Breach Icicle and decided it wasn't worth the risk. Those who have attempted it have seldom gotten as far as the Icicle's base, and those who have managed to reach the pillar have turned back after realizing the ferocity of the falling rocks and bits of ice. As if to seal the deal, climate changes in equatorial Africa have caused the glaciers of Kilimanjaro to recede and the Breach Icicle to become, if such a thing were possible, even more fragile.

Scott and Wes came down Kilimanjaro with Kishingo and spent several days visiting Francis's family at their home near the mountain. They drank *mbege*, a local beer made of fermented bananas and millet seeds and served in hollowed-out gourds. Friendships were sealed, and in the years to come Wes would count on Francis as a guide and business partner as Wes's East Africa climbing and safari offerings grew into a company of his own.

Yet Scott could not relax and simply enjoy the moment. He had been committed to climbing Kilimanjaro and doing the Breach Wall Direct, and now that the climbing was done, he was anxious to be on his way. He wanted to get to another climb, or at least return to Seattle and start planning the next adventure.

"By the time we got back to Arusha we finally had this whole Tanzania thing figured out," Wes told me of the end game of their Kilimanjaro trip. "We had our currency declaration form forged so we could get around the government. I was ready to stay in town as long as it took to get enough fuel to drive to the Serengeti and back." But he couldn't convince Scott to stick around.

"Come on," Scott told Wes, "we climbed the mountain. Let's get out of here."

"Bruce, don't you want to go out to Ngorongoro and watch lions and elephants and have a great time? Don't you want to drive around in the Serengeti?"

Scott's answer was no. He was ready to get home and see Jeannie, plan the next adventure, and figure out the next climb.

"How can you come all the way to Africa and not go see an elephant?" Wes asked.

As seemed so often the case for Scott, he was on a schedule. Sometimes it was a calendar imposed upon him by others, but more often it was his own internal clock restlessly ticking away, driving him toward the next adventure and then the one after that. Stopping on horizontal ground seemed not to be in his constitution.

The two agreed that in the future Wes would run Mountain Madness adventures in Africa with the help of Francis Kishingo and Scott would take clients to the rest of the world. They were also wrapping their heads around another climb to do together—a fast, lightweight ascent of a mountain in Nepal called the Fang. Its summit was a mile higher than either of them had ever climbed, and they were convinced that ascending the Fang would open up good things for them and for Mountain Madness. In any case, it was sure to be great fun. But if they thought the Breach Icicle had been a test, they had no idea of the challenges that lay in store for them in the Himalayas. Compared with what was to come, the Breach Icicle had been a piece of cake.

CHAPTER 10

Annapurna Fang

*The mountain is considered to be very difficult to climb,
and its summit has been reached only once, by an Austrian
team in the spring of 1980.*
    —Elizabeth Hawley, Kathmandu journalist and documenter of
                                                    Himalayan climbing

THE FIRST TIME I heard the story of the Fang was in 1984 as the
three of us sat in the living room of the Fischer-Price house shortly
after Scott Fischer and Wesley Krause had returned from the Himalayas. Rapidly gaining back most of the body weight he had lost,
Scott Fischer had filled a plate with a couple of tortillas and a heap
of scrambled eggs covered with salsa and a scoop of plain yogurt.
Wes Krause kept his foot moving, bending it this way and that as he
had been instructed by his physical therapist. The angry red scar up
the back of his leg had begun to heal, but it was still fresh enough to
be tender and the ankle had nowhere near its full range of motion.

A few months ago, more than two decades after Scott had finished that plate of tortillas and eggs, I heard the story again. This
time I was sitting in Wes Krause's home near Bozeman, Montana,
where he and his wife Melly Reuling and their children were enjoying a yearlong sabbatical from their home and adventure travel
business in Tanzania. The kitchen of their Montana house was tem-
porarily dominated by a large aluminum tub containing half a dozen
baby chicks and two small ducks cheeping in the straw under a heating lamp, a project of the Krause children, Eliza and Makari. Eliza,

age eight, had spread paper and paints all over the kitchen table and was deep into artwork that was as yet identifiable only to her.

As Makari watered the potted plants he hoped to nurture through the Montana winter, he contemplated his most recent brush with authority. Accustomed to living in Tanzania where a ten-year-old boy needs a few tools, he had taken his knife with the four-inch blade to a recent grade school play practice, intending to while away the time when he wasn't required to be onstage by honing the knife with a whetstone. A teacher had seen him and, in this age of terrorism and school lockdowns, had gone fairly ballistic. Wes was much more sanguine about the event, reminding Makari that he wasn't in Tanzania anymore and a bit of discretionary disarmament before heading to school could go a long way toward honoring the customs and belief systems of the local culture.

Before setting off to climb Kilimanjaro's Breach Icicle in 1984, Wes and Scott had already been looking ahead to what they might try next. Scott's eye was on Everest, but at the time he had no real Himalayan experience and Wes had never been to Nepal. They wanted to start somewhere, though, so agreed they would get themselves to Nepal and climb something big. Anything, as long as the summit was high and the cost of the permit was low.

Friends returning to Kenya from trekking in the Annapurna region west of Kathmandu showed Wes photographs of the mountains they had seen. Among them was a peak called Varaha Shikhar that, because of its distinctive shape, was nicknamed the Fang. It was part of the same gigantic massif as Annapurna I, the world's tenth highest peak.

Wes relayed the word to Scott in Seattle that the Fang looked like a perfect climb for them. The base could be reached fairly easily. At 25,000 feet, the summit was wicked high, but not so lofty that they would need to carry bottled oxygen. Perhaps best of all, Wes discovered that a Fang permit for the autumn of 1984 would cost just $900. He sent off the paperwork, and the Mountain Madness Fang expedition was soon on its way to the Himalayas.

The Fang had seldom been attempted. In 1979, an Austrian team turned back when one of their members fell to his death. An

Italian expedition attacked the peak later that year with 250 porters, 15 high-altitude Sherpas, and 20 climbers. They were repulsed after a month of bad weather and severe avalanche danger and, like the Austrians before them, they also suffered a fatality. The Austrians returned the following year and were successful as Joseph Mayer, who described himself as a restorer of church steeples and an alpine guide, and Hermann Neumair, a roofer of church towers, joined high-altitude Sherpa Ang Chepal on the summit. Two years after that a French expedition stalled out in the face of storms, and no other climbers had approached the mountain until the Mountain Madness Fang expedition arrived.

The only route description the Mountain Madness team could find was a report by the Austrians written in German. They deciphered enough of it to discover that the Austrians had spent thirty-five days completing their ascent. Scott and Wes figured they could do it much more quickly with a light, self-contained expedition with no established camps along their route.

They invited Joe Hladick, a NOLS friend, to round out their team. They estimated it would cost just under $4,000 to climb the Fang, minus the permit fee and their airfare. To that end, they raised $1,000 in cash donations and received another $1,500 from the newly instituted NOLS Instructor Development Fund. The Sierra Designs equipment company gave them clothing, tents, and camping gear, and they were beginning to feel as though they had the whole expedition planning scheme figured out. What they didn't already know, they could learn along the way.

Wes received a letter from the Nepalese government encouraging the climbers to use the Kathmandu-based Sherpa Cooperative to coordinate the logistics of the expedition. He wrote back to stress that they wanted their Fang trip to be alpine-style climbing with no Sherpa support above base camp. "The Sherpa Cooperative told us they would put together the whole expedition," Wes told me. "They would hire the porters, buy the food, prepare the loads, and take care of everything. Of course, by the end there were kind of a lot of them."

Scott and Joe were the first to arrive in Kathmandu, and Scott enjoyed showing Joe around the city he'd last visited nearly a decade earlier on his journey from Europe with his friend Rainbow. They rented bicycles to cruise around, visited Freak Street and the Thamal section of town, and ate at Joe's Place. "Sure brings back memories," Scott wrote in a journal he was beginning to keep for the trip. "We met some folks, did the Kathmandu thing."

After Wes arrived, they went to the Ministry of Tourism for their Fang permit and were told that the price had more than doubled. In addition to the two porters for each climber and the four base camp staff members they had planned to hire, they also learned they were expected to hire additional porters for the members of the camp staff, and since those people would need to be fed, too, the expedition needed to arrange for a cook tent. Eager to be light and nimble, they suddenly found themselves employing twenty-one porters, a cook, a mail runner, a *sirdar* who would oversee the activities of the porters and camp staff, and a liaison officer who would track the expedition's progress and file reports with the Nepalese government's Ministry of Tourism.

They also sat down for an interview with Elizabeth Hawley. A Reuters reporter working in Kathmandu since 1960, Miss Hawley had documented Himalayan climbs long enough that by the early 1980s she was legendary for her thoroughness, her pointed inquiries, and her knack for finding mountaineers in Kathmandu before their expeditions left town and soon after they had had returned. "She asked a lot of questions," Scott wrote in his journal.

The Annapurna region of Nepal had been opened for trekking in the 1960s by Colonel Jimmy Roberts, a British commander of Gurkha soldiers who had stayed in Nepal after World War II. He had been the equipment manager for the British expedition making the first successful ascent of Mount Everest, and served the same post in 1963 for the first American expedition to succeed on that mountain. In the 1960s he began taking clients on treks around Annapurna. He called his company Mountain Travel, and it represented the real beginning of trekking in the Himalayas. A guidebook he prepared for his Sherpa trekking staffs introduced the concept of serving "bed tea" each morning as clients awoke in their tents, a custom still practiced in the Himalayas and on Kilimanjaro.

Scott, Wes, and Joe left Kathmandu in mid-September and began their approach to Annapurna Fang as the monsoon season was ending, accompanied by P. B. Thapa of the Sherpa Cooperative. "It was a riot hiking with him," Wes told me. "He knew somebody in every village, usually some sweet Sherpani. We'd hang out in a little guestee and drink tea. He definitely got us hooked on Himalayan trekking." It also got them acquainted with P. B., who would be involved with Mountain Madness trips in the Himalayas for years to come. The experience was similar to that of Scott and Wes meeting Francis Kishingo on their Kilimanjaro climb a few months earlier and making a friend who would become their longtime business partner in Africa.

Near the village of Lete they left the Annapurna Circuit trail and hiked across plowed fields toward the Fang, a sharp incisor of a mountain protruding above an immense, snowy ridge stretching for several miles. "We were looking up and saying, oh my God, that thing is huge!" Wes recalled. "We'd been to Alaska and climbed there a fair bit, but those Himalayan peaks were an eye-opener."

Scott's awe with his surroundings was tempered by a bad case of bed bugs. "The second night out we were camped on this really high ridge between two drainages," Wes said. "We could see the Fang right ahead of us, the first time we got a look at the whole ridge. It's getting cold, we have this beautiful view of the Fang, and there's Bruce with his clothes off, washing with kerosene to try and get rid of the bed bugs before he can go to sleep."

"I'm bumming on the bed bugs," Scott noted in his journal.

When they reached the Base Camp they were surprised to discover it was at an elevation of just 11,500 feet, and that they couldn't ask the porters who had come with them to continue up the steep tundra to the Advanced Base Camp they wanted to establish 5,000 feet above. Scott, Wes, and Joe resigned themselves to ferrying loads of gear to the higher camp, and enough food to last twelve days.

Food consisted mostly of dehydrated meals with somewhat dubious nutritional value. They also had a tent, a modest selection of pitons, carabiners, and other rock-climbing hardware, and snow pickets—aluminum stakes three feet long that could be driven into the snow and used as belay anchors. For rope they carried 600 feet of thin Perlon line and several other ropes that, when tied together, gave them an additional 600 feet. "And then," Wes said, "we decided to just go for it."

Going for it meant climbing 4,000 feet to the top of the ridge, following the narrow crest for two miles to the Fang's summit tooth, and then climbing that. And then coming down. And doing it all before exhausting their food supply. "None of us," Scott said, "had any experience on a mountain of this scale."

They soon discovered the snow that coated the steep face of the ridge was very loose. "Real deep trail-breaking in sugar snow that does not hold steps," Scott wrote. "Instead of quick climbing we faced four full days of arduous, waist deep trail-breaking on a fifty-degree slope." At night they prepared packets of mountain food. "Tasty, but meager," he reported.

It didn't get any easier when they had deposited their gear and provisions on top of the ridge and gotten a look at the route ahead. The two miles of high-altitude technical ridge travel would be along the thinnest of knife edges with a drop of a vertical mile on either side. They would need to be roped together the entire way, establishing belay anchors to protect themselves in case of a fall.

Then the most minor of mishaps threatened to end the expedition. As he was scooping snow from the ridge to carve a platform for the tent, Joe lost his grip on the team's shovel and watched it careen down the mountain. In an environment where steepness abounds and a level niche is a rare phenomenon, the shovel had been critical for establishing flatness. No freakouts, but can three guys live on a ridge like this without a shovel? Scott wondered.

They cooked a packet of dehydrated sweet and sour shrimp while they thought about it. Joe was having difficulty adjusting to the altitude and decided the Fang wasn't for him. He bid his friends farewell, descended the ridge, and made his way back toward Kathmandu.

"We were seriously contemplating turning around, too," Scott said, but figured he and Wes could use their cook pot to scoop out tent platforms. Carrying heavy packs, they started moving up the thin ridge toward the distant Fang summit, driving snow pickets into the narrow crest and using them to anchor the rope to protect themselves if they fell off either side. Along the way they had to negotiate steep fins of rock and snow. At times they were forced to cling precariously to the face as they traversed below obstacles.

Late in the day they cached the packs, returned along the rope, and spent the night in their tent. They broke camp the next morning and carefully moved the rest of their supplies up to the packs, collecting the aluminum anchor pickets as they passed them. Pitching the tent where the packs had been left, they hoisted the loads to their shoulders and again moved out, setting anchors and laboriously working their way forward as far as the rope would allow. Again they cached the packs and again returned to the tent to melt snow for water, cook a little dinner, and crawl wearily into their sleeping bags. The next day they did it all again, and the days after that, too. Moving from morning until dusk they could, with luck, advance along the ridge in the sky about 1,200 feet a day.

Dragging all that rope through the snow and hauling heavy packs through the thin air of such high elevations gradually wore them down. To add to his struggles, Scott was suffering increasingly severe diarrhea. "We just cannot continue to work at this rate," Scott noted in his journal after a week on the ridge. They had food for only more three days, and most of that was in the packs they had left the previous afternoon closer to the tooth of the Fang. They estimated that if the weather held, the summit was still two hard days of travel beyond the packs.

They awoke the following morning to find themselves pinned down by a fierce Himalayan storm. "At times we look up to see only thick clouds being driven over our peak with incredible force by winds that must be 80–100 miles an hour," Scott wrote, "then the sky will break some, blue will poke through in places, and it won't look nearly so hostile." They were tempted to move forward to the packs and their food, but that would mean rolling up the tent and taking it with them. Without a shovel to level a platform for it, their chances of making an emergency bivouac were slim. "Survival is the thing up here," Scott scribbled. "We just cannot get caught between camps. It's a bummer how hard these decisions are to go or not to go."

The storm abated, and afer another night without food they moved ahead to the packs and searched in vain for a tent site. They didn't need much, but the angle of the ridge top was so severe they found nothing they could use, even after digging at the ice and frozen rocks with their cook pot. Frustrated, they retreated and pitched the tent where it had been the previous nights. They portioned out their provisions and, despite their hunger, ate as little as possible for sustenance.

"Our tent at that last site was at something like 24,000 feet, but the ridge went on forever and we were still a real long way from the top," Wes told me. "We were basically out of food, so in the morning we decided to just get to the summit." They pressed along the ridge through the following day and, far from the tent, burrowed down into the snow when it got dark, then arose to finish off the Fang.

"We had abandoned our tent and we were out of food and we were climbing up that damned ridiculous ridge," Wes remembered. "We were close enough to the summit we were pretty sure we could make it." And then they got into real trouble.

"It was incredibly windy and I was up ahead in these horrific, terrible snow conditions, trying to climb egg shells of rime ice," Wes told me. "We had to chop it away with our ice axes or stomp it down to get some footing, and it was really slow going.

"Scott was belaying me on a crusty, nasty pitch that had lots of overhanging stuff. I was about three hundred feet in front of him. He turned his head to look off the edge, and the wind blew the contact lens out of his eye, so now he's Cyclops."

That, finally, was enough. Wes shouted to Scott that he was coming down, that the Fang wasn't going to happen. "I packed the snow by stomping on it to consolidate it as best I could and then drove in a picket," he recalled. "I clipped the rope to it and I started rappelling back down."

The snow under Wes's feet felt a little unstable and then a lot unstable, and then he felt nothing underneath him at all. "A huge chunk of the ridge just evaporated and I tumbled away with it."

The stake he had set as an anchor had held his weight while he was rappelling, but when he fell off the ridge, the force channeling up the rope came onto the picket from a different direction and it flew out of the snow. Fifty feet, a hundred, two hundred, Wes was sliding down the face of the Fang with nothing but a mile of air beneath him, picking up speed as he dropped, bouncing off snow and rock, and then the rope went taut. The force of his fall screamed through the nylon fibers to the end of the rope tied to an aluminum stake that Scott had buried in the snow and was standing on with all his weight. Against all odds, that anchor held.

"It was my worst climbing nightmare come true," Scott said, "watching my partner disappear off the ridge and down onto the face where I couldn't see him."

Hanging from the rope by his seat harness, Wes was startled to discover that he was still alive. Below him the closest flat ground was a mile away, and above him were 300 feet of almost vertical rock and snow bisected by the rope that connected him with Scott and any hope of a future beyond the present moment. God, I'm fine! he thought. *This is amazing!* He had fallen off the Fang and he wasn't dead. Everything was going to be okay.

Wes righted himself and made his first tentative moves to climb, then realized his right foot didn't work. The points of the crampon strapped to his boot had caught on the snow while he was falling and had wrenched his foot upward, and for some reason his calf muscle had balled up below the back of his knee. Slowly he made the one-legged climb to the crest of the ridge.

The two men sat beside each other, perched at 24,000 feet on a ridge so narrow they couldn't take a step either to the left or the right. They hadn't eaten in days. Scott was ill and Wes could move only by hopping on one foot. "Scott was shitting his brains out and I had a foot that didn't work," Wes said. "It was getting so epic."

They decided at least to try returning to their tent. That took them two days, with another overnight bivouac in the snow without shelter or food. They found a little oatmeal and some powdered milk in the tent, but nothing more. The route atop the ridge to the point where they could safely descend stretched out before them, a distance they realized they had neither the strength nor the time to travel. Their only chance was to bail off the ridge and rappel a mile down the North Face. Before they could do that, though, Scott had to retrieve the rope they had left anchored across a complicated section of the ridge as they had neared the tent.

"I made sure that I had Wes's knife so that if I fell and was hurt and hanging I could just cut the rope," Scott later wrote in his journal. "No way Wes was going to be able to save me. Obviously no room for error. It was a day of a lot of thinking. Appreciation of family, friends, life. Got to be so careful."

Together again, they sorted the ice screws, pitons, and sling that could be used as rappel anchors, and realized they might have just enough hardware to make it. They drove a stake into the snow on top of the ridge, tied all the ropes together, and used a carabiner to clip the middle of the line to the stake.

"We would set up the best anchor we could," Wes said of their descent method. "I would tie myself to that anchor and get down in the snow in as stable a position as I could find. Scott would tie in to one end of the rope and I would lower him with the backpacks half the rope length, about six hundred feet. When he'd found a place he could stand, I would throw off the other half of the rope and rappel down that half. Once we had a new anchor set, we would pull down the rope and start the whole process again."

Where there was strong ice, they could twist in an ice screw. If the ice was weak or there was only snow, they used the cook pot to dig down to bare rock, then searched for a crack where they could drive in a piton and trust to it the weight of each man as he made the next rappel. One by one they sacrificed their pitons, slings, carabiners, and ice screws, leaving behind the hardware they had used for an anchor as they brought down the rope.

"At least twice doing six-hundred-foot rappels we went over these overhangs and it was thirty feet back to the wall," Wes told me. "If a rappel had ended with one of us dangling away from the wall at the end of the rope, it would have been a disaster. We would have been stranded. But we were lucky. At the end of each rappel we managed to reconnect with the face."

Darkness fell and they scooped out space to rest in their sleeping bags on a ledge midway down the face. "We had a horrible bivouac," Scott said. "My coldest night, and I was really shitting. My feet were so cold I put on my boots in the morning without warming my feet. I knew I was freezing them, but in the interest of survival I didn't do anything except concentrate on going down."

Through much of the next day they continued to set anchors, rappel, find footing, and anchor in again. When they were sure they were within 1,200 feet of the base, they used their last hardware to set an anchor, tied one end of the line to it, and threw the full length of the joined ropes down the mountain. Each man rappelled down, and they stood again on flat ground. "About two p.m.," Scott wrote, "we were off the accursed mountain."

"We left the rope hanging," Wes told me. "We were so outta there, stumbling back through the boulder field toward our base camp. I'm limping and Scott's shitting blood. Big head, little body, all withered away, he looked like a trout that had been in a stream without enough food."

The sirdar of their expedition ran to meet them with apples, biscuits, and cheese. He explained that the contracts for the rest of the support staff had expired and everybody else had gone home. The sirdar had used binoculars to watch them rappelling off the Fang. "I wanted to come and help you," he told the exhausted climbers, "but you know, I didn't have any way I could get there!"

"Well," Wes told him, "it was good that you were thinking about us."

They reached the village of Lete and stayed four days to recuperate. "As soon as we finished one meal we ordered another one," Wes said. "When the people told us there weren't any more chickens or any more eggs in the village, we decided it was time to leave."

They made their way to Jombsom where they hoped to board a plane. Bad weather had grounded the aircraft and many trekkers who had been on the Annapurna Circuit were waiting for flights out, so the weary men rested and ate for three more days before going to Kathmandu. They had been relishing the idea of staying at the Kathmandu Guest House or one of the other nicer places in the city, but the better lodges were full. They ended up far from the main thoroughfares frequented by Westerners, renting a place down a winding alley. Their room had no windows and barely space for two narrow beds. As they began to unload their packs, there was a knock at the door. It was Elizabeth Hawley.

"My God, how did you even know we were back?" Wes asked her. "And how did you know we were staying here?" She didn't say, but Wes and Scott assumed that because it had taken the two of them so long to return from the Fang, some of their Nepalese staff had gotten word to Miss Hawley. How she had learned where they were staying, though, remained a mystery.

Elizabeth sat on the edge of one of the beds, opened her notebook, perched her glasses partway down her nose, and interviewed them about their climb. She wanted facts, correct spellings of names, and accurate elevations and dates. Under "Accidents and Achievements" she wrote, "Krause twisted ankle while coming down from high point on Oct. 10." She thanked them, wished them luck, and was on her way.

"Some of the guys from the Sherpa Cooperative who had been with us earlier on the trip came around to see how we were, too," Wes remembered. "We told them we were pretty hurting. I had this bum leg and Scott had lost about half his body weight. The guys said, 'Well, at least you came back alive. That's more than many, you know.'"

Wes rented a bicycle and rode through the streets of Kathmandu to a hospital. His ankle had become huge. "It didn't really hurt, but I couldn't use it, couldn't push off my toes." A nurse took an X-ray and told him there was nothing that an elastic bandage wouldn't help. "I thought, well, I guess I'm a wimp after all," Wes recalled. "Here I was thinking there was definitely something wrong with my foot just because I couldn't make it work."

Five weeks later when Wes finally got back to the States, a physician checking his Achilles tendon discovered it was ruptured. His fall had ripped apart the tendon and his calf muscle was no longer attached to his heel. "Can you be in the hospital in two hours for surgery?" he asked.

No, Wes told him, he was scheduled to be in Tanzania in two weeks to take clients up Kilimanjaro. He had the surgery anyway. The following spring, after months in a cast and extensive rehabilitation, he was back on Kilimanjaro, and among his first clients was the surgeon who had repaired his tendon.

"The Fang got the better of us this time," Scott concluded in his writing. "While we climbed well, our lack of knowledge about the Himalayan climbing scene made our trip more difficult than it should have been. But we learned, and we'll not make the same mistakes again. And next time, we'll reach the summit of the highest mountain in the world." His optimistic prediction was off by only a decade.

In the kitchen of his Montana home, Wes finished retelling his Fang story. We sat quietly for a while watching the chickens hopping up onto the rim of the aluminum tank and then traversing unroped to the freedom of the kitchen counter. I knew that Wes, Melly, and their children had recently gone back to Nepal and trekked the Annapurna Circuit, camping near Lete where he and Scott had recovered from their climb so long ago.

"I looked up at the Fang," Wes told me, "and thought, what the hell had I been doing up there? There's not any question that if you keep doing that stuff enough, the odds are just so hugely against you. To go back to a place where I could so easily have died on that mountain and now to be there with my kids, I had to wonder what I had been thinking back then. At the time it had been fine, but I could not imagine putting myself into that kind of situation again."

He had pointed out to his children the route he and Scott had followed to get up on the ridge and the very long way they had traveled to get close to the Fang. He showed them the highest elevation they had reached and the face where the two of them had saved themselves with their long, desperate rappel.

"I was talking with them about what it had been like on the Fang and showing them everything," Wes said, "and they're looking at me and saying, 'Dad, you guys had to have been out of your minds.'"

CHAPTER 11

Rockin' with the Ruskies

Too much fun! You are having too much fun!
—Soviet Chaperone at the Caucasus International Mountaineering
Camp of the USSR

IN THE SHADOW of Elbrus, the highest peak in Europe, we're in the disco of a Soviet tourist hotel dancing with the sweet Soviet ladies. The women call it shakin' and after several bottles of *piva*—high-octane beer tasting like home brew—it's a good description of what's going on. Everything is loose and easy until a man in a black suit and dark glasses cuts off the stereo. "Too much fun!" he warns, wagging his finger at us. "You are having too much fun!"

At first we laugh it off, but the man is serious. We promise to keep our fun in check and he revs up the music again, then returns to the shadows to watch us stretch the boundaries of acceptable Soviet behavior, having more than our share of fun and adventure in a country being run like an eighth-grade study hall.

This is what it was like to travel with Scott Fischer in the early years of Mountain Madness. I had been working in the Mountain Madness office in the basement of Scott's house several days a week, answering the telephone and typing on the computer, and Scott invited me to come on a Mount Elbrus expedition—as long as I paid my airfare and covered my expenses. Wes Krause was going, too, along with two paying clients. Financially the numbers didn't even begin to add up, and yet we were soon on our way, flying sleek Scandinavian Air Service planes from Seattle to Copenhagen and then to Moscow. There we boarded an old Aeroflot airliner with bald tires on the landing gears and cigarette smoke rolling out of the cockpit, and flew a thousand miles south to an airfield at Mineralnye Vody.

Near the borders of Turkey and Iran, the Caucasus Range stretches from the Black Sea to the Caspian Sea, a high, jagged wall separating Europe from Asia. I knew from my reading that the Greek gods had chained Prometheus to a mountain in Caucasus as punishment for revealing to man the secrets of fire, and here Jason and the Argonauts had believed they might find the Golden Fleece. The maps showed mountains with magnificent names—Shkhelda, Ushba, Nakra, Donguz-orun, Chatyn-tau—and the tallest, Mount Elbrus. Rising to an elevation of 18,481 feet, it is the highest mountain in Europe and thus one of the Seven Summits, the collection composed of the loftiest peak on each of the seven continents.

In the 1980s the Caucasus Range was rarely visited by Westerners. Earlier flurries of activity in the late 1800s and 1930s resulted in European and American climbers completing many major first ascents in the region. Since then, war and revolution, distance and political differences had shrouded the range in mystery, rendering its granite peaks and glaciated volcanoes little known to climbers beyond the Soviet sphere.

In the mid-1970s, International Mountaineering Camps hosted by the Soviet Sports Committee began offering climbers of many nations opportunities to test the Caucasus' challenging routes and to scale Elbrus, and thus we found ourselves bouncing along in the back of an old bus toward a tourist hotel at the base of the mountains. Imagine Estes Park, Colorado, circa 1950, with the rudiments of a tourist industry against a backdrop of spectacular alpine terrain. In all, eighty climbers had come that summer to the 1986 Caucasus Climbing Camp of the USSR. They arrived from Austria, Bulgaria, Hungary, Poland, Czechoslovakia, Italy, and included the five of us with Mountain Madness. Each team was assigned a Soviet mountain guide and, if necessary, an interpreter. The camp also offered logistical support and had both a rescue team and a local physician on call.

"Sasha will help plan your climbs," Marina told us as we settled into the Spartan hotel rooms. A striking young woman, Marina was our translator, Sasha our guide. Trained to interpret for foreign businessmen visiting Moscow, Marina used her annual vacation leave to come to the Caucasus. Sasha spent his winters teaching mountaineering in a Leningrad high school and his summers at the climbing camps. We soon suspected that an attraction to one another, more than the attraction of the mountains, might be what brought Sasha and Marina to the Caucasus each year, a notion given credence when we realized Sasha spoke perfectly good English.

On an order form written in some approximation of English we checked off the food items we wanted, then followed Sasha and Marina into a storeroom near the hotel kitchen to draw five days' provisions for our Elbrus climb. "Your chicken," Marina said, handing us a skinny bird barely plucked, its head, legs, and guts intact. "Sugar." Sasha rolled a sheet of paper into a cone, poured in a kilo of granules, and passed it across the counter. So it went down the checklist—a slab of beef, a large glass jar full of yogurt, a head of cabbage, a fistful of salt.

"You got any plastic bags for this stuff?" Wes asked. He was sporting a huge mustache that started just below his ears and swept out in front of his face. A group of Czechoslovakian climbers we had met in the hotel were calling him *Sumec*, their word for a fish with mustache-like feelers. Wes would put his hands alongside his ears and flap them like gills while he mouthed the air, and the Slovaks would collapse with laughter. For him there was never any bad news, simply opportunities to wing it, to keep moving forward, to work out solutions to problems as they arose. The problem of the bags, for example.

"No bags," Marina told us. "You did not ask for bags."

"Well, I'm asking now."

"Now is not the time for asking," Marina replied.

"So," Scott said, "if we had written *bags* on the list of what we wanted, we could have some bags now?"

"Now there are no bags."

"Right."

We stowed the food in the nylon stuff sacks and ditty bags we'd planned to use for carrying our toothbrushes and spare socks and tents. Sasha added to our pile of provisions by handing us an old, dented pressure cooker that, with its safety valve welded shut, looked more like the product of a Soviet nuclear weapons program than a benign kitchen item.

Leaving Marina at the hotel, Sasha led us on the long ride up creaky gondolas and ski lifts to the 12,000-foot level of Elbrus. From there we strolled another 2,000 feet up a gentle snowfield to Pruitt 11, a three-story metal hut resembling a Jules Verne submarine run aground in the snow. Constructed in the 1930s to shelter Soviet soldiers engaged in high altitude training exercises, the hut had been given over to tourists, most of them Russians. A hundred or more would ride the lifts and make their way to the Pruitt 11 each summer afternoon, spend a raucous night singing, cooking, drinking, and dancing, then descend to make room for the next day's hundred. Most we saw were poorly equipped for the cold and unprepared for foul weather. Having no sunscreen, they shielded their faces with white towels or by wrapping gauze around their heads.

The top floor of the shelter was reserved for climbing teams. We unloaded our packs next to those of Czechoslovakians who were hoping to make a ski descent from the Elbrus summit. It was our intention to approach Elbrus by climbing on the first two days from the hut at 14,000 feet to an elevation of about 16,000 feet, returning at night to the hut. That would allow our bodies to acclimate to the thin air. With the gear we stowed up high, we could establish a camp and spend a night just below the Elbrus summit.

Sasha argued that we should go all the way to the top and be back before dark. "Teams of weak Hungarian women do it in a day!" he exclaimed, hoping we would be properly embarrassed. "Two Czech women are up there right now!"

"We like to camp high," Scott explained. "We want to wake up and see the sun rise."

"But what is the purpose?"

Much to Sasha's exasperation, we went ahead with our plan. The route up the mountain's glaciers was marked with wands, and as long as we were careful not to wander off the beaten track, we would not need to use ropes. By the end of the second day, we'd cached all the gear we needed for a high camp and had come back down to Pruitt Hut. Sasha told us he was deeply concerned that the

Czechoslovakian women farther up the mountain had not been responding to radio messages.

That night a storm swept across the Caucasus. Thousands of feet above us near the Elbrus summit, one of the Czech women collapsed from pulmonary edema. The stricken woman's partner fought her way through the storm to summon aid at the hut, and at dawn Sasha led a Soviet rescue team up the mountain. Flying ice and punishing winds drove them back, and we waited in the hut while the storm raged. Nine climbers had already died on Elbrus during the year, a startling toll for a mountain that seemed to offer no substantial difficulty save for its elevation and weather.

More Soviet climbers came up to the hut to beef up the search team, but the storm prevented them from going farther. They were strong and eager, but poorly equipped with thin nylon parkas, khaki canvas gaiters, and lots of sweaters. "You trade your boots? I have titanium," one of them asked us. He opened a bag and spilled out a dozen lightweight ice screws intended for anchoring ropes to the frozen faces of mountains and waterfalls. No, we told him, we needed our boots for climbing. Another Soviet asked if we would swap our parkas for titanium screws, and soon we were besieged by Soviets eager to swap screws for gear. The screws had been made by machinist friends of the climbers who told us they had nothing else to trade.

"In our country, they don't make good climbing equipment, so we must get American gear at the mountaineering camps," one of them explained. "If we let this chance pass, we have to wait another year." We agreed that at the end of our stay we would do some dealing.

The Czechoslovakian climbers were subdued, sharing with us their concern for the Czech woman. No one was sure quite how to react. "A climber's in trouble on the mountain and we can't go get her," Scott said. "Does that mean we shouldn't eat and drink and visit? What do you do when you're pretty sure somebody's not coming back?" We ate and drank and visited, but our thoughts were always on what might be happening near the top of the mountain.

The storm abated three days after it had begun. Plumes of snow still spun off the Elbrus summit, but the Soviets were able to reach the woman where she lay face down in the snow. They wrapped her body in a nylon tent fly and lashed it to an aluminum sled, then used ropes to guide the sled down to Pruitt 11. Cold and tired, they hurried inside to drink black tea sweetened with jam. The body lay in state, surrounded by the quiet, clear beauty of the Caucasus Range.

We ascended Elbrus the following morning. In their zeal, the rescuers had carried our high camp cache down the mountain, leaving us with only the provisions we could carry for a single day's climb. After six hours of steady effort we reached the top of Europe. It had been a long and gorgeous walk-up, and as we stood on the summit it was difficult to believe that a few days earlier the Czech woman had died close by.

We stayed in the hut for a final night and then went down into the sweet-smelling forests of the valleys far below. At roadside stands we spent a few rubles on spicy beef shish kebabs and warm, fragrant loaves of bread. When we reached the hotel in the middle of the day, Marina was all aglow. "I am so happy my men have come back to me," she gushed, hugging us all but mostly Sasha.

Sasha and a tall Russian climber named Losha invited us to their hotel room for vodka to celebrate our ascent. Some of the Czech climbers crowded in, too. "Very good," Sasha proclaimed, spilling the liquor into our glasses and looking us in the eye. "More?" He poured again. "Eh?" Another splash. We drank it down, the Soviets cheered, and Sasha opened another bottle. It quickly became a vodka showdown with Communist and American livers having it out over shots at high noon.

"The Russian, he drinks like this," explained one of the Czech climbers, taking a quiet sip with his elbows tucked against his body, "But the Czech, he drinks like this!" He extended his elbow and took another drink, then uttered a sigh of pleasure.

"And the American drinks like this," Scott shouted, extending his elbow, throwing back a shot of vodka, and then roaring, "Yah!" From then on, everyone in the room roared "Yah!" with each elbow-raising drink.

Sasha told us that Losha, respected by the other Soviet climbers as one of their best all-around mountaineers, was preparing for a climbing competition, an annual event that meant a great deal in the regimented world of Soviet climbing. Success in the contests could help a climber maintain his position as a state-sponsored guide and qualify him to secure a job teaching mountaineering. The best climbers were proclaimed Soviet Masters of Sport, an honor that carried with it many perquisites.

"But Losha has no good boots," Sasha told us as he poured more vodka. "He has no good parka or wind pants. Your Bob is the same size as our Losha. We would like to trade ice screws for all of Bob's equipment."

We drank another round of vodka and shouted, "Yah!"

"Hell," Scott said, "we'll trade you Bob *and* all his gear if you give us Losha and let us take him home to America."

"No, we must keep our Losha!" Sasha protested with alarm. "You cannot have our Losha!" I can't say that I was all that excited about the bargain either, though it would have been interesting to be labeled a Soviet Master of Sport.

Awash with alcohol, we made our way unsteadily downstairs to the hotel dining room for a lunch heavy on potatoes, meat, and more vodka. Partway through the meal Wes pushed back his chair and rose from the table. "A little walk, I think," he said, his words slurred. "I could use a walk."

The rest of us continued to eat, interrupted a few minutes later by the hotel man in the black suit and sunglasses. "Excuse me," he said, "but your friend seems to be lying on the lawn."

Scott asked if that posed a problem. "Yes," the man told us, "yes it does."

Well, then. When Scott stood up the rest of us did, too, and we marched a wavering route through the lobby and out the front door, trying to get in step with one another to make our procession a little more official. Wes was lying on his back on the cool, green grass in front of the hotel, his eyes closed and a peaceful smile pushing up the ends of his mustache. Holding each of his wrists was a *babushka*, a Russian grandmother. They were scolding him and trying to drag him off the lawn by yanking on his arms, but he was too heavy for them to budge.

We gathered around and looked down at him. "Wesley, are you

okay?" Scott asked. Yes, he said, his eyes still closed. The babushkas reefed again on his arms and again managed to move him nowhere.

"You want us to do anything for you?" No, Wes replied, couldn't think of a thing. The babushkas continued to haul at him, but he seemed to be anchored to the turf.

"He's all yours," Scott told the Russian ladies, and we paraded into the hotel, past the man sitting in the lobby in his black suit and sunglasses, and back to our table to finish lunch.

In the days that followed, I backpacked with several of the Czechs and some Russians over the high passes separating Europe from Asia while Scott and Wes made an unsuccessful bid with one of the Mountain Madness clients to climb Ushba, the most spectacular peak in the range. Its twin 15,000 foot summits rise like Siamese Matterhorns. The approaches are guarded by long, glaciated valleys and busy icefalls, and the climbers had found themselves not well enough equipped to take on the steep, snowy ridges leading to the summits.

With just a few days left in the Caucasus, Scott convinced me to climb with him at least partway up Ushba. We were joined by Jana, a woman who had come to the Caucasus with another expedition. She had decided that the Mountain Madness team was having more fun than the climbers in her group, and so had switched allegiances and thrown in with us.

The three of us spent much of the first day going up an icefall, a pitch of glacier tumbling down a steep, narrow chute of the mountain. Roped together for safety, we navigated around crevasses and past balanced blocks of ice, the teeth of our crampons biting into the hard snow. At the top of the icefall we reached the level snowfield of the Ushba Plateau where we made our camp. Enjoying distant views of Elbrus, we cooked dinner and spent the evening looking up at the route leading above the Plateau toward the heights of Ushba.

A warm front moved through during the night, and as we lay in our sleeping bags we could hear the icefall below us reacting to the rising temperature by softening and shifting, cracking and booming. "We'd better get down the icefall while we can," Scott told us in the darkness. "We sure don't want to be on it when the sun hits it."

At first light we quickly packed our gear, roped up, and started the descent with Scott in the lead, followed by me, then Jana. The icefall had changed dramatically, our route of the previous day freshly bisected by yawning crevasses. The footprints of our ascent led right to the edges of new chasms and then, on the far side, continued again. Urging us to be quick about it, Scott led the way around the widest crevasses, jumped the narrow ones, and had us making good time until he suddenly plunged up to his shoulders into a hidden crevasse. One of my crampons was planted tightly in the ice when the jolt on the rope pulled me off balance, twisting my ankle and sending me careening down the ice. "Self-arrest!" Scott shouted as I shot past him, and I managed to embed the point of my ice axe into the slope just as the rope between us tightened and Scott braced himself to help stop my fall. Jana was in a full-on tumble of body, pack, crampons, and gear as she careened over me and then hit the end of the rope and lay still.

Scott was out of the crevasse and beside me in a moment. With a handful of snow he rubbed blood from my forehead. "You hurt?" he asked. "You okay?" As far as I could tell I was all in one piece. "Next time don't self-arrest with your face," Scott told me, and slid down to check on Jana. She'd had a history of injuries to her foot and feared she might have broken her ankle. When she got up, though, she could bear weight on her leg and seemed more shaken than injured.

The icefall was still groaning around us, and we could see the sunlight moving across the valley. "Let's go, let's go, let's go!" Scott urged. We reassembled ourselves and moved on, reaching the valley floor an hour later. Now it was my ankle that hurt, and without the icefall to worry about I realized that it hurt a lot. There was enough swelling that my foot had become tightly jammed inside my boot, and I knew that if I loosened the laces I would never get them tied again. Because of the swelling, the boot was acting almost as a walking cast. Scott took much of the gear out of my backpack and stowed it in his own to lighten my load. In a bottle of water he mixed powdered milk and a couple of sugar packets and had me drink it for energy and hydration, then we started hiking along the edge of the glacier as it curved down the valley. We hiked all day, getting back to a road and then to the Soviet hotel just after dark.

I went to my room, pulled off my boot, and watched discolored swelling balloon around my ankle. The hotel physician arrived. Despite the pain shooting through my foot, I couldn't help but notice that his assistant was a beautiful Russian girl wearing jeans and a red flannel shirt, her hair braided into long pigtails. The physician looked at my ankle, opened his bag, and took out a tin containing a camphor-laden balm that he massaged into my foot. It hurt like hell, but in the meantime, the girl had cradled my head between her breasts and, in the ultimate of pain-pleasure scenarios, was gently washing the wounds on my forehead. I assumed that the moment the physician stopped massaging my leg, the girl would be done with me, too, and I certainly didn't want her to go away. But then the man began wrapping my foot and ankle with an elastic bandage, pulling it as tightly as he could, and I yelped. "Leave this on for thirteen days," he told me as he closed his bag and got ready to go. "In thirteen days you will be healed."

I wanted to argue for thirteen days of forehead bathing, too, but the girl simply applied a large bandage to my skin and followed the physician out the door. I endured the thirteen-day tight wrap for, at most, thirteen minutes, then tore off the elastic band and in both pain and relief hobbled down to the hotel disco where the music was playing and Sasha and Marina were slow-dancing with each other to Iron Butterfly's "In-A-Gadda-Davida." Scott handed me a beer and the Russian climbers came by to remind us it was titanium trading time. The man in the black suit and dark glasses was on duty, sitting in the full blare of a stereo speaker, going deaf while he watched to see that we didn't have too much fun.

But we fooled him that night as we had all month, rockin' with the Ruskies in the heart of their own land. It was a good skill to have, but as Scott and Wes were about to discover, you can only mess with the Soviets so many times, and perhaps the mountains themselves, before they start to catch on.

CHAPTER 12

It's All Fun Until Somebody Dies

People dying is just part of the risk you take.
—Stacy Allison, Everest mountaineer and Pik Kommunizma team
member

IT IS A HARD, cold, and seemingly obvious fact that mountaineers sometimes don't come back alive. There are all manner of high country hazards. Avalanche. Thin air. Cold. Storm. Hunger. Exhaustion. Injury. Illness. Gravity. For many alpinists the dangers increase the attraction of their sport. There is a greater sense of living on the edge, of having one's senses fully alive because to do otherwise could be to lose one's senses all together.

Until 1986, with fifteen years of serious climbing behind him, Scott Fischer had never been with someone in the mountains when they had died. There had been plenty of close calls. Scott and Wes Krause had saved one another from disaster on Mount Drum in Alaska and in Nepal on the Annapurna Fang. Near the summit of Argentina's Aconcagua, Scott had come upon a Japanese climber named Toshi who was alone and succumbing to altitude sickness. Scott hoisted the man over his shoulder and toted him down the mountain far enough for thicker air to do its magic. Toshi recovered and the term *to Toshi* entered the Mountain Madness lexicon, as in, "I was climbing really well, but then the route got steep and I Toshi-ed out." Or, "I was in the gym trying to beat Fischer at pullups, but after twenty I just Toshi-ed."

What happened on Pik Kommunizma was different. Nobody joked about it afterward. No new terminology memorialized the event. It was the first and only death of a Mountain Madness client on a team that Scott was leading, and the man died cradled in Scott's arms.

Located in what was then the Soviet Republic of Tajikistan, the great peaks of the Pamir Range rise above 23,000 feet, and Pik Kommunizma, the highest, reaches almost 24,600 feet. The peaks intrigued Scott as an expedition destination because they were remote, challenging, and in a foreign land. He had made several trips to the Caucasus mountains to scale Mount Elbrus on the border between Russia and Soviet Georgia, and was eager to develop climbs there and in the Pamirs as staples of the Mountain Madness expedition menu. He had such high hopes for becoming a regular presence in the mountains of the USSR that he had enrolled in a Russian language class in Seattle.

The extreme elevation of the Pamirs also made them ideal for a 1986 springtime warm-up for a Mount Everest attempt Scott was hoping to organize for the following year. A number of climbers had expressed an interest in the Everest climb, and Scott invited them to come with him to test themselves on the heights of the Pamirs.

Wes Krause joined the Pamirs team as deputy expedition leader, the Achilles tendon he had injured while on the Annapurna Fang the previous year nearly healed. Stacy Allison signed on, too. She had met Scott in Zion a decade earlier and been deeply impressed by his willingness to help her learn how to climb. Her skills had continued to progress, and she had been to the top of Ama Dablam, a spectacular peak near Everest. Other Everest hopefuls who signed on to go to the Pamirs were Montana lawyer Geo Schunk, NOLS veteran Liz Nichol, and George Karhl, an acquaintance of Stacy.

Scott also marketed the Pamirs trip as a Mountain Madness offering and sparked the interest of a close-knit group of climbers who had come through the ranks of the Colorado Outward Bound School. They included Mark and Brad Udall, sons of U.S. Congressman Morris Udall and nephews of Stewart Udall, a former Congressman and President Kennedy's Secretary of Interior. Mark was serving at the time as the executive director of the Colorado

Outward Bound School. His wife Maggie Fox, who was also coming to the Pamirs, was a Sierra Club attorney. The resume of their friend Steve Monfredo included ascents of Mount McKinley and Annapurna South, the latter a climb above 23,000 feet that he had completed with Mark Udall. The Outward Bounders were preparing for a Himalayan expedition to Cho Oyu, the world's seventh highest mountain. Like Scott, they saw the Pamirs trip as both a great adventure and a fine way to prepare themselves for their big climb the following year.

The rigid structure of Intourist, the Soviet Union's state-run travel agency, made travel to the remote Pamirs almost as straightforward as expeditions to the Caucasus and Mount Elbrus. Mountain Madness could book clients into Moscow and then leave the rest of the arrangements to the Russians. It was a way for the Soviets to cash in on the willingness of climbers to pay for the privilege of going to the high places, and was also a means to control what foreigners could do and see in the far-flung regions of the USSR.

The Mountain Madness team touched down for a few days in Moscow, then continued to the city of Osh in southern Kyrgyzstan. A small plane lifted them into the Pamirs where they transferred to old school buses for the long drive over rugged roads to the Intourist climbing camp. With interpreters, camp managers, and a dining facility, the camp was similar to what Scott and Wes had found the previous year at the Caucasus climbing camp, only with tents rather than a hotel. After the climbers had acclimated for a few days, military helicopters ferried the team to the Pik Kommunizma base camp at an elevation of 14,000 feet.

Scott was convinced that the climbers who had come with him to the Pamirs knew what they were doing and could take care of themselves. They were all experienced mountain travelers who considered themselves capable of setting out the following year for significant climbs in the Himalayas. Surely they would be able to manage the Pamirs without much difficulty and without the constant attention of a hands-on guide. Scott planned to lead by expecting the climbers to determine their own agendas and schedules. He and Wes certainly had theirs.

"We felt like, hey, these guys are all getting themselves ready for eight-thousand-meter peaks," Wes told me. "It's not like we had to worry about taking care of them and making sure that they're acclimatizing well enough. They should be totally self-sufficient and organized."

Scott and Wes were accustomed to climbing together and had full trust in one another, especially after their ascent of Kilimanjaro's Breach Icicle and their attempt at Annapurna Fang. They were attuned to their strengths, and each knew that if he was climbing quickly, the other would be matching him step for step.

"When we got to the base of Pik Kommunizma, there were two other mountains nearby that we wanted to climb, too, Lenin and Korzhenevskoi," Wes told me. "We just wanted to knock out Pik Kommunizma fast, so we were going to push pretty hard."

Stacy Allison interpreted their message as, *We're going to go up and if you want to come with us, then come with us. And if not, we'll see you up on the mountain.* "I think for Scott that was a real typical scenario when he and Wes were climbing together," she recently told me. "It's not that they were disrespectful of anyone else, it's just that they had their agenda and you either keep up or you don't."

The first challenge on Kommunizma was a snowy climb over the 17,000-foot Borodkin Ridge. Beyond the ridge lay the broad, rising expanse of the Pip Plateau, and then a final steep 4,000 feet of mixed snow and ice leading to the mountain's summit. The climbers felt the effects of the thinning air as they hauled their heavy packs up the ridge. Stacy noticed that Steve Monfredo was having a little difficulty, but concluded that his shortness of breath was the result of altitude and exertion.

French and Bulgarian teams were also making their way up the mountain, and there were Russian climbers on the route, too. A group of New Zealand alpinists that included a young climber named Gary Ball shadowed the Mountain Madness team onto the Pip Plateau, encouraged by the possibility of dining off excess provisions they believed were being carried by the Americans. To further lighten their loads the New Zealanders had decided to travel without tents, taking shelter each evening in a glacial crevasse.

"Three metres below the surface we hacked out a comfortable platform where we spent an enjoyable night eating stew then sleeping soundly," one of them wrote of a night on the mountain. "Outside, the Russians and Americans in residence at Camp II spent a restless night holding on to their tents as they were battered by the wind. They were surprised at dawn to see three red-suited Kiwis pop out of a hole and drop down to join them."

The winds were being stirred by a low pressure atmospheric system the Soviets in the main climbing camp had been monitoring at long range. They radioed Scott to alert him that bad weather was rolling toward Pik Kommunizma and recommended that the Mountain Madness team return to base camp and wait for better conditions. Scott and Wes studied the sky and, though they could see what appeared to be a weather disturbance on the horizon, felt no urgency to descend. They checked the security of their tents and settled in with the rest of their team, and the storm the Soviets had warned about unleashed on them for three days and nights. The Soviets radioed again when the sky cleared, sternly ordering the American climbers to come down immediately. Believing they had made it through the worst of the weather, Scott again adamantly refused.

The Udalls and the other Outward Bound climbers were willing to defy the Soviets by staying high on the mountain, too, but wanted to wait a day for the snow dumped by the storm to settle and become less of an avalanche hazard. Scott was convinced that the danger was not severe. He, Wes, and Stacy packed up their gear, crossed the rest of the Pip Plateau, and then ascended halfway up the slope leading toward the summit. At 21,000 feet they spent the night, then ascended another 2,000 feet the next morning and carved tent platforms on the steep slope for the expedition's highest camp. Looking down the mountain, they could see their companions crossing the plateau and climbing up to join them.

"This lone German comes trudging up, too," Wes recalled. "We'd met him back at the Soviet climbing camp, so we were sort of buddies. He wasn't carrying a very big pack. We told him we thought he should just move in with us, but he kept going."

By nightfall all of the Mountain Madness climbers were together again, pitching their tents, melting snow, and cooking dinner. They hoped to climb the final 1,600 feet to the top of Pik Kommunizma the following day, but not everyone was in the best of shape. Though he assured others he was fine, Steve Monfredo continued to cough, and his breathing was becoming labored and noisy.

When Scott awakened the team at 2:00 a.m. to get ready for the summit push, he discovered that Steve and his tent mate George Karhl had decided they weren't going any higher. Maggie Fox and Outward Bound climber Mike Carr had chosen to stay behind as well. The four would start down the mountain after daybreak.

Those going to the summit followed the beams of their headlamps and, in the darkness, found themselves plowing through waist-deep snow. "We're in the tracks that the German had put in above us," Wes told me, "when all of a sudden the tracks end. It had snowed during the night, and here's this little mound in front of us. We poke around, and sure enough he's under a space blanket, lying there completely covered with snow."

The German climber awoke, shook off the snow, and began getting himself together as the Mountain Madness team moved on. "We're breaking trail, getting close to the summit, and the German guy comes motoring up and passes us and plows right on through that deep snow," Wes marveled. "Man, that guy was strong!"

Brad Udall felt his feet becoming cold and, concerned about frostbite, turned back. Liz Nichol had gotten a late start from the high camp and though she felt good, she realized as the morning progressed that she wouldn't be able to catch up with the others as they neared the summit. "I remember thinking, this is fine going up alone, but I don't want to come down it by myself," she told me, "so I turned around."

The climbers with Scott reached the top of Pik Kommunizma where they photographed one another next to a portrait of Lenin that marks the summit. They had gone high without significant difficulties and they felt strong. Returning to the now-deserted high camp, they got on the radio to inform the remainder of their team that they had succeeded and were in fine shape. That's when they discovered that farther down the mountain, things were not going well at all.

Earlier in the day as the summit team was ascending above the high camp, Steve Monfredo had started down the mountain by himself, intending to descend to the Pip Plateau as his first step in getting off of Pik Kommunizma. He had become disoriented and had wandered off the route, taking much of the day to complete what should have been a four-hour journey. Expecting to catch up with him during his own descent, George Kharl reached the Plateau without having seen Steve. When Monfredo did finally arrive at the Plateau camp, George helped him into a tent and zipped him into his sleeping bag.

Maggie and Mike had started down together and were making good time when Maggie fell and severely fractured her leg. Brad Udall joined them as he returned from his summit bid and helped Mike splint Maggie's leg. Drawing on their Outward Bound training, they fashioned a pack frame into a stretcher and used it to ease her down to the Plateau.

Scott and Wes reacted with disbelief to the news they were hearing over the radio. It was late in the day and those who had been to the summit were tired. Even so, they packed their gear and descended through the darkness to join the others now camped on the Plateau. The Outward Bound climbers were working out the treatment and evacuation of Maggie, and a physician from a team tenting nearby did what he could with limited resources to treat the symptoms of high altitude pulmonary edema that Steve was exhibiting. It was obvious that the only effective treatment would be to get him to lower elevations.

With the help of several other mountaineers, Scott and Wes rigged up a sled the next morning and started moving Steve across the Pip Plateau. "In the beginning we're dragging him because it was easy terrain and steep, so we could go downhill pretty fast," Wes remembered. As the day wore on and they descended into richer air, Steve improved enough that he could walk while the others assisted him.

"We're expecting him to start recovering quickly," Wes said. "It was obviously an altitude-related problem and we had descended thousands of feet. Scott and I are pretty burned out and are ready to rest a little bit. Steve is showing some signs of improvement, though not as much as we'd hoped for." They made camp and settled in for the night, then continued the long journey through the following day. "Steve was still about the same," Wes said. "It was depressing that he hadn't gotten better, but at least he hadn't gotten worse."

The descent became more difficult as they crossed ribs of rock on the face of the Borodkin Ridge, but they were making good progress. "We were getting close," Wes told me. "The bottom of the mountain was right there. We're going to be down in two or three hours and the Russians will have a helicopter to meet us, so everything was all in place. Monfredo's coherent, not getting better, but we're thinking it's okay, he's not so bad."

Scott had his arm around Steve Monfredo's back to support him when Steve collapsed onto the snow. He had stopped breathing and his pulse was gone. "It was real sudden," Wes said. "We tried to resuscitate him, but he died right there, two hours from the helicopter." There was nothing else they could do but wrap his body in the nylon fly from their tent and lower him on down the mountain.

The helicopter arrived to take the body to Osh. "Okay, you must come, too," Intourist officials told Wes and Scott, motioning for them to get into the aircraft and explaining that the Soviets weren't about to fly a deceased American out of the mountains by themselves. Scott and Wes were informed that they were to attend the autopsy, too. The Soviets wanted everything witnessed and fully documented so that there would be no questions later about what had happened.

"They took us to a hotel in Osh and reluctantly got us a room and told us to stay in it," Wes recalled. "There was nothing the Russians hated more than having to turn Americans loose in those sorts of places, but they didn't have the staff they needed to put somebody on us." Awaiting the arrival of Maggie Fox and shaken by the loss of Steve Monfredo, they had no interest in whiling away the hours sitting in a hotel. A few minutes after the Russians had left, they slipped out to wander the streets of Osh.

"It was a little Russian village with a bakery over here, butcher shop there," Wes remembered. Most of the people they met had never encountered an American, and when they discovered the origins of the two climbers, they would laugh and clap their hands. "They had all their little bits in place and everybody seemed to be doing fine," Wes continued. "It was a real eye opener for us to see."

Maggie Fox was brought down the mountain in a sled fashioned from half a plastic equipment barrel, then flown to the hospital at Osh. The Soviets located Scott and Wes and summoned them to attend the autopsy of Steve Monfredo's body.

"It was really a bad deal." Wes paused, then said, "We had to watch the whole process, and everything that they found, they wanted us to look. *See, signs of edema here.* What a bummer." The results indicated that the deceased man's lungs had probably been damaged years earlier by pleurisy and that his heart, enlarged and elasticized, could have compromised his health regardless of the effects of going to high altitude.

The death of Steve Monfredo was a profound shock to the Outward Bound community and deeply troubling to the rest of the Mountain Madness Pamirs team. Scott didn't say much about it, but as he was telling me some of the details, he became solemn and then quiet. Steve's death had certainly given him pause.

High mountains are dangerous places where people sometimes die. Scott was quite certain it wouldn't happen to him. He expected that he could be strong enough, smart enough, and lucky enough to come home alive. If anything, though, he was about to up the ante by finally climbing on Mount Everest where dying could be a fairly common occurrence.

CHAPTER 13

Everest North Face

Hundreds of sleepy Sherpas
Hired at dawn, to carry
Tea and socks to Chomolungma.

—Gary Snyder

IN A WAREHOUSE in a Seattle suburb, Scott Fischer sat cross-legged among the heavy cardboard boxes, marking off the last items on the long checklist in his lap. Each box was impregnated with wax to protect its contents from the vagaries of the upcoming journey by ship, railroad, and truck, and the boxes were sized to be lashed in pairs to the sawbuck saddles of Tibetan yaks. They were loaded with enough food and equipment to sustain fifteen mountaineers for the months they would need to climb the North Face of Mount Everest.

On his way home, Scott stopped at a grocery store to pick up diapers and baby formula, a couple of items that weren't on his Everest checklist. For the moment, though, they were every bit as important as what he had been stowing in the boxes bound for the far side of the globe.

Scott and Jeannie's first child, Andy Fischer-Price, had been born on May 13, 1987, and Scott felt fully connected with his son the moment he saw him. He loved to be with Andy, holding the little baby in his large hands and trying to figure out what to make of this newest Bruce. The template of his own childhood, that of a suburban family with children growing up with supportive parents, was beginning to take shape for him, too. Any nervousness he might have had about becoming a father seemed to fade when he and

Andy were together, and life with a son was richer than he had ever imagined.

Nothing changes a family and one's outlook more than the arrival of a baby, but new as that was for Scott, the old drive to climb was still there, too. Two months after Andy's birth, Scott would be on his way to the Himalayas as the leader of an Everest expedition. He had gotten the permit for the climb long before Jeannie had become pregnant, and had invested well over a year to organizing the team and getting everything ready. When there had been just the two of them, he and Jeannie had been able to accommodate his long absences without much difficulty. This time he would also be leaving a child. It was a new kind of challenge for Scott, and those of us watching wondered how it was all going to work out as he sorted the boxes of his family and home with those of being the leader of the 1987 American Everest North Face Expedition.

Everest's North Face lies on the Tibetan side of the border that bisects the Himalayas and separates Tibet from Nepal. The first attempts to climb Mount Everest had been through Tibet, commencing in the 1920s with British expeditions seeking a way to get close to the mountain, and then trying to determine how to reach the top. The Kingdom of Nepal did not allow foreigners to cross its borders, so approaching Everest could only be done by trekking from India into Tibet and coming at the mountain from the north. Among those taking part was George Leigh-Mallory, an English school teacher and a gifted climber.

In 1924 Mallory and his climbing partner Sandy Irvine were last seen above 27,000 feet on Everest's Northeast Ridge. Dressed in woolen clothing, Mallory and Irvine were carrying rudimentary oxygen tanks and believed to be climbing strongly when they disappeared into the clouds.*

Other British teams going into Tibet tried without success to climb Everest in the 1930s. World War II spelled an end to Himalayan expeditions for more than a decade, and the invasion of Tibet by

---

*Seventy-five years later Mallory's body was found well below the crest of the ridge. Evidence indicated he had fallen a long way. There was no sign of Sandy Irvine, and no conclusive proof that either man had been to the summit of Everest.

China in 1950 closed the north side of Everest to climbers outside the Communist sphere. Nepal opened its borders soon after that, and the focus of Everest mountaineering moved to approaches from Nepal's Khumbu Valley. While several Chinese expeditions did venture onto Everest from the north, teams of other nationalities were not allowed to try the mountain from Tibet until the early 1980s.

As Wes Krause and Scott were leaving Nepal after their 1984 attempt to climb Annapurna Fang, they heard about an Australian team pioneering an Everest North Face route. The way they went was daunting, but the Australians proved it could be done. That was good enough for Scott. He applied to the Chinese government for a permit and received permission to attempt the Australians' route in the fall of 1987. It was an audacious undertaking at a time when putting together an Everest expedition was an enormous task, especially for someone who had never set foot on the mountain. Even so, Scott felt confident he was about to open the way to the top of the world. All he needed to make it happen was a climbing team, money to pay for the permit and expenses, and a lot of boxes full of exactly the right stuff.

Scott was not looking for a team of mountaineering all-stars but rather people who had proven they were independent, strong, and accustomed to living in the backcountry. He wanted a bunch of Bruces, and he looked first to veterans of the National Outdoor Leadership School. Among them was Liz Nichol, who had been a student and an instructor during the organization's earliest days. "Scott thought the NOLS experience was really valuable," she told me recently. "I accepted the invitation to Everest with the attitude of just going as far as I could go, and that would be fine for me. And I knew that would be fine for Scott, too."

In addition to Liz, four of the other fifteen climbers who joined the Everest team were also women, a high percentage at that time for expeditions. Stacy Allison and her friend Evelyn Lees had learned the basics of climbing from Scott in the late 1970s in Zion, and Stacy had been with Liz Nichol and Scott in the Pamirs in 1986 on the expedition he had envisioned as a tune-up for Everest. Melly Reuling and Mimi Stone were also from the NOLS world. "There aren't many times in your life when you can ditch everything for the months of an expedition and just be in the moment and go with the flow and have a good time," Melly said of deciding to go to Tibet.

As a young NOLS instructor, Melly had taught one of her first monthlong courses in the North Cascades with Scott as her co-leader. "He seemed pretty darn compassionate with people," she remembered of that experience. "Your classic nerdy, uncoordinated characters, Scott would usually make them feel good about who they were and teach them how to laugh at themselves. That's a pretty special thing, actually, getting people to just keep putting one foot in front of the other." They had climbed every peak they could reach and engaged in footraces across the ice floes bobbing in an alpine lake. "When somebody's having such a good time and is so full of fun and so clear about what he's doing, that's infectious," Melly said. "It's hard not to get caught up in that sheer force of joy-fulness in the mountains."

Melly went on to lead Mountain Madness trips, then headed for Africa to do academic research on elephants and to guide trips on Kilimanjaro and in the Serengeti with Wes Krause, a partnership that grew into a romance. With a long history of climbing with Scott, Wes was also eager for a shot at the world's highest mountain.

Other climbers who signed on for the Everest expedition had strengths that lent themselves to figuring out how to get the gear and raise the money. NOLS veteran Ben Toland had been marketing director for Sierra Designs and would serve that same role for the expedition. Q Belk, who had directed the NOLS East Africa branch, also brought marketing expertise to the table. David Black, an orthopedic surgeon with a background of climbs in Yosemite and Alaska, would be the expedition's doctor. Bob McConnell joined the team to manage base camp, drawing on his experiences as a colonel in the Army Reserves. Michael Graber, George "Geo" Schunk, and Peter Goldman filled out the climbing roster.

"We had a lot of good people going to Everest who were good climbers," Wes remembered. "Lots of them were NOLS people who had lived in the mountains for extended periods of time." The NOLS heritage of expedition behavior that had been instilled in them from their early days in the field attuned them to motivating people and looking for solutions to problems. They were all at ease with diverse groups and prided themselves on being able to act both democratically and on their own to make things happen. Surely, it seemed, a group of friends could draw on that to succeed in the Himalayas.

None of them had ever attempted Mount Everest, though, and few had traveled to the Himalayas. It was going to be a learning experience, from the basics of finding funding and securing food and equipment to moving the expedition and its boxes of supplies through China and Tibet and then up the Rongbuk Glacier to the bottom of Everest's North Face. If they managed to accomplish all that, there would still be the matter of scaling the two vertical miles of rock and snow separating them from the summit.

Every expedition setting off to climb Mount Everest has had its boxes. The British expeditions in the 1920s hired porters to carry their goods all the way from India around to the Tibetan side of Everest. Photographs of expeditions of the 1950s and 1960s and 1970s show long lines of porters toting heavy loads up the Nepal's Khumbu Valley toward Everest Base Camp.

The concept of what one needed to haul in for an Everest climb was revolutionized in 1978 when Reinhold Messner and his partner Peter Habeler reached the summit without breathing bottled oxygen, a feat that, like breaking the sound barrier, many had believed beyond human capability. Messner returned two years later to complete the even more astounding feat of climbing Everest alone and without supplemental oxygen, carrying little in his pack but a tiny tent, some extra clothing, a bit of food, and a camera. He left everything else at base camp including his girlfriend, perhaps as an added incentive to get himself down from the summit.

Few who came to Everest after Messner were interested in so minimalist an experience. Most expeditions still relied on building a base camp where yaks and porters carrying their boxes could go no farther. From there the climbers, their support staffs, or an alliance of the two groups would spend weeks ferrying loads on their backs up the mountain and leaving supplies at a series of camps each about a day's climb apart. The carries could be tedious and seemingly never-ending, but they had the beneficial effect of giving climbers time to acclimate to the extreme elevations of Everest's upper slopes. It was a race against the clock, though. High altitude deteriorates the human body. Without enough oxygen to fully assimilate nutrition, muscles melt away. Add to that the fact that the windows of relatively stable weather forming over Everest in the spring and autumn stay open only a few weeks, slamming shut with the ferocity of monsoon storms sweeping in from the Bay of Bengal.

Among the first tasks of the American Everest North Face team was developing a promotional packet describing the upcoming expedition and inviting individuals and companies to become involved in the success of the effort. Donors were promised postcards from the mountain and photographs of the ascent. Those at higher contribution levels could symbolically adopt one of the yaks who would be hauling the boxes to Advance Base Camp. The names of all the contributors would be copied onto a roll of microfilm to be left on the summit. Promotional materials also included the fact that with so many female climbers on the team, the expedition had a good chance of having the first American woman reach the top of the world's highest mountain.

Scott mailed one of the first packets to Vuarnet, a manufacturer of high-quality eyewear. In a cover letter he outlined the mission of the expedition and the importance of protecting the eyes of climbers to prevent snow blindness, and he asked if Vuarnet would donate twenty pairs of its best glacier goggles and a similar number of sunglasses. It seemed the height of hubris, but soon a box arrived at the Mountain Madness office containing all the glasses and goggles Scott had requested and a note wishing the expedition safe travels.

Buoyed by their initial successes, team members fanned out with their packets and fund-raising plans to make the expedition a reality. They attended sporting goods shows and organized fund-raising banquets and auctions. They encouraged people to buy space on a six-week Mountain Madness trek that would tour Kathmandu and then journey into Tibet to visit the climbers. Scott flew with Stacy Allison to New York and appeared on the *Today* show to talk about the upcoming adventure, and Stacy lived for a while in the Mountain Madness office while she brought order to the checklists of gear. Liz Nichol, who owned a natural foods store in Colorado Springs, found herself devoting much of her time to planning and securing the provisions for the Everest expedition.

The boxes slowly filled with sleeping bags, shovels, down clothing, batteries, tents, stoves, mittens, long underwear, and boots. Scott's friend Dan McHale built backpacks for Scott and some of the other climbers. Liz Nichol loaded boxes with dehydrated food, flour, coffee, corn nuts, honey, energy bars, jerky, and tofu, and that was just the start. There would be 460 boxes in all, totaling fifteen tons. When the time came to stack the boxes in a cargo metal container and have it driven to the Seattle docks and hoisted aboard a boat bound for China, everything was ready.

Expedition members had raised enough money to pay the Chinese government $100,000 for their permit and associated costs, and they had assembled provisions and equipment worth at least that much again. Financially they were still in the black, a remarkable achievement for any large mountaineering expedition. They gave the boxes several months' head start, and then the climbers were on their way to the Himalayas, too, from their homes in Montana and Colorado, California, Washington State, and Tanzania. At the Seattle airport Scott said good-bye to Jeannie and Andy, and set off for Everest.

Liz Nichol flew with Scott to Beijing to finalize the paperwork with government authorities. They picked up an interpreter who would travel with them, and the liaison officer who would act as a go-between with the government and the team and see that the climbers stayed within the bounds of their permit. The boxes they had shipped from Seattle were there, too, and they traveled overland with the boxes to Lhasa, the capital of Tibet, and on toward the Himalayas.

The rest of the team flew to Nepal rather than China. In Kathmandu they shopped for local foodstuffs and made last-minute gear purchases, then traveled for several days by bus and truck toward Tibet. Scott met them at the border to see that everything went smoothly as they passed through customs, and soon they were on their way across the Tibetan Plateau toward the north side of Everest.

"Dealing with the Chinese was a real experience," Wes recalled. "They've got our stuff in their trucks out in that huge Tibetan expanse. We'd come into a little village and there would be one pseudo hotel with a wall around it. They'd tell us this is where we're staying, here's some food out of cans. There wasn't much, and we had paid hundreds of dollars a day per person to be escorted through Tibet in Chinese manner. They didn't want us outside the compounds at all, so we had to sneak out to see what the real world was like there."

Much of the real world they saw in the coming days was watching the approach of Mount Everest as they crossed the Tibetan Plateau. Sitting atop their boxes in the backs of Chinese trucks, the climbers sometimes wore face masks to protect themselves from the dust. The rutted road meandered across the stark landscape, the brilliant blue of the sky throwing the snowy wall of the Himalayas into luminous relief ahead of them. Everest seemed to grow in height as they neared the mouth of the Rongbuk Valley. Flanked on either side by high ridges, Everest's North Face stood before them as a massive shard of white cut by the shadow of the Great Couloir, a huge gulley furrowing down from the summit.

The trucks strained through road washouts and river crossings. One vehicle broke down, delaying the expedition's progress until Scott could arrange for a tractor and wagon to move the boxes forward. What little road there was ended at 17,000 feet of elevation at the terminal moraine of the Rongbuk Glacier, and the trucks could go no farther. The team unloaded the boxes and the trucks went away, replaced by yaks. Tibetan herders lashed the boxes to the saddles and the caravan headed up the valley to the site of the expedition's Advance Base Camp at 18,400 feet. Several miles beyond, where the Rongbuk Glacier presented obstacles beyond the abilities even of the yaks to negotiate, the herders and climbers stacked the boxes containing the gear and provisions slated to go farther up the mountain.

"The yaksters were a wild bunch of cowboys, really fun," Wes told me. "As we got to know them better, we set up a big mess tent where we were playing music, dancing, drinking whiskey, taking pictures. We all got to be buddies, having a great time together." It was a friendship the climbers quickly realized was predicated on keeping a close eye on their visitors to make sure that contents of the expedition's boxes didn't end up in yak herder pouches and bags.

The team established Camp I at 19,200 feet on the Rongbuk Glacier, as close to the bottom of the North Face as they dared go and still stay clear of avalanche debris hurtling down the mountain. There were no porters to haul loads as there would have been on the Nepalese side of Everest. Instead, the Mountain Madness climbers themselves moved the contents of the boxes a pack load at a time the several miles from Advance Base Camp to Camp I. They used skis to speed their many trips up the valley and back down again, sweating through the long carries as sunlight reflecting off the glacier and snowfields turned the route into an oven.

As they ferried loads, team members could look far above them and study the mountain they had come to climb. The lower portion of the North Face is curtained with rock and ice, and the middle of the mountain is covered by an immense snowfield the 1984 Australian expedition had christened White Limbo. The snowfield is prone to frequent avalanching and is steep enough that an unroped climber who slips while traversing it can slide thousands of feet down to the glacier. Above White Limbo is the Great Couloir, the gulley leading nearly to the top of Everest.

The team decided to establish three intermediate camps on the North Face. Camp II would be above the cliffs at an elevation of 22,600 feet. Camp III at 25,000 feet would be high on White Limbo. The final camp, Camp IV, would be in the Great Couloir at 26,500 feet. Climbers setting out from there would have another 2,500 feet to ascend to reach the top.

"We wanted to get enough food and fuel in every camp for four people for five nights before anybody went to the summit," Wes told me. There was plenty to do, starting with getting up the mountain to build the camps. Much of the grunt work would involve unloading the boxes hauling backpacks full of provisions and gear to the higher camps, but there was no clear designation of who would take responsibility for each task or how it would be done. "We always felt that to come up with this elaborate plan of how the expedition was going to unfold was ludicrous," Wes explained. "You just don't know until you're up there how things are going to go."

Scott had made it clear from the beginning that he did not intend to micromanage the expedition. He'd played a major role in the preparations and logistical organization for the trip, but once they reached the mountain, he expected team members to make their own decisions about what they could do to move the effort forward. They were going to go for it, and through sheer willpower and the combined efforts of everyone doing what seemed most appropriate at any given time, they would make it happen.

"You all go as friends and figure that if we can't do it without a leader, then it can't be done," Stacy Allison told me. "We thought we knew what we were doing, but we *didn't* know, and you *always* need a leader. You need someone to coordinate people and logistics, and we didn't have that."

"It was naïve and totally heartfelt and kind of sweet, very grass roots," Melly Reuling remembered, "but in hindsight, it would have been better to have some veterans along, somebody who had been there before and knew a little bit more."

One decision that Scott did make was that he and Wes would immediately begin pushing the route up the mountain. They would be a team again as they had been on the Fang and Kilimanjaro, climbing fast and making the hard moves on the tough pitches, leading the charge if not the expedition. They started up the North Face toward the site of Camp II and, at least to the perceptions of some of the others, never really came down.

"The climbing on the North Face gets tough right away," Wes recalled. He and Scott found themselves confronted with rock that in places was nearly vertical. They anchored ropes so that other climbers could clip their ascenders to the lines, both to pull themselves up the cliffs and to protect themselves from going very far if they were to fall. Hauling food and equipment up the ropes was much more grueling than carrying packs on the Rongbuk, and as Camps II and III took shape, there were many loads to be schlepped up the mountain. When they arrived at the high camps, climbers could dump the contents of their packs and descend, or they might stay awhile to help advance the route or to work on the snow caves that would serve as the high camp shelters.

Snow caves are remarkable structures. A tent can be set up in a fraction of the time it takes to excavate a cave, but a good snow cave is nearly bombproof. Aerodynamically sound, it is unaffected by even the strongest winds. Snow acting as insulation traps the body heat of climbers in a snow cave and helps them stay warm. Avalanches that would wipe out a tent site will thunder over a well-placed cave, leaving it intact. While storms might bury the entrance under many feet of snow, a cave and its contents—and anyone hunkered down inside—will remain safe.

With mountaineering shovels, the North Face climbers tunneled into a drift in the lee of a cliff at Camp II and, deep under the snow, carved a domed room large enough to shelter four people and their provisions and gear. With Camp II established, Scott and Wes led the route up White Limbo, using aluminum stakes to anchor ropes on the open expanses of the huge snowfield. Near the top of the snowfield they began digging the Camp III snow cave.

Down on the Rongbuk Glacier, expedition members operated on their own timetables, each deciding when to go up the mountain, what to carry, and what they might do to help once they got up high. Some found that one trip to Camp II was as much of the route as they felt comfortable climbing. Others ferried numerous loads all the way to Camp III.

"It was really dangerous," Melly recalled. Avalanches were less likely to occur at night when the mountain was frozen hard, and so team members turned on their headlamps and carried loads up the fixed lines in the darkness. "You'd hear the ice chunks just winging past you all night long. If one hit you in the head that would be it. Pure and simple bad luck."

The extreme physical effort, personal danger, and the dynamics of many people living for several months in the close confines and primitive conditions of remote camps on the Rongbuk Glacier began taking their toll. As the weeks went by, some came to resent what they saw as Scott and Wes living high on the North Face while others were relegated to moving the contents of the boxes up the mountain. For a few, cooperation turned to competition as they maneuvered for a shot at the summit. What team would assemble itself for the final ascent? Would carrying lighter loads help a climber maintain strength and increase the chances of later success? Or would carrying a heavier pack impress Scott and Wes and increase the odds of joining what was shaping up as the two of them and several others making a run for the top?

We're just up here trying to climb this mountain, so let's just keep doing what we need to do, Wes thought. *There's no use worrying about who's going to get to the top because we're not even close enough yet for anybody to get there.*

Perception has enormous power, though. Melly pointed out that establishing and stocking the upper camps in a timely manner was a phenomenal success, but that she and Wes had opposing views about how it had been done. "We were on different parts of the mountain the whole time," she remembered. "Wes and Scott were just up there, getting fed by all of us. They would come down to Camp II and here was some more stuff. They were totally out of the fray of the logistics down lower."

Others were not so concerned. "To me it didn't matter because I wasn't really headed for the summit," Liz Nichol told me. "The stakes weren't so high for me. Just being there was all gravy. I thought the way Scott did it was great, but for others it probably wasn't."

What no one could deny, though, was the danger, a fact driven home when the Mountain Madness trekkers arrived in base camp. Among them were Scott's mother Shirley Fischer and Hank Reuling, Melly's dad. It is not the sort of data historians of Himalayan expeditions usually keep, but it may well have been the first time the leader of a Mount Everest expedition had his mom show up at base camp to see how her boy was doing.

With the help of P. B. Thapa, the Kathmandu-based trip organizer Scott and Wes had met during their Fang expedition several years earlier, Scott had put together the trek as a feature of the Everest North Face expedition, and his mother had jumped at the chance to join. She trained for her trip to the Himalayas by wearing a backpack while she walked around a golf course near her home, and by doing lots of yoga. When she arrived in Kathmandu to begin the six-week trek, one of her fellow travelers asked, "What are you are going to do when you get to base camp, stand on your head?"

She thought she just might, but first she had to get there. The trekkers traveled through rain and mud to the Nepalese border, then bounced across the Tibetan Plateau in a bus and then a truck to the end of the road. Hiking up the Rongbuk to Advance Base Camp, Shirley felt strong and healthy.

"When I saw Everest, my God, it was almost a spiritual experience!" she exclaimed. "It was awesome. The height, everything about it, I couldn't believe it."

Scott came down from Camp III to spend several days with his mother, and she was delighted to see him. She sat next to him in the dining tent eating rice and yak stew, drinking tea and studying her son's face burned by the sun and the wind. She talked with others on the team and found their enthusiasm and dedication to the expedition contagious. Scott handed her a pair of binoculars and guided her gaze up the North Face so that she could watch climbers high on the mountain. And while she did her daily yoga, there was plenty to inspire her without the need to resort to headstands.

"It was great to be with Scott, to better understand his passion," she said of their time together. Even though she could hear the avalanches and feel the cold wind blowing off the mountain, she saw the expedition as further validation that climbing was central to Scott's existence, a fact she had known for years. It was what he most wanted to do. It was what he *had* to do. "I shared Everest with Scott. An incredible experience."

Melly's father was greatly enjoying being with Melly, but was not so sanguine about his daughter's safety. "I had gone up the North Face four times and been as high as Camp III," Melly told me. "It was pretty miserable up there. In the deep freeze and very windy. Having those ice blocks coming down, it's so obviously such a crap shoot." She had also developed a nagging respiratory infection that was affecting her breathing.

Hank Reuling watched the mountain and listened to the roar of falling ice. He spent time with expedition members seemingly willing to do whatever was necessary to climb Mount Everest, and then he sat down with Melly. "You wouldn't risk your life to get to the top, would you?" he wanted to know.

She listened to his concerns, thought of her growing uneasiness about the route, and realized that she had gone about as far up the mountain as she was able or willing to go. "No, it's just not worth it," she told him. "Nothing is that important."

Others, though, continued to press upward. From Camp III, Scott and Wes climbed through deep snow into the Great Couloir and found a spot for Camp IV where they left a cache of gear and the oxygen bottles the two of them planned to use when they went to the summit. Carrying loads that high took much longer than they had expected, and they descended very late. "I'd suffered a retinal hemorrhage, so could only see a little through one eye," Wes told me. "Scott had his dark glasses on and hadn't brought his other glasses. It got pitch black and we can't see at all. We're coming down the Great Couloir, the blind leading the blind."

They realized that all was in readiness for a summit bid. The caves at Camps II and III were fully stocked. There was no cave at Camp IV, but the cache of supplies they had left included a couple of tents ready to be set up for the night a summit team would need them. Scott and Wes headed down toward Advance Base Camp to get ready for their climb to the roof of the world.

"That was the plan from the beginning," Wes told me. "We're going to get everything in place, we're going to come down and rest for three days, we're going to put together the strongest summit team we still have, and we're going to go." They had determined that in addition to themselves, the first team that would try for the top would include Stacy Allison and Q Belk.

An expedition that invites its members to act on their own initiative, though, might be in for a few surprises. As Scott and Wes were climbing down the fixed ropes, they met Michael Graber and Mimi Stone climbing up. The two had been helping carry loads and realized that the route to the summit was wide open. With Scott and Wes on their way to Advance Base Camp, Mimi and Michael knew that no one would be using the snow caves for the next four or five days, and they were launching their own try for the top. Their decision to act independently didn't sit well with some of the rest of the team, but Wes and Scott eventually came to see it in positive ways.

"We figured, it's all sorting out," Wes recalled. "There were gobs of food and fuel up there. Mike and Mimi were carrying their own oxygen, so they weren't cutting into anybody else's attempt."

After several days of ascent the two reached the Camp IV cache Scott and Wes had left in the Great Couloir and pitched a tent. The next morning they were confronted by terrific winds that turned them back at 27,800 feet, still 1,200 feet from the summit. Descending through the high camps, they met Scott, Wes, Stacy, and Q. on their way up.

"They had been safe, they didn't do anything crazy, they didn't jeopardize the rest of the expedition by climbing into a situation they couldn't get themselves back out of, and they got back down," Wes said of Mimi and Mike. "It was pretty hard to criticize."

Heavy snow was falling as Scott, Wes, Stacy, and Q. reached the cave at Camp II, but they weren't overly worried. They were certain it was too early for the monsoon to be moving across India and into the Himalayas, and that the storm building around them would probably blow itself out overnight. But it did not abate, not that night or the next or the one after that. Snuggled into their sleeping bags with their headlamps turned off to conserve their batteries, the four climbers lay in the darkness and listened to avalanches booming down the mountain. Now and then the climbers would punch through the snow clogging the tunnel to let fresh air into the cave and to have a look outside, but all they saw was more of what had become a raging blizzard. Had they been in tents instead of a cave they would almost certainly have had to bail off the mountain in severe conditions.

The storm eased on the fourth day and the foursome set off for Camp III. Wind scouring loose snow from the North Face had reduced the threat of avalanches, but the storm had torn out the fixed ropes, too, leaving only a few twisted stakes. Far below they could see that snow had filled the Rongbuk Valley for miles past the glacial moraine where the trucks had dropped their boxes. Their teammates reported by radio that six feet of snow had fallen on Advance Base Camp, burying the tents and encasing the dining shelter in ice.

The summit team reached the elevation of Camp III and found no trace of the entrance to the snow cave, but they knew where to dig and soon opened the tunnel. "There it was, our perfect little hangout," Wes recalled. "We moved right in, no problem." They melted snow for hot drinks and crawled into their sleeping bags, happy that the storm was behind them. They planned to reach Camp IV the next day and, after a night in the tents, complete their climb of Mount Everest.

Two hours before sunrise they awoke to find it very cold even inside the cave. They pulled on layers of pile, their goose down suits, and their face masks, then pushed through the tunnel and out onto a mountainside being pounded by ferocious winds. "Every time we tried to climb any higher it was totally desperate," Wes said. "We couldn't stay warm out there even just putting on our crampons." Three mornings in a row they got ready to climb, and three mornings in a row they were confronted with winds so strong they could do nothing but burrow back into the snow cave and lie in their sleeping bags to wait.

Team members on the Rongbuk were enduring a growing desperation of their own. The deep snow had made the camps miserable, and as the prospects of success on Everest faded, so did any remaining cohesion holding the expedition together. Those most eager to go home packed their gear and left.

"Once the momentum was lost, everybody bailed," Wes remembered. "People were on the radio yelling at us up at that high camp, still hoping we'd get to the top, but weather had gotten so bad they all wanted to leave. We knew it was going to be an epic getting out of there."

On their fourth day at Camp III, Scott and the others finally gave in to the reality that there was no longer any chance they could reach the summit. Their supplies were dwindling and so were their energies. It appeared that the monsoon season had arrived, and the weather refused to give them a break. They stowed the remaining gear from the cave into duffel bags and launched them off the mountain. The following day they did the same with what had been left in the Camp II cave. The bags careened thousands of feet to the bottom of the North Face and rolled out onto the flats near Camp I where their teammates were able to retrieve almost everything.

Scott and Wes joined the depleted number of expedition members to break down Advance Base Camp, knowing that the recent snows would prevent yaks from coming in anytime soon to haul loads. They packed up what they planned to carry with them and put everything else back into the waxed boxes. Scooping away the snow, they cleared a spot to stack the boxes, covered them with a tarp, and left them to fate.

Carrying backpacks and pulling make-shift sleds piled with gear, they skied away from Everest, reaching the road near the Rongbuk Monastery a few days later. Most of them went from there toward Nepal, taking their time and enjoying the adventure.

"We got back to Kathmandu maybe a week after leaving base camp," Wes remembered. "We were walking from the bus station to the hotel and these rickshaws passed us on the street with all our waxed boxes in them." Entrepreneurial Tibetans and Nepalese had managed to retrieve the boxes out of the snows of Advance Base Camp and get them all the way to Kathmandu as quickly as Wes and his party had managed to cover the miles themselves.

"Obviously, making something like that happen depended on who you know," Wes concluded, "and we didn't know anybody."

He felt a certain satisfaction that the gear they had brought down the North Face and had left in the boxes would soon be showing up in the secondhand stores of Kathmandu for someone else to use.

Having come to Tibet through China, Liz Nichol and Scott had to go out that way, too, in order to settle the expedition's accounts. Officials in Beijing brought him the final bill. Among many fees he felt had been piled on was the cost of rebuilding the engine of the truck that had broken down several months early on the way to Everest. "Hey, you guys should be paying *me*," he argued, pointing out the hardship to the expedition and the need to hire a tractor and wagon. The rational of the Chinese, though, was that if Scott hadn't hired the truck in the first place, it wouldn't have broken down, and so he was responsible for its repair.

Scott refused to pay, but the Chinese were holding his passport. "Okay," they told him, "no problem. Go back to your hotel and we'll talk about it again tomorrow." He could rant about unfairness all he wanted, but in the end he had no choice but to pay.

Every Everest journey is a learning experience, and Scott had learned a great deal about how to put together an expedition and move it to the mountain. The North Face had also tested his determination not to shoulder the mantle of buck-stops-here decision making. Some team members were critical of his management style, believing Scott should have stepped in and insisted on a more orderly and traditional approach to directing the expedition. On the other hand, had it not been for stretches of truly horrendous weather, several teams might well have succeeded in ascending one of Everest's more difficult routes. There had been no fatalities and no significant injuries, and everyone came home safe. There's something to be said for expedition leadership that can take a degree of credit for all of that.

It was time for Scott to pay off the Chinese and leave Beijing behind. Time to leave the boxes, too, and the Himalayas. Everest would be there if he ever had another chance to try climbing it. For the moment, though, he was most interested in getting back to Seattle to see his young family.

CHAPTER 14

The Nutrition Expedition

It's okay! We're all up here together!
—Scott Fischer alone on Everest's South Col

I'M DRIVING ACROSS Seattle with Scott Fischer on a winter evening in 1988 and Scott is jazzed, buzzing along the highway full of enthusiasm and energy, full of the Bruce force, and it's not just because a pack of Cub Scouts awaits him and his slide show about climbing in the Himalayas. He's been back in Seattle for four months after leading the 1987 American Everest North Face Expedition, and the phone at the Mountain Madness office has been ringing off the hook. "Some Baylor University students called the other day," he tells me. "They've got a month in Russia scheduled and they need a guide to take them climbing. I'm pretty sure that could be me." Another group of climbers has inquired about going up some peaks in Bolivia.

A local guide service is up for sale and Scott feels he has the inside track to buy it and its lucrative contract to lead trips for the outdoor equipment company Recreational Equipment, Inc. He's thinking again about going up against Rainier Mountaineering, Inc., the only company allowed to lead climbers on Mount Rainier, and trying to force the National Park Service to grant Mountain Madness a guide concession, too. "It's the mountain in our backyard," Scott says, "and I can't lead trips there? Come on." He's also angling for something to open on Alaska's Mount McKinley, where for many years the six guide concessions have been in the hands of the same companies, none of them his.

"Things are happening," Scott continues, rocking back and forth in the driver's seat as we speed through the darkness. The American Alpine Club has asked him to speak at a banquet in Seattle the following night. Best of all, he and Stacy Allison have been asked to meet with a Seattle-based group of mountaineers looking for a couple of climbers to fill out their roster for a 1988 autumn attempt on Everest. Scott is certain he will be invited to join the team and that in six months he will be back in the Himalayas standing on the top of the world.

To add to the mix, Scott and Jeannie's son Andy is closing in on his first birthday. Scott delights in spending time with Andy, bringing him to the Mountain Madness office and towing him around town. The ease between father and son is obvious. Scott adores Andy and is taking the role of being a dad seriously even as he continues to figure out how to accommodate this big change in his busy life.

"I love my wife. I love my baby boy," Scott tells me. "But I'm at the height of my climbing career. I don't do these expeditions now, I'll never do them. I'm going back to Everest, that's all there is to it. I'm going to climb that mountain."

At the Cub Scout meeting, Scott passes around his ice axe and lets the boys try on the down suit he wore on Everest. They are in awe, and they want to know if he has ever fallen. "Yep," he tells them, and they are convinced. They ask if he has ever been afraid. "Yep," Scott says, but the looks on the Cub Scouts' faces suggest they aren't so sure about that answer. He fires up a slide projector and illuminates a wall with photographs from his Everest expedition, and then we drive back to Scott's house where he discovers he had put the wrong dates in his calendar. The American Alpine Club banquet had been that night, not the next evening. Stacy Allison had filled in for him.

I have been sensing all evening a subtle change in Scott, some small bit of remove, his brain disengaged from the present and from the surroundings of the moment as if a part of him were still in the Himalayas. He had dedicated three months to climbing the North Face of Mount Everest and had almost tagged the summit. One more day of good weather and he's sure he could have blasted to the top. It had been months of life reduced to the clarity of mountaineering, the clean lines of success and failure, of going up or coming down, of living on the simplicity of purpose in the Himalayas far removed from the world below.

He had come home from Everest with all his fingers and toes intact, a box of photographic slides, and a severe case of wanderlust. I'm fascinated, as I have always been, that climbing Everest means so much to him that he's willing to risk so much, or at least able in his mind to reduce risk to a phenomenon that doesn't necessarily apply to him. He clearly believes that if he turns down the invitation to join the next Everest expedition, he'll be watching a prime season of his climbing career slip away.

On the other hand, some of Scott's closest friends were deciding to approach mountains in ways that flirted less with the prospects of mortality. Many from the National Outdoor Leadership School were choosing to untie from their climbing ropes and go in other directions. They were building careers as attorneys, teachers, and physicians, earning business degrees, getting married and starting families.

For some, the 1987 North Face expedition was their last high-altitude hurrah. Wes Krause and Melly Reuling were finding plenty of satisfaction taking people on Kilimanjaro climbs and game-viewing safaris in East Africa. Michael Allison had been invited to go to Everest with Scott's team, too, but took his name off the roster when his wife became pregnant. "It wasn't my scene," he told me, "and Bonnie was going to have a baby." He began looking at adventuring as a series of weekend trips closer to home and leading a Mountain Madness trek now and then. Doing the math, he reasoned that the accumulation of his shorter outings more than equaled the time he would have spent in the field had he instead continued going on infrequent but extended expeditions to Alaska and Nepal.

For Scott, though, life was all about meshing family and business and everything else with his need to climb, a drive sharpened by the setbacks of the next few weeks. The deal fell through to buy the guide service with REI connections, and while the Mountain Madness phone continued to ring with inquiries about trips, few of them materialized into adventures for which clients were willing or able to pay the full fare. I knew from my own Mountain Madness experiences that acquaintances covering their airfare and expenses were always welcome to come along even though that did nothing to improve the company's bottom line.

The real blow was the outcome of the interview with organizers of the upcoming Everest expedition. Scott had sent in his application and, without asking her ahead of time, had included Stacy Allison's resume along with his. "I'm going to get us on another climb!" he told her over her protests that it was too soon to think about Everest again. "Stacy, let's go to the interview."

Stacy was offered a place on the team. Despite acknowledging Scott's obvious skill and high-altitude experience, the organizers felt that Scott was not a good match for the group they were assembling, and did not ask him along. He encouraged Stacy to accept the invitation that had been extended to her, but was exasperated that he had been rejected and that the door to Everest had closed.

"He was too threatening," Stacy told me. "People think Scott had all this self-confidence, but a part of him lacked confidence, and he could come across as being arrogant. He had just led an Everest expedition and the leaders of the 1988 trip thought that they might have a hard time getting him to fit in with their team and take direction."

When Stacy went to Everest in the autumn, Scott led a trek of Mountain Madness friends up the Khumbu as far as Kala Patar. Stacy hiked down from Everest Base Camp to see him just before she became the first American woman to stand atop the world's highest mountain. He was happy for her and proud that he had introduced Stacy to climbing, had taught her the basics, and had been responsible for her getting an interview with the 1988 expedition. Now she had climbed Everest. He could hardly wait to get back on the mountain himself, if only he could find a way.

Then the Mountain Madness telephone rang and the doorway to Everest was suddenly kicked wide open again.

Walt McConnell, a New Jersey physician, had been dreaming of climbing the mountain since the late 1970s when he had seen it while trekking in Nepal. In 1981 he had tried to get on an Everest team being organized by the American Medical Association, an expedition that interested him both because it was doing scientific research and because its leaders had figured out a means of funding their Himalayan adventure. McConnell didn't have enough climbing experience to make the roster of the AMA climb, a fact he set out to rectify by enrolling in a climbing school. He also continued to trek, expanding the range of his trips to include mountains in Mexico and South America. By 1987 he was again enthused about accompanying a research expedition to Everest, but this time he would put it together himself.

Among the scientists Dr. McConnell invited to join his expedition were Bob Reynolds, a researcher associated with the U.S. Department of Agriculture's Beltsville Human Nutrition Research Center in Maryland, and Frank Butler, an ophthalmologist, Navy SEAL, and active-duty captain with the Navy Medical Corps. Dr. Reynolds was interested in studying the absorption rates of various food groups at high altitude. Dr. Butler's primary field of inquiry was the effects of increased pressure on the eyes of divers. If it meant a chance to go to Everest, he was willing to devote a couple of months to documenting the effects of decreased pressure on the eyes of mountaineers.

Walt also invited two Mexican climbers he had met during his treks. Sergio Fitch-Watkins was a seasoned guide for the Mountain Travel adventure company who described himself as an alpine guide and philosopher. Ricardo Torres-Nava was a mountain guide trained as a pharmacist. Neither Ricardo nor Sergio had climbing experience in the Himalayas.

Dr. McConnell applied for a permit and discovered that in addition to charging each expedition a fee of $3,000, the Nepalese Ministry of Tourism also required that any group asking to climb a big mountain give evidence of its technical expertise by obtaining an endorsement from a recognized mountaineering group in its home nation. There were two in the United States at the time, the American Alpine Club and the American Mountain Foundation.

McConnell approached the American Alpine Club first. Glenn Porzak, a Boulder, Colorado, attorney and the club's president, told

Walt that the AAC had already credentialed an Everest expedition for the spring of 1989, one that included Porzak himself as a team member, and would not be able to endorse a second expedition.

The American Mountain Foundation was headed by Mark Hesse, a climber with deep connections to Outward Bound. With several Himalayan expeditions to his credit, Hesse understood uthe challenges of getting up a big Himalayan peak. He noted that while Ricardo Torres-Nava and Sergio Fitch-Watkins had spent plenty of time in the mountains, no one on Walt McConnell's roster had ever ascended higher than the 23,000-foot summit of Aconcagua, South America's highest peak. He told McConnell that he wouldn't endorse Walt's expedition until proven high-altitude climbers were added to the team, and he had in mind two men he was sure would fit the bill. One was Wally Berg, an acquaintance of Mark's through Outward Bound. The other was Scott Fischer.

Walt telephoned Scott to tell him about the permit for an Everest expedition in the spring of 1989, just six months away. He explained that the team would be weighted heavily toward scientists and researchers, and that the primary intent of the trip would be to study nutrition at high altitude. "We're calling it the On Top Everest 89 Nutrition Research Expedition," he told Scott, "and we need some professional climbers to join us." There was no salary, but all of Scott's expenses would be paid and he would have a shot at going to the summit. Dr. McConnell wanted Scott to understand that because it was a scientific expedition, the research would come first. Putting a climber on the Everest summit would be, as they say in the scientific world, "ancillary." Scott, as they say in the mountaineering world, replied, "Hell, yes!"

Walt McConnell also dialed the number of the Colorado Outward Bound office and asked for Wally Berg. "I've heard a little bit about you and I want to talk with you about my Everest expedition," Walt told him. Wally had recently returned from the Himalayas, too, having climbed Cho Oyu at the same time that Scott and his Mountain Madness expedition were on the North Face of Everest. Since then he had been working on ski patrols in Colorado, putting together Outward Bound courses, and trying to figure out what to do next.

Wally also jumped at the invitation to go to Everest, and encouraged Walt to invite his friend Peter Jamison to come along, too. Wally and Peter had been students together at Fort Lewis College near Durango, Colorado, and both had worked extensively for Outward Bound. In 1983 Peter had climbed Mount Everest by the same South Col route that the On Top Everest expedition planned to use.

With Scott, Wally, and Peter on board, the expedition had the high-altitude climbers it needed in order to get the endorsement from the American Mountain Foundation and then the Everest permit from the Nepalese Ministry of Tourism. The scientists refined the research they intended to conduct and approached the Department of Agriculture for funding. A military officer involved in the negotiations demanded to know the rationale behind the request. "What the hell are you doing going to Mount Everest?" he asked Dr. Reynolds. "You can't grow corn or wheat at the top of the mountain."

"No," Reynolds told him, "but I haven't seen any American military personnel standing on top of Everest either."

Eventually the Department of Agriculture provided $250,000 for the expedition scientists to set up their research, collect information on Everest, and conduct post-expedition analysis of the data. The sponsorship harkened back to the glory days of big national expeditions going to the Himalayas in the 1950s and 1960s, but even a quarter of a million dollars would stretch only so far for an expedition as large as Dr. McConnell had envisioned. Team members needed to raise another $250,000 to cover the remainder of the costs. In what was becoming standard practice for the expeditions of the 1980s, they sold T-shirts, hustled corporate sponsorships, and, as Bob Reynolds put it, "stood outside of REI stores with a tin cup."

Scott, Wally, and Peter flew to Maryland in September 1988 for the first gathering of the On Top Everest expedition. "Scott and I had a real affinity for each other," Wally said of meeting Scott for the first time. "We thought the same way, had the same ideas, and we were both enjoying the 'professional climber' aspect of this. Somebody was buying us plane tickets to fly back east for a meeting about going to climb Everest. The recognition of being professional climbers was very important to us, and we appreciated that."

Walt McConnell introduced Bob Reynolds as the team's scientific leader. To help out at what would be perhaps the world's highest scientific station, the team had invited two scientists from Holland, the world's lowest nation in elevation, to be base camp research assistants. Walt also noted the presence of Ricardo Torres-Nava and Sergio Fitch-Watkins. Finally he introduced Scott, Wally, and Peter as the expedition's professional climbers.

Dr. Reynolds explained that once they began trekking up the Khumbu Valley, the climbers would eat only the food provided to them by the scientists. When they ascended above base camp, they would from time to time drink H_3O—"dual-labeled" water laced with isotopes—and would collect their urine in specimen bags to bring down to base camp for analysis.

"I told them that it was informed consent, that no one had to participate in the research," Bob Reynolds remembered. "Of course, if you don't want to do the research, then you just don't go to Everest." Not surprisingly, everyone in the room agreed to the research.

The expedition's nutritionists put together precisely measured menus and boxed everything for shipment to Nepal. Much of the food was donated by manufacturers—Campbell's Soup, Nabisco, Nestlé, Oscar Mayer, and Quaker Oats, among others. For good measure, Alka-Seltzer signed on as a sponsor, too.

"The idea was that during the expedition if we ate potatoes, they wouldn't be Khumbu potatoes carried up on yaks like climbers normally get to eat," Wally Berg told me. "They were French's Dehydrated Potatoes. The nutritionists had complete data about all the mineral content and everything else in the food. Of course, you can imagine after a few weeks in base camp we were all craving yak cheese and rice and just good local Khumbu food, and there were some minor revolts about that."

As a government-funded research project, the expedition's food could be shipped to Asia via diplomatic pouch. Bob Reynolds had the help of Milton Frank, the United States ambassador to Nepal, to usher the provisions to Kathmandu. "Since I was with the government I had access to the embassy," Dr. Reynolds explained. And while one might think of a "diplomatic pouch" as a shoulder bag containing sensitive documents protected from inquisitive foreign agents, in this case it was many crates of food trucked from Maryland to Los Angeles and then flown via Malaysia and Delhi to Kathmandu, the dehydrated potatoes and energy snacks presumably shielded from the curious eyes of any local spies.

Scott, Wally, and Peter returned to Maryland several times to undergo baseline studies at the Beltsville Human Nutrition Research Center. "We had bone densities done and our body fat measured," Wally recalled. "We slept in chambers that monitored our physiology overnight, everything from respirations to pulse. They were getting very precise and thorough measurements about our metabolism."

When climbers travel, they often pull on their outdoor clothing, fleece vests, and hiking boots as soon as possible. Scott and Wally preferred to wear pressed khaki pants, sports coats, and shirts with collars. "We enjoyed looking professional, looking like we were part of the real world," Wally told me. "We thought of ourselves as athletes and found it very gratifying and exciting that the world valued who we were and what we did as mountaineers." If they had duffels crammed with camping gear, they would ship them ahead and go through airports with carry-on bags. "We'd hauled around enough backpacks in our lives and we knew we were going to carry them again," Wally said of their choices of luggage. "We were looking for ways to set ourselves apart from everybody else."

Wally was also becoming familiar with Scott's exuberance and the effect he had on others. "There was a great deal of enthusiasm bubbling from Scott for his whole world, and people appreciated that. He was a great spirit. There was a magnetism involved with it, just in how he carried himself."

Scott had always been able to put himself into new situations and prevail. He was better at that in the mountains, though, than in a conference room. "We would go to these things in the East," Wally remembered, "and I think in hindsight he was more unpolished than I realized at the time. He would go overboard with the self-depreciating humor and sometimes would seem like the kid who had moved to Lander, Wyoming, too soon. But there was an innocence and pure enthusiasm for what he did that carried the day anyway."

At the final organizational meeting, Walt McConnell announced that Malaysia Airlines had signed on as an expedition sponsor and would donate airfare for the team members and free shipping of the cargo as far as Bangkok. The only condition was that the expedition members were expected to help celebrate the twenty-fifth anniversary of the airlines by stopping off in Borneo to climb Kinabalu, Malaysia's highest mountain.

Scott realized he couldn't go. The Kinabalu climb would add a few days to the time he would be gone from Seattle and he was trying to plan his schedule to make more time to be with his family. As an airline pilot, Jeannie certainly understood that work could mean being away from home, but in her case it was seldom more than an overnight layover between flights. Since Scott's absences could stretch into several months, he and Jeannie were trying to put together a formula that Scott would follow: number of days each year away from Seattle on long expeditions, days on shorter trips, and days at home. Climbing Kinabalu would put him over the calendar limit.

With everybody along except Scott, the American members of the On Top Everest expedition flew to Kuala Lumpur and then to a small airport on Borneo near Kinabalu. "It was the first time I'd encountered something like that, where we were met at the airport and people were taking our pictures because we were climbers," Wally Berg said. "It was a wonderful, fun time."

The Kinabalu summit day was a rainy round trip jog to the top at 14,000 feet, followed by a banquet hosted by the Malaysian Minister of Tourism. The following morning the team flew back to Kuala Lumpur where, from the balcony of their hotel, they could watch the contestants of the Miss Malaysia competition strolling in the lobby. "It gave us something to think about when we got to Everest Base Camp," Bob Reynolds told me.

There were no climbers that spring on the Tibetan side of Everest. Protests by Chinese students that would result in the Tiananmen Square massacres in May were already building in March, and the government was beginning to close the borders. Expeditions that had been granted permission to climb Everest's north side, which was under Chinese control, were told their permits were revoked. Some of the groups, including an American expedition called the American Men and Women on Everest that had held its permit for several years, learned of the cancellations just days before they were to depart from the United States.

Although Scott had been in Tibet two years earlier, 1989 was the first time for him to be with an expedition pitching tents among the boulders and pools of glacier melt at Everest Base Camp in Nepal. The closest vegetation was miles away down the Khumbu Valley. Above Base Camp to the east rose the Khumbu Icefall. To the north stood Everest's enormous West Ridge, dipping down to a pass called the Lho La that was itself several thousand feet of technical climbing higher than Base Camp. The Lho La and the West Ridge mark the border between Nepal and Tibet.

Sherpas for the On Top Everest expedition had set up several large tents to shelter the scientific gear. They pitched a cook tent, and with plastic tarps arranged over rocks stacked to form walls had created an expansive shelter for dining and socializing. Six other expeditions were settling in at base camp, too, bringing the climber total to more than a hundred. Add the Sherpas, support staffs, and the yak herders hauling in supplies, and the number of people at base camp on a given day could double or even triple.

Not far from the On Top Everest encampment were the tents of a Yugoslavian expedition and those of a team of Polish climbers. The Poles were planning to climb to the Lho La, establish an advanced base camp at the top of that pass, and attempt a route on Everest's West Ridge.

Also at Everest Base Camp was a group of climbers who had bought spaces on a permit acquired by Dick Bass, a Texas oil man who in 1985 had been the first person to climb the highest peak on each continent. His 1989 permit offered space to climbers able to take care of themselves and to pay for their expenses and a portion of the permit fee. Hailing from the United States, Britain, Australia, Sweden, and Belgium, those who took him up on the offer included Glenn Porzak on his second try at Everest, and Edmund Hillary's son Peter, who at age forty was embarking on his eighth Himalayan expedition and third attempt to relive his father's journey to the top of the world.

"That was something that was beginning to happen, the idea that various people would come together on one permit," Wally Berg told me. "Basically it was people who had in common that they had all been trying to climb Everest for years."

Another team was made up of New Zealanders Rob Hall, Gary Ball, and several Sherpas. Scott had met Gary Ball during the 1986 Mountain Madness trip to climb Pik Kommunizma in the Soviet Union. After that journey Gary had begun joining forces with his fellow countryman, most notably in 1988 when Hall and Ball made their first try at Mount Everest and were turned back by bad weather. In the evenings the New Zealanders often shared meals with members of other expeditions and passed the hours playing the board game Trivial Pursuit in the dining tent of the On Top Everest expedition.

"That was a formative time for all of us," Wally Berg remembered. "Friendships were being forged. There was a lightness to it, a newness because most of us had not yet climbed the mountain. Everybody thought they were known mountaineers, or were on their way to becoming known, but I also think it was embarrassing for a lot of people that they still hadn't succeeded on Everest."

While no one in 1989 was using the words "guiding" and "Everest" in the same sentence, the pieces to do that were falling into place. Climbers could already buy their way on to a permit and then trust in their own skills to ascend as high as they could. It would be a small step beyond that for expedition leaders to charge a fee to less experienced clients and then shepherd them to the summit.

"The commercial era on Everest was just about to happen," Wally continued. "One of the significant things that kept it from starting right then was that Gary Ball and Rob Hall had not climbed Everest. Nor had Scott Fischer or Peter Hillary. I hadn't climbed Everest." No matter how experienced they might be on other peaks of the world, climbers couldn't legitimately advertise themselves as Everest guides if they hadn't yet proven that they could even get themselves to the top.

Rising 2,000 feet of elevation over the course of a mile of travel, the Khumbu Icefall was the first obstacle for the mountaineers to overcome. When Peter Jamieson had come to Everest in 1983, the climbers themselves had established a route through the tangled and frozen terrain. "The icefall is other worldly, not like part of the planet," Peter told me. "Ice, towers. Things collapsing and shifting without warning. You start to get a little comfortable and then suddenly realize this is not a place you're meant to be."

By 1989, expeditions were hiring Sherpas to install the route. Their primary tools were ropes anchored to the ice and left fixed in place to protect climbers, and aluminum ladders lashed together to serve as bridges over crevasses or leaned against frozen cliffs. The "Icefall Doctor" was an older Sherpa in charge of developing and maintaining the route. He never went beyond the top of the icefall and he was typically extremely religious, praying throughout the day and throwing sacred rice over his shoulders on repeated trips among shadowy cliffs and icy pillars that could, at any moment, crash upon him.

Even with the Icefall Doctor in charge, Wally, Scott, and Peter helped put in the Khumbu Icefall route, joined in that effort by Rob Hall and Gary Ball. "We kind of assumed we had knowledge that the Sherpas needed or that we should be there to watch what they were doing," Wally explained. "I made something like fourteen trips into the icefall before I finally got all the way through it."

Walt McConnell named Scott the climbing leader for the expedition, entrusting him with decisions about how camps higher on the mountain would be established and stocked with supplies, and then who would use the camps for summit attempts. It was a much more structured role for Scott than the loose organization of his expedition two years earlier on Everest's North Face, but Scott seemed willing to oblige if it would lead to success on the mountain. He insisted that everyone practice climbing skills on ice cliffs close to base camp and rescue techniques in nearby crevasses. Now and then he would pull out a photograph of his son Andy, show it to some of the team members, and tell them, "This is why I don't take chances when I'm climbing."

Fourteen members of the On Top Everest expedition thought of themselves as climbers. "Scott drilled us for two weeks before we could even go into the Icefall," Walt McConnell said. "That eliminated a couple of the people." Several more were eliminated by Scott's insistence that before going higher on the mountain, each person had to carry two loads of supplies through the Icefall to Camp I. Another to go was Sergio Fitch-Watkins, who felt the expedition wasn't a good fit for him and departed for Kathmandu.

The remaining climbers with summit aspirations split into several factions. Scott, Wally, and Peter saw themselves as the primary summit team. A second group included several of the researchers—Walt McConnell and Bob Reynolds in particular—and Ricardo Torres-Nava, who had arrived at base camp well after the rest of the expedition.

"Ricardo felt like he was being slighted, but Scott and Wally and I were already up there at Camp I and Camp II hauling loads and putting in camps," Peter Jamieson told me. "We'd done the icefall. My attitude was, you're not up here working so you really can't complain." Wally considered Ricardo a likable fellow who wasn't in the best of shape and seemed to be content hanging around base camp. As climbing leader, Scott had required those who wanted to go high on the mountain to haul loads, and Ricardo had missed that part of the effort.

The scientific research kicked into gear as climbers returning to base camp from above went to the research tents to have their body fat measured, blood analyzed, and eyes checked. They drank the H_3O dual-labeled water and then collected all of their urine for the next seventy-two hours.

To avoid crawling out of warm sleeping bags, mountaineers have long been accustomed to peeing into plastic bottles, so managing urine was not a challenge for Peter, Wally, and Scott. This time they would use brown plastic bags with their names written on them, leave the filled bags outside of their tents to freeze, and then get the bags to base camp. The Sherpas weren't enthused about carrying around bags of another man's frozen pee, explaining that they wouldn't do that even for their parents and ancestors, so the climbers themselves schlepped most of their bags down the mountain. Researchers at base camp thawed and analyzed the urine to gather information on how thoroughly the dual-labeled water was being metabolized at higher elevations. They also shipped vials of urine via diplomatic pouch back to Bethesda, Maryland, for further study.

(Nearly a decade later on a subsequent Everest climb, Wally Berg happened upon one of his urine containers, still intact and frozen, at a high camp. He gave fleeting thought to toting it down the Khumbu and sending it to Bethesda for analysis, but decided that the statute of limitations had probably run out both on the research project and on high-altitude brown bag urine humor.)

By early May the upper camps were in place—Camp I at the top of the Icefall, Camp II a few miles up the Western Cwm, and Camp III carved into the ice midway up the steep face of Lhotse, Everest's neighbor, at the head of the Western Cwm. Above Camp III, the Sherpas had passed a distinctly colored layer of sandstone called the Yellow Band and left tents, provisions, and oxygen bottles at the site of Camp IV on the South Col, the pass between Lhotse and Everest.

Scott, Wally, and Peter set out for the expedition's first summit attempt, making it known that once they got to the South Col they would be going on alone without the help of Sherpas. The high-altitude Sherpas hired by the expedition didn't take the news well. They had played a major role in hauling loads all the way to Camp IV, and were motivated to reach the summit, too. One of them, Phu Dorje Sherpa, had stood atop Everest six months earlier on the expedition that had included Stacy Allison's successful ascent. Even so, the three American climbers were convinced that climbing with as little support as possible was a more honest way to scale big mountains. It was how Scott's Mountain Madness team had approached Everest's North Face in 1987, and the way Wally had climbed Cho Oyu. They had no doubt, however, that breathing supplemented oxygen above the South Col would improve their chances of success.

The three got a sluggish start from the South Col, leaving at dawn rather than in the middle of the night. Almost immediately they waded into thigh-deep snow. "I started having these memories of being there in 1983 when we left late and had similar conditions, and after summiting we were lucky to get back alive," Peter told me. "I didn't think I wanted to do that again." He turned around and began descending to the South Col. Wally and Scott continued to climb, but somewhere above 27,000 feet they turned back, too, realizing that having Sherpas along might have increased their chances of success because there would have been more mountaineers to break trail through the snow.

The three climbers returned to base camp to rest and to be poked and prodded and told that, thanks to their efforts to get as high as they had, the expedition's research objectives had been realized. "That was good," Wally told me, "but we were very much in the mode that the team also needed a summit success and that as the professional climbers we would be the ones to get it."

A week later they headed up the mountain once more. They again climbed above the South Col without Sherpa support and again encountered tough going. Peter turned back even sooner this time as the weather deteriorated. "Scott and I ended up somewhere in deep snow, not going fast enough," Wally said. "I remember us just about crying our eyes out. Scott especially was very emotional. We talked about it being his son Andy's second birthday, but we weren't going to climb Everest. It really broke Scott's heart that he couldn't get to the top."

Poor weather was limiting their visibility and they knew they shouldn't go higher, but Scott continued alone for another 500 feet of elevation gain. "He just couldn't will himself to walk downhill," Wally recalled, "but ultimately he did."

During his descent Scott radioed Peter several times to ask for help in finding the route, concerned that he might have become lost. "He was struggling a bit to find his way back down," Peter told me. "It got a little hairy."

They were all together on the South Col by 8:30 a.m. With most of the day still ahead of them and the weather getting worse, they decided to go down the Lhotse Face toward the richer air of the lower camps. "I was quite a bit ahead of Scott coming down the fixed line that crosses the Yellow Band," Wally told me, "and I see Peter Hillary and some other climbers coming up. We exchange hugs and Peter says, 'Let's go, man! Let's all go to the summit to-gether!' Why we weren't smart enough to go together in the first place and combine our strength astounds me now. That was a big mistake." Wally told Peter Hillary that he and Peter Jamieson and Scott were finished with Everest for the year, that they'd had two shots at the top and now they were tired and needed to descend. He wished Hillary luck and trudged downhill again.

"I was just getting to the steep part of the Lhotse Face where you're able to go pretty fast and I remember being aware of what was probably going to happen," Wally said of the next few min-utes. "Sure enough I look up and there on the traverse across to the Yellow Band I see Peter Hillary and Scott Fischer talking. And then I see Scott turn around and start climbing back up toward the South Col." Scott had decided to make a third try for the top.

Wally continued down to Camp II where he got out of his climb-ing gear, drank fluids, ate food, and took a nap. He awoke late in the day and walked over to the New Zealanders' camp where, much to his surprise he found the climbers who had passed him that morning on their way to the South Col. Peter Hillary explained that when they had reached the Col they had crawled into their tents and pulled out their sleeping bags and stoves, then started melting snow for drinks. The storm continue to worsen, and they realized that nobody would be climbing Everest the following morning. Rather than exhaust their supplies and themselves by waiting out the weather on the Col, the group decided to return to Camp II. They geared themselves up and, as they left Camp IV, shouted over to Scott in his own tent that everybody was going down.

"At the South Col the few feet from one tent to another can be a world away," Wally told me. "It's such an extreme environment. It's noisy because of wind. No one is moving well. People are on oxygen. Stoves are going. It's hard to communicate. Some of them may have thought they yelled to Scott, but the point is we're all down at Camp II, it's nearly dark, and Scott's the only person left up there."

Wally established radio contact and told Scott to come down. Over the howl of the wind and the wild flapping of his tent, Scott shouted into his radio, "No, we're going to go for it, man!"

"He was psyched," Wally remembered. "He thought he was going to get to climb Everest the next day. I told him, 'Scott, it's not happening! The weather's too bad!'"

Wally felt physically drained from his own exertions of recent days and weeks and was concerned about Scott's situation. "I'm giving him information, but he's being Scott and he's telling me more than I'm telling him," Wally said. Scott was adamant that in a few hours he would be on is way to the summit, and Wally was just as stern in warning Scott of the growing danger.

Then, as if to settle the debate, Scott declared, "It's okay! We're all up here together!"

Wally looked around Camp II at Peter Hillary and the other climbers Scott thought were in South Col tents near his own and suddenly realized Scott didn't know that he was by himself. "Several of us flashed on this image of Scott Fischer up there with George Mallory and all the other ghosts of Everest climbers who never came down," Wally remembered. "The weather was really bad and even though we were pretty worried about Scott, it was a bizarre, black humor moment when we all had that same thought."

Wally handed the radio to Peter Hillary who explained to Scott that Peter and his team were at Camp II with Wally. The reality finally sank in. Scott stayed in his tent until dawn and then he, too, retreated down the mountain.

With the professional climbers back in base camp, the On Top Everest expedition made one more attempt to get somebody to the summit before heading for home. Walt McConnell, Ricardo Torres-Nava, Ang Danu Sherpa, and Phu Dorje Sherpa ascended to the South Col and got a 3:30 a.m. start. Unlike the deep snow that had confronted Scott, Wally, and Peter on both of their summit bids, the wind had blown the route clear of loose drifts. The team found their crampons crunching into ice and their progress steady, but not far above the South Col Walt's headlamp went out. He removed his gloves and fumbled with it, felt his fingers growing numb, and watched the lights of the other climbers pulling away from him. Realizing in the darkness that if he went too far to the left he would plunge into Nepal and too far to the right would send him tumbling into Tibet, Walt sat until daybreak. When the sun came up he went back to Camp IV to await the others' return.

Up above, Ricardo, Ang Danu, and Phu Dorje climbed into deepening snow near the South Summit. They found better conditions farther on, and around 3:30 in the afternoon arrived on top of Mount Everest. Ricardo was the first citizen of Mexico to scale the mountain.

Their success was soon marred by tragedy. Ricardo slipped as they descended below the South Summit, slid fifty feet, and saved himself with his ice axe. Danu suggested they rope up for safety, but Phu Dorje refused and hurried down the mountain on his own. Following in his tracks, Ricardo and Danu came upon Phu Dorje's ice axe stuck in the snow. He had a habit of not putting the sling of the axe around his wrist, and they assumed he had accidentally left the tool behind. When they got to the South Col camp just after dark, though, they discovered that Phu Dorje had not returned. Neither man had the energy to climb back up the route to search for him. Phu Dorje had been twenty-six years old, and his son was about the same age as Scott's son Andy.

The death of Phu Dorje was a prelude to the greatest tragedy on

Everest up to that time. With Ricardo and Danu back in base camp, most of the members of the On Top Everest expedition began packing their gear and making their way down the Khumbu Valley toward Lukla to catch flights to Kathmandu. Along the way they were engulfed by the rains of the leading edge of the monsoon season. Heavy snow fell on Scott and Wally who were still at Everest Base Camp, and the peaks became loaded with a dangerous, avalanche-prone snow pack.

Among the only climbers still on Everest were members of the Polish team that had succeeded in making its way up the West Ridge. Two had reached the summit, and all had returned to their Advance Base Camp at the Lho La, 2,000 feet above Everest Base Camp. The route down from there was nearly vertical, so the Polish team decided to head for home by going over the shoulder of Khumbutse, the mountain to the west of the Lho La, and follow easier terrain into the Khumbu Valley. As they started up Khumbutse, though, a massive avalanche occurred, visible from Everest Base Camp. Four of the men were buried and another was badly injured and died the next day. The surviving Polish climber suffered broken ribs and, though able to walk, was stranded alone atop the Lho La. He could go no farther and help could not come to him.

"You can stand on the Lho La and almost throw rocks on the tents down at base camp if you want to," Wally told me. He and Scott could talk to the Polish climber on the radio. "We could *see* him, but we couldn't get to him."

Wally pointed out that those who had died in the avalanche were five of the best Polish climbers of their generation. "When people talk to me about *the* Everest tragedy, they usually mean what happened in 1996, but here you had five well-known and respected Polish climbers dying. Even today there are people in Poland who can rattle off their names."

A year earlier or a year later, helping the surviving Polish climber would have been relatively easy. Someone from the normally crowded Everest North Face Base Camp could have hiked a few miles up the Rongbuk to the Lho La and offered assistance, but the Tibetan side of Everest was still closed to foreigners. Rescue climbers trying to go straight up to the Lho La from Everest Base Camp in Nepal were soon thwarted by deep snow and extreme avalanche danger. "We mulled over the problem," Wally said. "We talked to this guy on the radio, we kind of kicked our feet in the moraine, and we wondered what else we could do."

Rob Hall and Gary Ball had reached Kathmandu when word arrived of the deaths of the Polish climbers and of their stranded teammate. They volunteered to drive into Tibet and hike up the Rongbuk Glacier to the Lho La, but needed permission from the Chinese to cross the border. In normal times that could take months, and these were anything but normal times. Bob Reynolds reminded them that he had access to the United States embassy. Reynolds met with the U.S. ambassador who called the Soviet ambassador who was at that moment playing tennis with the Chinese ambassador, and asked that the Chinese grant the permit. Since Poland was still in the Soviet sphere and the Polish expedition had standing with the USSR, the Soviet ambassador seconded the motion and the Chinese ambassador agreed to provide a letter directing border guards to allow a rescue party through.

Hall and Ball piled into a vehicle with two Sherpas who knew the Lho La region and with Janusz Majar, a Polish climber who also happened to be in Kathmandu. They wheeled onto the Kodari Highway and covered the distance to the Tibet border in half a day. Beyond that, the road climbed over a high pass, dropped down onto the Tibetan Plateau, and then ascended several more passes before reaching the Rongbuk Monastery north of Mount Everest. They hoisted their packs and walked up the Central Rongbuk Glacier, bivouacking briefly for a little sleep. As they neared the Lho La they shouted the name of the surviving Polish climber and were startled to see the man crawl from a tent nearly buried in the snow. His radio batteries were dead, and he had assumed that soon he would be dead, too. The rescuers helped him down to the monastery, then drove to Kathmandu. They had been in Tibet just fifty-five hours and away from Kathmandu a mere four days.

"It was a big thing, what happened," Wally Berg recalled. "Hall and Ball got to the Polish climber within an hour after his fuel had run out for his stove and he wasn't going to be able to melt anymore water for drinking. They rescued him and they got great attention and satisfaction out of that. Back home in New Zealand they were heroes." The Himalayan Rescue Association honored the two, as did the Mountaineering Club of Gdansk, Poland.

Ricardo Torres-Nava also found himself famous. As the first from his nation to climb Mount Everest, he was named Mexico's Sportsman of the Year. He married a television producer and launched his own career as a broadcast personality.

"You can imagine what all that did to Scott," Wally remembered. "He and I had thought of Ricardo as this nice enough guy who was just sort of hanging around base camp, and then he summits. Scott would say, 'You mean *that* guy's climbed Everest and *I* haven't climbed Everest?' It was hard on him, definitely."

The time Scott had arranged to be away from his family was nearly up. Despite his failing to summit Everest, there was a silver lining. As he and Wally were leaving base camp, Glenn Porzak invited them to join him the following year for his American Everest-Lhotse expedition. Most on that team would be scaling Everest, Porzak explained. He wanted Wally and Scott to be the designated Lhotse climbers who, after they had climbed the mountain next to Everest would have a shot at the top of Everest itself. In one trip Scott and Wally could become the first Americans to summit of the fourth highest peak in the world, and then climb the highest.

A little success on Mount Everest would be a good thing for Scott. It didn't have to be much. He didn't need to have a medal minted in his honor or be named a sportsman of the year, he just wanted to stand on top of the world. He had been away from home for ten weeks, and as he journeyed back to Seattle, he was sure that the following spring he would finally leave his footprints on Everest's summit.

But of course nothing on that mountain is ever certain.

CHAPTER 15

The Wrong Mountain

Climbed the wrong mountain!
    –Scott Fischer returning to Seattle from the Himalayas

"I REMEMBER WELL talking with Scott about you in the late eighties and early nineties," Wally Berg says as he fills my cup with more black tea. "It's surprising that our paths never crossed. I assumed that they would, knowing that you were doing things with Scott and Mountain Madness and so was I."

I'm sitting at the dining room table with Wally in his home near Canmore, Alberta, Canada, showing him a photograph of us taken more than a quarter of a century ago as Wally and I were building trails in the mountains of northern New Mexico. We have been reminiscing about our summers as college students when we had both migrated to being trail crew foremen at Philmont Scout Ranch, one of the few jobs at the national camp of the Boy Scouts of America that had allowed us to run our own show in the back-country for weeks at a time. There had been little need for us to come down from the mountains except to pick up more food to supplement the trout we were catching from the cold, rushing waters of the Rayado River. Since then, Wally had devoted his life to mountaineering and had become one of the most respected mountain guides of his generation.

"There are some pretty big parts of Scott's life that I am uniquely qualified to help you relate," he continues. "This is a good opportunity to get some memories about Scott down before I lose any more brain cells to old age and high altitude." Among his happiest memories is of an ascent that at the time Scott all but dismissed—their climb of Lhotse.

At nearly 28,000 feet, Lhotse is the world's fourth highest mountain. If it were anywhere but next to Mount Everest, it would probably be more famous and sought after as a peak to climb. Many mountaineers going up Everest actually ascend Lhotse much of the way, climbing Lhotse's West Face to 25,000 feet before veering off to the South Col, the pass that separates the two peaks. To climb Lhotse, mountaineers don't make that turn, they simply keep going straight up. Do not turn left, do not pass the South Col, do not go to the top of the world's highest peak.

For those who have not yet succeeded on Everest, almost none could resist the pull to go toward the highest summit rather than ascending the peak that is merely the fourth highest. By 1990 nearly a hundred people had stood atop Everest. Fewer than twenty had reached the summit of Lhotse.

Glenn Porzak held a 1990 permit to climb both Everest and Lhotse. For him and others on the 1990 Everest-Lhotse team, Lhotse was an interesting part of the puzzle because it had never been climbed by an American, but it was almost an afterthought for those with Everest fever. After spending time with Wally Berg and Scott Fischer in the spring of 1989 at Everest Base Camp, Glenn had invited the two to join the 1990 expedition as the designated Lhotse climbers. Once the primary goals of reaching the two summits were achieved, he expected that the expedition would continue to function long enough for Scott and Wally to have a shot at climbing Everest, too.

Accepting the invitation was easy for Scott. The fact that his expenses were again being paid was important both to his budget and to his self-esteem in being recognized as an international mountaineer. Life at home was good with Jeannie flying for Alaska Airlines and their son Andy thriving as his third birthday neared. Jeannie was pregnant again, planning to give birth in October. She and Scott had fine-tuned their agreement on how many days he could be away from Seattle so that he could fit in the Everest-Lhotse climb.

Six expeditions settled into base camp on the Nepalese side of

Everest for the 1990 spring climbing season. Many of the usual characters were back for another try at the mountain, but not Mexico's Sportsman of the Year Ricardo Torres-Nava. He'd already climbed it. Not Dick Bass. He'd reached the top five years earlier. But Rob Hall and Gary Hall and Pete Hillary and Wally Berg and Scott Fischer were all in camp again, and climber Pete Athans was there as co-leader of the Everest-Lhotse team. Everest had become central to their lives. They had spent so much time together in the high camps of the Himalayas that they had developed strong friendships and impressive alpine resumes, yet among them they could not boast a single Everest summit success.

A few who had been up Everest were back for more. Australian Timothy Macartney-Snape, who had reached the summit in 1984, had set out this time from the surf of the Bay of Bengal to walk across India and then into Nepal with the intent of going on foot from the ocean to the top of the world, a "Sea to Summit Expedition." On the Tibetan side of the mountain, Jim Whittaker, who in 1963 had been the first American to climb Everest, was back to lead the Everest Peace Climb. The previous year's political turmoil in China that had caused the government to close Tibet to outsiders had subsided, and the Chinese had re-opened Everest's northern routes to expeditions including Whittaker's large team of American, Soviet, and Chinese climbers.

Controlling the climbing schedule on the Nepalese side of the mountain was the Royal Nepal Army expedition. Their leader informed the other expeditions in base camp that the army would take responsibility for establishing the route through the Khumbu Icefall and would then make the first attempts on the summit. The remaining expeditions would be welcome to ascend, but not until the military climbers had completed their mission.

The Nepalese Army of that time was made up primarily of Nepalese Gurkhas accustomed to living at lower elevations than the Sherpas. Even so, Scott and Wally recognized Sherpas from previous seasons in the Himalayas now wearing army uniforms. Lakpa Gelu, the Sherpa Icefall Doctor in 1989, was again chanting his prayers, throwing rice over his shoulder, and going into the Khumbu

Icefall to direct the setting of the route; this time, however, he was wearing the khaki shirt of a soldier.

Perhaps most surprising to the climbers was the arrival of Ang Rita Sherpa, a legend in Himalayan alpine history. He had already ascended Everest five times, and would eventually reach the top with ten different expeditions, but in 1990 Ang Rita had been away from the mountains for some time. Rumor around base camp was that during a festival in Ang Rita's home village there had been a fight, a monk was killed, and Ang Rita was convicted of murder and imprisoned. When he appeared at base camp wearing a Royal Nepal Army uniform, the word spread that the army expedition had sprung Ang Rita. "We started calling the situation Ang Rita's Freedom Trail," Wally Berg told me. "If he could get the Nepalese Army up Everest, he would never go back to prison."

The army was efficient in its approach, and on April 23, Ang Rita and three of his teammates reached the summit. A few days later the Army expedition headed down the Khumbu, and the other teams were free to climb.

As they waited in base camp, Scott and Wally considered their strategy for reaching the top of Lhotse. They would follow the es-tablished Everest route through the Icefall and up the Western Cwm to the base of the Lhotse Face, and then continue along the route several thousand feet higher to the site of Camp III. They talked about whether to cover the remaining 4,500 feet from Camp III to the Lhotse summit in one long push, but decided to establish a mid-way camp directly above Camp III near a bulge of rock they called the Turtle. They also planned to use supplemental oxygen on sum-mit day. There was an appeal to climbing without it, but they felt that breathing bottled air would help them maintain their fitness so that after climbing Lhotse they could recover quickly at base camp before beginning their journey up Everest.

Peter Athans and Andy Lapkass, two of the team members slated for Everest, each carried a load up to the Turtle for Scott and Wally, helped chop a tent platform into the ice, and left a tent and a cache of supplies. It was a tremendous support for what Scott and

Wally were attempting, and an effort for which they were very grateful.

On May 9 nearly all of the American Everest-Lhotse expedition climbers assigned to Everest reached the South Col. Peter Hillary, Rob Hall, and Gary Ball where there, too, and before midnight they all set off for the summit. The night was cold and the snow deep, but the sky was clear. A full moon lit their way. At 7:15 the next morning, Glenn Porzak and his team had reached the top.

An hour later Peter Hillary, Rob Hall, and Gary Ball arrived and made a call to a radio station in New Zealand where Peter's father, Sir Edmund Hillary, was waiting with New Zealand's prime minister for word of the expedition's success. Tim Macartney-Snape reached the summit, too, a full 29,035 vertical feet higher than the Bay of Bengal waves where he had begun his journey.

As the summiteers were returning to the South Col, Scott and Wally were relaxing at Camp III and preparing for an early morning start to reach their high camp at the Turtle. "We felt great, we felt strong, we were very excited," Wally told me. Then a late afternoon radio call came in. Unable to contact base camp directly, climbers on the Col were relaying their communications through Wally at Camp III. Glenn Porzak needed to get an urgent message to Charlie Jones, the expedition's base camp physician.

"Mike can't breathe," Glenn said, referring to his teammate Mike Browning, who had just come down from the Everest summit. The expedition physician warned that Mike was probably suffering from pulmonary edema and needed to come down from the South Col right away, but those who had been to the summit that day were too exhausted to escort him to the lower camps.

Scott and Wally wolfed down the last of their Top Ramen noodles and pulled on their outer clothing. After years with NOLS and Outward Bound, it was second nature for them to assist a climber in trouble. "When we heard what was happening on the South Col, we never gave it a second thought," Wally said. "We just started lacing up our boots."

While they were preparing to climb toward the South Col, Peter

Hillary arrived alone at their camp. He knew that if he could get himself well down the mountain the same day he had been to the top of Everest, he would have a much better chance of avoiding the physical problems of having been at high elevation. The radio Peter was carrying was on the same frequency as the one Rob Hall and Gary Ball had in their tent on the South Col. Wally borrowed the radio and called Rob and Gary. "Look, Mike Browning has pulmonary edema," Wally told them. "You need to go over to his tent and see what's happening. See if you can help get him started down."

Gary Ball had suffered from pulmonary edema on the South Col the previous year and understood the danger. He and Rob helped Mike on his feet and outfitted him with an oxygen bottle, then started him down the fixed ropes with a Sherpa to guide and assist him. "Mike's about my build," Wally said. "It was fairly easy for the Sherpa to short-rope him down the lines."

Moving as quickly as they could, Scott and Wally climbed up the Lhotse Face. Darkness fell and they kept going, meeting the Sherpa with Mike Browning at the Yellow Band.

"The Yellow Band is a long, long way from Camp II," Wally recalled, "but Mike was very weak and we knew we had to get him all the way down there that night." Scott went first, using his body to prop up the ill man. Wally followed, further controlling the speed of descent by holding the rope tied to Browning's harness. They reached Camp II around 3:00 a.m. and continued to treat Mike for pulmonary edema.

The effort took its toll and put Scott and Wally off their schedule by twenty-four hours. They had been moving nearly the entire night and needed to recover at Camp II while Sherpas and other climbers escorted Mike the rest of the way to base camp. The two climbed back to Camp III the following day, rested a few hours, then continued to ascend until they reached their camp at the Turtle. Early the next morning they set off to scale the rest of Lhotse.

"It was a beautiful day of climbing," Wally recalled. "I was with somebody I trusted totally and it was mutual. Scott and I had a great deal of respect for one another's strength. We climbed fast."

They were roped together, but even though the Lhotse Face is extremely steep, they rarely put in anchors for protection.

"Wally is incredible," Scott would later say. "Together we just totally smoked Lhotse."

"I've never liked the use of the term 'alpine style' applied to Himalayan mountaineering," Wally told me, "but we'd had full support from the rest of the team and now we had the chance just to climb."

The day was cold and overcast, and visibility was poor. They took turns leading as they climbed into a long, steep couloir that guided them to a rocky notch seventy-five feet below summit. A short pitch of cliff climbing brought them to the top of the highest rock of Lhotse. There was nothing above but a fin of wind-packed snow rising another twenty-five feet into the sky.

"It was a really unstable-looking sliver of snow," Wally told me. "We talked about whether we should get up on it or not. Of course we wanted to do it, so we straddled the edge and shimmied on up there." Had they slipped off either side, they would have fallen nearly two miles before what was left of their bodies stopped tumbling.

Wally and Scott leaned away from each other to create a little artistic space as they photographed one another sitting atop the snow atop Lhotse, then Wally got out his radio and called base camp. He knew that most of the climbers who had summited Everest would be awaiting word that the American Everest-Lhotse expedition had lived up to its hyphenated title.

"I have an announcement to make," Wally said into the radio. He could sense the anticipation two vertical miles below, and he continued, "It's May 13, Andy Fischer's birthday."

"That's great," Glenn Porzak radioed back, then let the radio go quiet while everyone around him waited.

Wally grinned at Scott and clicked the transmit button again. "Something else I want to add is that Scott and I are on the summit of Lhotse." There were cheers in base camp for the first Americans to summit the world's fourth highest mountain.

The two eased off the fin of snow. The sky had cleared enough for them to look north and see the route up Everest they were certain they would be climbing soon. They talked about it as they came down the couloir, went past the Turtle, past Camp III, and on to Camp II where they intended to rest the following day. The day after that they would climb to the South Col for their Everest summit bid.

Scott radioed base camp to report their late afternoon arrival at Camp II and to share the plan of taking a day to recover before starting up again. Glenn answered, telling Scott and Wally that there wasn't going to be time for them to climb Everest after all. He felt that the route through the Khumbu Icefall was deteriorating and it was time to begin taking out the ropes and ladders and storing them in anticipation of the next climbing season.

"Basically I'm sure at base camp anyone who was honest would say that we made our announcement that we were on the summit of Lhotse at 11:30 a.m. and by 11:35 they were heading for home," Wally told me.

Glenn couched the radio discussion in possibilities. If Scott and Wally wanted to go for the top of Everest immediately, they might have just enough time to make it, but Wally felt strongly that after the all-night rescue they had performed and then the Lhotse climb, they had to rest before attempting to ascend to 29,000 feet. He also recognized that with the upper camps deserted, there would be no one in a position to help if he and Scott ran into trouble. "We didn't discuss it much further," he said.

Scott and Wally came through the icefall the next day and were enthusiastically greeted at base camp their expedition teammates. The Sherpas had baked them a cake and, in frosting, had written WALLY/SCOTT/CONGRATULATIONS.

"We talked a little more about trying to wait things out and give the guys who had climbed Everest a chance to climb Lhotse and the Lhotse guys a chance to climb Everest," Glenn explained to me recently, "but the weather was bad and the icefall was getting bad."

As Wally and I sit in his home with our cups of coffee and tea, he can evaluate the Everest-Lhotse climb from the vantage of fifteen additional years of experience. "I know Everest mountaineering much better now, and I've been leader of a number of expeditions since then. We had already pushed our luck in 1990, and a lot of amazing things had happened, including the Nepalese Army ascent, our Everest climbers, the rescue of Mike Browning, Scott and I on Lhotse, and Macartney-Snape walking all the way from the Bay of Bengal. Nobody got hurt. We'd had plenty of success. I have a better understanding now of why the team thought it was time to go home without giving Scott and me a chance for an Everest attempt."

A lot of people climbed Everest that spring. Rob Hall, Gary Ball, Peter Hillary, and Peter Athans had all summited and could begin positioning themselves as Everest guides, but Scott Fischer and Wally Berg weren't going to be part of that, at least not yet.

"The Lhotse climb was one of the golden moments of my life," Wally tells me. "It was fun. Scott and I got to be together again, we got to maintain our renegade status in the comfort and support of a large, well-organized expedition, and we got to be the first Americans on Lhotse."

I tell him that I had gone to the Seattle airport with Jeannie and some other friends to greet Scott upon his return from Lhotse. "We had balloons and signs and we were excited to celebrate his accomplishment, but after Scott cleared customs his first words to us were, *Climbed the wrong mountain!*"

"It's too bad he didn't have the confidence or the patience to put Lhotse in a different perspective," Wally replies. "Being met by a crowd at an airport is a big deal that's only happened to me once or twice. It's good to be able to enjoy the moment and understand the importance of what it is. But the Everest thing became a negative burden on Scott's shoulders. He just couldn't say, 'Yeah, we climbed Lhotse!' because Everest was Everest and he still hadn't been to the top."

CHAPTER 16

F.O.S.

Even then, in the midst of expedition planning and dreaming of the mountains, Scott's real passion shows through. He suddenly looks up from the route photos and exclaims, "You haven't met my kids, have you? You've got to meet my kids, they're amazing!

—Phil Powers, NOLS instructor and administrator

Go up the creaky wooden stairs to the Mountain Madness office in the building on the corner of SW Alaska Street and SW California Avenue, and you would have felt as though you were standing at the portal to adventure. On sunny days, the two large rooms were illuminated by big south-facing windows overlooking the heart of West Seattle's business district. A smaller room held office supplies, stacks of Mountain Madness T-shirts, and shelves of brochures, permission forms, and trip descriptions. In a storeroom were enough tents, ice axes, crampons, and other gear to outfit a fairly large mountain expedition.

Go under the chin-up board above the door leading to Scott Fischer's office, and you would have found a room dominated not by the desk of a business owner, but rather by a homemade table covered with photographic slides. Lit from below, frosted plastic panels recessed in the table illuminated several dozen Kodak transparencies, and hundreds of other slides would have been scattered about. Tacked to the walls were enlargements of Scott's photographs showing breathtaking scenery from some of the world's wildest places. Portraits of Sherpas and climbers were there, too, and pictures of Scott's family. There was no particular order to the photographs. The places, the expeditions, and the F.O.S.—the Friends of Scott and the Family of Scott—had become as thoroughly mixed as had all the other elements of his busy life.

If you found Scott in the office he probably would have been talking on the telephone, energized about the next big adventure. Despite missing out on climbing Everest the previous spring and with no prospects for returning to the heights of that mountain anytime soon, 1991 was unfolding as a good year, beginning in the autumn of 1990 when Jeannie had given birth to their second child, Katie Rose.

Jeannie's pregnancy had been difficult. Katie Rose was born six weeks early, a tiny being dropping into Scott's life. The first nights the family was at home, Katie Rose's temperature fell, not a good sign for a premature baby. Jeannie was exhausted and frantic. "I was totally freaking out," she remembered, "and Scott told me to go to bed. He said he would take care of her."

Scott sat on the couch with his baby in his arms. "Now, Katie Rose, I need to talk to you," he said to her. "We need to warm you up." He undressed her, laid her on his chest, and wrapped the two of them in a blanket. It was exactly what he would have done in the mountains to treat someone suffering from hypothermia, and was the first of many nights he would bundle up with his daughter to keep her cozy.

Scott nicknamed her "K2" after the world's second highest mountain, and arranged his calendar to stay close to home for a while to be with Katie Rose and with four-year-old Andy. He also renewed his efforts to make Mountain Madness a success; one key to that had been inviting Karen Dickinson to manage the office.

A native Washingtonian whose family had deep roots in the valleys east side of the Cascade mountains, Karen had become interested in the administration of adventure travel while working on a business degree at the University of Washington. She found Mountain Madness in the telephone book and had interviewed Scott while doing research for a class paper. The more they talked, the more Scott saw in her a solution to a problem that had troubled him for years. He had never had much interest in the details of running a company, and he concluded that it would be good to have Karen join Mountain Madness to take care of everything that someone with training in business should be able to do. He offered her a part-time job with a small hourly wage.

"Scott was real smart," Karen told me recently. "That wasn't where his business skills fell apart. They fell apart because he would rather go climbing."

Mountaineer Brent Bishop, who would develop several companies of his own, later observed that the business and public relations worlds vexed Scott. "Things that came so easily on climbs didn't happen in the business settings," he recalled. "Show up at base camp and cruise or bum, just climb the thing, Scott was best at that. But running a business is a lot of grunt."

Sitting down for a lunch meeting with Wes Krause and Scott, Karen told the Mountain Madness founders she was enjoying working for them, but that she needed to find a full-time position with a firm that had the resources to pay her a decent salary. Wes announced that he had been thinking about making some changes, too. He and Melly Reuling had married and were living in Tanzania, investing their energies in running Kilimanjaro climbs and game-viewing safaris. To better manage affairs halfway around the world they had established African Environments, a subsidiary company of Mountain Madness that led Kilimanjaro climbs and East African safaris for clients sent to him by the Seattle office. They were also generating commerce with other travel companies eager to have African Environments provide logistical support for their own programs in Tanzania and Kenya.

"I was ready to figure out some way to make more money, maybe buy a house someday," Wes remembered. "I'd borrowed money to buy a Land Rover for Africa trips, and I wanted to get more vehicles so things could continue to grow."

Wes suggested that he spin off African Environments as a separate entity. "That will be my company, and you will have Mountain Madness," he told Scott. African Environments would contract with

Mountain Madness to continue serving their clients, but Wes would take control of the budget and future of the Africa enterprise.

It all sounded good to Scott. He would still be able to rely on Wes to take care of people he sent to Tanzania and Kenya, but without involving Mountain Madness in the day-to-day operation of the East African scene. With Karen managing the office, Scott believed he could leave many of the business matters to her while he focused on what he did best—organizing expeditions, getting people enthused about coming along, and leading trips.

Karen was interested, too, but pointed out that Mountain Madness didn't always have the money to pay her. She suggested that she and Scott agree upon some sort of equity arrangement that would allow her to become part owner of the company. They shook hands and decided that they would work out the details later. *Later* turned into months and then into years. "We were content with how we had structured this ownership thing," Karen recalled, though they never got around to signing any documents.

The handshake understanding seemed fine for both of them until Scott died, then questions arose about who owned various percentages of Mountain Madness. "When he was suddenly gone, it looked insane. How did we go so many years without getting an arrangement formalized?" But that would be later. In 1991, having Karen manage the office seemed a way for Scott to spend less time with spreadsheets and expense accounts and immerse himself more fully in the adventure side of his adventure company.

Scott's mountaineering life brought with it long absences from Seattle, sometimes months at a time. Integrating the need to travel and to climb with the needs of his family was an even greater challenge than organizing the operation of the Mountain Madness office. He and Jeannie continued to work at it, looking for ways in which the family could accommodate two high-powered partners, one an airline captain and the other an expedition guide.

On board Alaska Airlines flights, Jeannie was accustomed to the structure and responsibilities of command. She had the final word for decisions that affected the safety of an airplane and its passengers traveling at half the speed of sound and six miles above Earth. Scott, too, was engaged in decisions with a life-and-death urgency that could be as immediate as those being made by his wife. He was taking people to places on the planet as remote as the thin air through which Jeannie guided her aircraft, and making choices that could have implications in the mountains just as serious as those she made during her hours aloft.

From the beginning the long absences would make their marriage unusual, but the two had proceeded with their eyes open and an eagerness to make it work. One responsibility Scott had taken upon himself was finding places for them to live. "I just need to be within twenty minutes of the airport," Jeannie reminded him. "Anything else is fine." He had found their first house in Seattle and did the packing and unpacking to get them moved. He had located their second rental house, too, and with the encouragement of friends savvy in the ways of real estate had settled on the house in West Seattle that he and Jeannie purchased.

After Andy was born and then Katie Rose, Scott also accepted the task of placing ads in newspapers and doing the initial interviews of potential nannies and caregivers to help out when he or Jeannie was away from home. "We both were on our own when he was gone," Jeannie said of those times. "We were both running our own show, both used to being in charge." Scott would have his expeditions operating the way he wanted and according to a schedule of his own making. Jeannie would become accustomed to having the household running in accordance with her rhythms and expectations.

When he returned from a long trip, Scott sometimes invited his climbing companions to use the Fischer-Price house as their Seattle base of operations while they got themselves squared away for life after an expedition. "They'll just be here for five or six days," Scott would say. "We're going to talk about Mountain Madness business and make some plans."

"Absolutely not!" Jeannie would tell him. She knew that she and Scott would have their hands full trying to blend their own schedules back together, and that a bunch of climbers under the same roof, all of them running on post-expedition energy, would do nothing to reduce the stress.

"You don't understand," Scott would argue. "These people have been tied to the end of ropes with me in life-and-death situations. I think they can stay at my house!"

They came to recognize a recurring pattern. "When Scott came back after being away for three or four months, we were both trying to be captain of the house and to be the expedition leader of the house, and it didn't work," Jeannie told me. "He would be coming out of a different time zone and he wouldn't get the kids to bed at the time I had been tucking them in. The house just wouldn't operate properly and we would be at each other's throats." It could take a month for them to get back onto the same schedule. "We knew that for a few weeks before and after Scott was away we would argue and say we wanted to divorce each other, but ultimately neither of us ever wanted to be without our family. We would always agree that we wanted to stay together, and then we would work it out."

To help ease transitions, they came up with a list of rules they wrote on cards to carry in their wallets. No more than one long expedition a year. No climbers in the house after a trip. Jeannie was verbally quicker than her husband and faster to size up a debate, so they included a rule that he would have time to think through his stand on an issue before coming back with an organized reply. Perhaps most important was that they would make no binding decisions in the month leading up to Scott's departure for a long absence or the month following his return.

"There's nothing harder than being married to a mountain climber," Jeannie observed. "But I knew when he was eighteen and I was nineteen that he was a climber. I didn't just go into this, and neither did he." She reminded me that when they had married they had talked about how different they were from one another and that the marriage might not last. "Scott loved his children so much," Jeannie continued, "and the bottom line was that in spite of the challenges, we loved each other very much, too, and would always figure out a way to make it work."

Though he couldn't get anything going for Everest that year, Scott was organizing a Nepalese trip to test out an expedition plan he hoped to incorporate into company brochures as a centerpiece of Mountain Madness Himalayan adventures. A few miles south of Mount Everest at the head of the Hinku Valley is Baruntse, a massive 23,688-foot mountain featuring four peaks linked by extremely steep ridges. It was remote enough and difficult enough that at the time fewer than two dozen climbers had stood on its summit. It was also not so high that supplemental oxygen would be necessary. Near Baruntse and 2,000 feet lower is Mera Peak. The route up Mera is technically less demanding than that on Baruntse, but the elevation and the challenges of glacier travel would still put climbers to the test.

Scott's idea was to have four teams of Mountain Madness travelers fly from Kathmandu to the airstrip at the village of Lukla. Rather than hiking the well-traveled trail through the Khumbu Valley toward Namche Bazaar and Everest Base Camp, the groups would go over a pass above Lukla and drop into the more remote Hinku Valley. One team of climbers would set off for Baruntse while another would ascend Mera. Composed of trekkers more interested in hiking than climbing, the other two groups would trail the climbers to their base camps. All the trekkers and climbers would conclude the expedition by rappelling down to the Khumbu Valley from a 19,000-foot pass called Amphu Labtsa, and then enjoy the easy descent through the Khumbu villages and past the tea houses to Lukla for their flights to Kathmandu.

More than most Mountain Madness adventures, Scott was bringing along the Friends of Scott, a bunch of the Bruces he had known and trusted for years. Wes Krause would come from Africa to help lead on Baruntse. Wally Berg, who had been with Scott on Everest expeditions the previous two years, agreed to head up the Mera Peak effort. The expedition was laced with others from Scott's NOLS days, too, including Michael Allison and Craig Seasholes, a former NOLS instructor who had been living in Nepal. Some of the clients were also friends. Dale Kruse and Dave Mondeau had attended many of Scott's ice-climbing seminars in Colorado. Peter

Goldman had been on the Everest North Face expedition in 1987. Wes Krause's father-in-law Hank Reuling, on his second trip in the Himalayas after trekking to the Everest North Face expedition base camp, was bringing along some of his buddies and looking forward to spending time with Wes.

Gorgeous weather prevailed and almost everything went off perfectly as the teams made their way from Lukla into the Hinku Valley, though Scott nearly took himself out of commission soon after the trip began. "I was doing yoga in camp the first night out," Michael Allison told me. "Scott was stretching and said he could sit in the Lotus position. He pulled his ankle over one knee and then was cranking his other leg up and snap! It sounded like a twig breaking." Scott had ripped a meniscus in his knee and would need surgery when he got home to repair the damaged cartilage. As long as he was in the Himalayas, though, he was determined to ignore the pain.

The Mera climbers camped at Mera La, a pass at 17,000 feet that positioned them to follow Wally Berg to the summit. Craig Seasholes and Scott joined them at the pass after they came down from the top and hiked with them for several days across a very high lake-studded basin to the Amphu Labtsa. When they looked down the Khumbu side of the Amphu Labtsa, they saw far below them the frozen body of a man who had fallen during a previous climbing season, and they realized their descent would involve much more than a simple scramble. Through a long, exhausting day they used ropes to lower climbers, trekkers, and Sherpas 300 feet down the rock face, and then sent them with Wally Berg and Michael Allison into the Khumbu.

"Scott, Craig, the whole crew, we all worked to set up a full-on technical descent of the Amphu Labtsa," Wally told me. "Having a group of experienced mountaineers there made it feasible, but it was still a big deal."

That done, Craig and Scott went the other way from the top of the Amphu Labtsa to Baruntse Base Camp, completing the hike with speed and efficiency despite Scott's sore knee. "I was being real careful picking my way through the rocks," Craig recalled, "and

Scott is just bounding down the gulleys. He was like a skier comfortable on double black diamond runs."

"We're just cruisin', just burning high test!" Scott had shouted to him as they raced along.

Aside from Scott's knee, the expedition's only other complication involved Wes Krause's delayed departure from Tanzania. He had been trying to purchase property from a Maasai woman who was reluctant to sign the final papers. By the time the negotiations were completed and he had flown to Nepal, Wes was a dozen days behind the other Mountain Madness trekkers and climbers. He spent a night in Kathmandu and connected with P. B. Thapa, the Nepalese trip organizer he'd met in 1984 when he and Scott had come to climb the Fang.

Thapa had been working with Scott to expand their business opportunities in the Himalayas, a cooperative arrangement P. B. acknowledged by placing Mountain Madness signs in the windows of his Kathmandu office. He and Scott felt they could not yet put together a commercial expedition to the summit of Mount Everest because Scott had still not been to the top. For the present, there did seem to be market for treks to Everest Base Camp and for more adventurous journeys like the Mera and Baruntse expedition under way with the Friends of Scott.

P. B. booked Wes on a flight to Lukla where he was met by a couple of Sherpas to hike with him to the Baruntse Base Camp. "It was a perfect trip for me, trekking at my own pace," Wes remembered. "You go over that pass and into the Hinku Valley and there were no people there. It was a little bit of wilderness and that was neat." The father of one of the Sherpas was staying in a yak herder camp that they passed, so they moved in and drank tea with him for an evening. A few days later Wes reached Baruntse. He had gone from his home at 4,500 feet in Africa to almost 18,000 feet in the Himalayas in less than a week, but despite having little time to adjust to the high elevation or recover from jet lag, he seemed no worse for the wear.

"I've just seen so many birds that are on my life list," Wes told

Craig Seasholes as he arrived at Base Camp, "and now I get to climb Baruntse. This is so great!" Wes was excited simply to be there, to be moving fast, to be experiencing new country and joining in an adventure with his friends. Observing the birds along the route had been every bit as important as cruising and burning high test, and no less interesting than everything else that was going on. His delay in reaching Nepal did mean he wouldn't catch up with his father-in-law who had already rappelled off the Amphu Labtsa and was heading down the Khumbu, but Wes could see him another time. For the moment he was in the middle of a terrific adventure, and that was fine with him.

Dropping his pack, Wes used his birding glasses to watch two specks moving against the snow high on Baruntse. Dave Mondeau and Scott had set out the previous day to anchor ropes on steep ice above base camp and establish a high camp where they had spent the night. When Wes saw them, they were making their way across a precipitous ridge.

"It was a real narrow ridgeline with snow flutes down to a rock face and cliff," Dale Kruse told me of his own crossing of the traverse a couple of days later. "Any little misstep and you're going to slide down and over the rock face. It's hardly worth being roped up. If one guy falls, there's not enough anchor to hold an ice axe and you're going to pull yourself off."

"If you knew you weren't going to die, you could go across fast," Craig Seasholes recalled, "but if you thought about it too much, it was going to take you awhile."

Scott led Dave Mondeau near the top of the ridge, the slope beneath them falling away at such a sharp angle that Dave became convinced they had to be on the wrong side of the crest. Surely the other side would be less severe. Scott disagreed and kept going, stomping out a trail as he worked his way forward. Dave was persistent, though, unable to shake the nagging feeling that the other face of the ridge must offer a safer way to go.

"Dammit, we're on the right route!" Scott said, emphasizing the point by chopping at the corniced ridge top with his ice axe until he had punched a hole through the snow. Mondeau peered into the opening and looked thousands of feet straight down the ridge's opposite side.

"Okay," he said as he settled once more into Scott's footsteps, "I think this is the route, then." They moved to the end of the ridge and up to the summit. The spectacular weather continued to hold, and they could see far out into the surrounding sweep of the Himalayas.

The following day Wes joined Craig Seasholes, Dale Kruse, and several others to climb to the high camp. "We'd been at base camp a week getting used to the altitude," Dale told me. "Wes had been there one day and he led us right up the mountain. I know he had some headaches, but he was so strong and he took us right up there."

"I'm kind of a fan of that whole acclimatizing thing," one of the other climbers told Wes, "but that's just me."

Leaving their high camp after midnight, the climbers ascended in the darkness until the shapes of Makalu and the other peaks nearby glowed golden with the first light of the dawn. They came upon ropes Scott had anchored in place and followed them to the beginning of the traverse across the ridge. The morning was very cold and all but Wes, Craig, and Dale turned back. The three followed the tracks of Scott and Dave, and reached Baruntse's summit in the middle of the day. "Wes was kind of hypoxic by then," Craig told me. "Dale was really strong. It was a great climb."

The Baruntse climbers reunited at base camp, packed their gear, and rappelled down the Amphu Labtsa into the Khumbu. From there it was a rambunctious parade from one Nepalese teahouse to the next. "All of us were fully acclimated by then and eating like crazy," Craig Seasholes remembered. "We'd made it up the peaks and now we were heading for home. It was just great fun, but then it was always more fun to be around Scott than it was not to be with him."

While they sitting in the sun having lunch in the village of Dingboche, an attractive woman hiked past wearing a fuzzy Tibetan hat covered with embroidery and gold brocade. The Bruces couldn't let that alone, and after teasing her about the hat, invited her to join them for a beer. She introduced herself as Lene Gammelgaard, a Danish adventurer who had been trekking in the upper Khumbu.

"Hiking with Wes and Scott could be pretty entertaining," Craig observed, "and she jumped right on the fun with Mountain Madness." Lene became part of their procession down the Khumbu. When they reached Lukla, they discovered that flight schedules were disrupted and climbers were facing potential delays of four or five days before they could fly to Kathmandu. Most of the Mountain Madness team decided to keep hiking, descending past villages and along terraced mountain fields for several more days to Jeri where the trail ends and a highway crowded with buses and cars gave them easy access to rides the rest of the way to Kathmandu.

Lene kept pace with them all the way, buoyed along in the adventure and the positive energy of the Madness, but Scott's knee was hurting and he decided that catching a flight out of Lukla could get him started on his way home a little more quickly to see his children.

Back in Seattle, Scott would hold Katie Rose and Andy close and know that being with them was the best experience in the world. He would tell Karen about the success of the most recent adventure and begin thinking about marketing something similar to clients who would be able to pay more than what he had charged a bunch of Bruces on the Friends of Scott sliding scale. Jeannie would have the Fischer-Price house flying along just the way she wanted, and she and Scott would argue their way back into rhythm, careful for at least a few weeks not to make any big decisions.

Coming home had seldom been a smooth transition for Scott, but having a baby daughter and a young son to enjoy made it easier to flip the switch and shift from the globe-trotting life of a mountain climber to the more sedate pleasures of being a family guy who goes to the office every day. At least it was easier for a little while. For Scott, the switch was never going to stay in that position for very long.

CHAPTER 17

K2 in '92

You want to make deposits at the First National Bank of Karma whenever you can just in case someday you need to make a big withdrawal.

—Scott Fischer

JEANNIE PRICE HAD landed the Alaska Airlines Boeing 727 at SeaTac, tossed her captain's hat onto the backseat of her car with the FLYAK license plate, and was driving over the last hill on her way home when she saw her five-year-old son Andy standing on the peak of the roof of the Fischer-Price home. She knew that her husband and his climbing partner Ed Viesturs, recently back from their K2 expedition, were re-roofing the place, but she had not expected Scott to be so irresponsible, so utterly without regard for Andy's safety, as to let the boy run around on top of the house. Is it too much to ask, she thought to herself, for Scott to keep their little boy just a bit safer than that?

She wheeled the car into the driveway, leaped out, and shouted, "Scott! Dammit, what's Andy doing up there?"

Scott looked over from the far side of the roof and then Ed's head popped up, too. Neither man was near Andy.

"Hey, it's great!" Scott called down. "We've got this thing wired! Come up and take a look."

Still furious, Jeannie climbed the ladder leaning against the eaves. When she reached shingle level she could see that Scott and Ed had tied a climbing rope around the top of the chimney, stretched the rope the length of the roof, and secured the other end to an exhaust vent. They had cinched a piece of webbing around Andy's waist to serve as a harness and used a carabiner to clip the boy to the rope. He had free range of the roof while Ed and his father worked. If he did happen to fall, Andy would go no more than a couple of feet before the belay line caught him.

Jeannie saw the wisdom and appreciated that Scott, after his long absence, was so engaged with Andy, but the household was in the usual turmoil it always assumed when Scott returned from a trip, and this time he had been away a long time. It had been hard on him, hard on Jeannie, and especially hard on Andy, who was still attending kindergarten when his dad had left in late spring and hadn't seen him again until autumn when first grade classes were under way. Katie Rose was two, and while she seemed not as affected by the long absence, Scott had missed twenty weeks of his young daughter's life.

Scott was scheduled to have surgery to repair the mess that his shoulder had become, but first he and Ed had to get a new roof on the house before the rainy season sank its soggy claws into Seattle. Once the days turned chilly and gray there would be plenty of time to spend with the children and to think about how so many threads of his climbing life had become entwined on the world's second highest mountain.

A year earlier on his way through Kathmandu after the Mountain Madness trip to Baruntse and Mera Peaks, Scott had run into Ed. It was not unusual for climbers to find one another in the Nepalese capital. Mountaineers often stayed at the Garuda or one of the other reasonably priced hotels in the city's Thamal District. They ate meals at Mike's Breakfast and the Yak n' Yeti, restaurants that catered to the palates of climbers who, after a month or two of camp food, Khumbu potatoes, and yak meat, were eager for a plate of huevos rancheros or a rack of lamb, or anything else prepared by a chef in a kitchen rather than a Sherpa in a tent. In the evenings they drank beer and swapped stories at the Rum Doodle, a bar with walls featuring autographs of those who had stood atop Everest.

Although they both lived in Seattle, it was the first time the two mountaineers had met. Ed had come to the Pacific Northwest from

Illinois to study veterinary medicine at Washington State University. Drawn to the Cascades, he was soon hooked on climbing and landed a job as a guide on Mount Rainier. A few years later he helped lead Dick Bass on a McKinley climb that was part of Bass's project to be the first to climb the highest peak on each of the seven continents.

Ed made his first trip to Everest in 1987 with an expedition that in the spring attempted the same route up the North Face that Scott's Mountain Madness expedition would try the following autumn. He was back the next year with another team on Everest's Kangshung Face, an effort abandoned after avalanches swept their fixed ropes and supply caches off the mountain. Two years later Jim Whittaker included Ed on the 1990 International Peace Everest expedition. Climbing from Tibet without breathing supplemental oxygen, Ed was one of nineteen expedition members to get to the top of the world. (Five days later Scott Fischer and Wally Berg would summit Lhotse from the Nepalese side, just a few miles away.) Ed was on Everest the following year, too, going up the mountain by the South Col route.

In Kathmandu, Scott and Ed told each other about their recent Himalayan adventures and shared what they hoped to do in the future. Ed was beginning to set his sights on summiting the world's fourteen peaks higher than 8,000 meters and doing each without using supplemental oxygen. Climbing them all would be a marathon requiring years to accomplish and tremendous skill, endurance, and luck. (Cataloging them as "the 8,000 meter peaks" was tidier and had much more appeal than calling them "the 26,246 foot peaks.")

Scott found the idea intriguing, but having yet to summit any of the mountains on that list, he had in mind the much simpler goal of climbing just one of the 8,000-meter giants, K2. He'd managed to secure a 1992 permit for K2's North Ridge, and a slate of climbers had expressed interest in joining the expedition. Ed said he would like to come along, too, and Scott promised to keep him in mind.

Back in Seattle, Scott learned that his potential K2 teammates were realizing they couldn't commit the time, the money, or both to the expedition. Without others to share the expenses, Scott gave up the permit and signed on as a member of an expedition being organized by Russian mountaineer Vladimir Balyberdin. Scott encouraged Ed to do that, too, envisioning that the two of them could be a climbing team embedded in the larger expedition. Space on the permit would cost them each $8,000. Neither man had that much money, but if Ed were interested, Scott was sure they could figure out the finances.

To raise cash, Scott advertised a thirty-five day Mountain Madness trek to K2 Base Camp that would precede the climb. "Cost includes $1,000 tax deductible contribution to the expedition," a Mountain Madness brochure concluded. In other words, money for Scott and Ed to get themselves to the mountain. The two climbers also encouraged their friends to help sell 1992 SOVIET-AMERICAN K2 EXPEDITION T-shirts, a sure sign that a trip to a big mountain was in the works.

"Scott and I were at different places in our lives," Ed Viesturs recalled of that time. "He had kids and he was running a business that was just breaking even. I was young and single and didn't have any of those obligations. I think a big thing for him was if he went off somewhere, he had to try and make money while he was doing it. Getting his guiding going and doing international trips was a priority."

Flying first to Islamabad, Pakistan, the climbers continued to Skardu, the capital of Baltistan, on the banks of the Indus River. There they met the Mountain Madness trekkers and rode with them in the backs of trucks along dusty, winding roads to Askole where ten days of hiking began. They ascended into mountains of increasing ruggedness and loft, shadowed by dozens of porters carrying food and gear. Their route took them below the Trango Towers and Mustang Tower, and within sight of Masherbrum and dozens of other imposing peaks. Much of the way was alongside the Baltoro Glacier, the ice veined with bands of crushed stone flowing a few inches a day toward the Indus River. The sense of remoteness increased with each passing mile, matched by the starkness of the terrain and the height and angularity of the mountains around them, and then at the confluence of the Baltoro Glacier and the Godwin Austen Glacier, they got their first look at the mountain they had come to climb. If any view were to give an mountaineer pause, this was it.

Encompassing a greater area covered with ice than any region on Earth other than the Arctic and Antarctic, the Karakoram Range is separated from the Himalayas to the east by several powerful rivers including the Indus. It also includes dozens of the world's highest peaks including K2. Named *K2* as the second mountain in the Karakoram to be surveyed, it is only about 780 feet lower than Mount Everest. Its neighbor Broad Peak was originally K3, the name changing when climbers noted the wide expanse of that mountain's summit, but K2 retained its austere name. There is nothing broad about it anywhere. Soaring nearly two miles straight up from the glaciers, it is arguably the steepest major mountain on the planet. There are no foothills, no gradual rise of terrain. K2 is simply and fully there.

"K2 is harsh, it is brutal, and if you can't handle it, then you get off and you never come back," Stacy Allison told me recently. "It does not let up at all." A K2 expedition leader in 1993, she had also stood atop Everest and could compare the world's two tallest mountains. "On Everest at Camp II you can kick back and hang out, have a beer if you want, but on K2, when you're on that mountain, you have to be focused the entire time."

Climber Charley Mace has also summited both peaks. "In some regards Everest is the easiest eight-thousand-meter peak," he told me. "It's the biggest, but it also has the biggest infrastructure. You've got icefall doctors to fix the route. Ladders to get up there. Ropes all the way to the summit. There's oxygen. When I guided Everest I never set up a tent. On K2 there were porters to base camp and that was it. The rest was up to us."

The first to attempt scaling K2 was Luigi Amedeo, the Duke of the Abruzzi, an Italian nobleman who launched a large expedition in 1909. No one with him ascended higher than 20,000 feet, but the Duke lent his name to the Abruzzi Ridge, a possible way up the mountain that had shown promise as a gateway to the summit.

Scott knew that in 1938, long before establishing the National Outdoor Leadership School, Paul Petzoldt had hiked up Baltoro Glacier with the first American expedition approaching to K2. The team pioneered the Abruzzi Ridge route and placed its highest camp at 24,700 feet. Petzoldt pressed on to 26,000 feet where he had seen the way open to the top. He would later say that if he and his fellow climbers had been able to carry more food and fuel to their higher camps, they might have summited.

The route that Petzoldt and his teammates had found was to become the most frequently attempted way up K2. In 1954 an Italian team used it with success, climbing the last pitches that Petzoldt had predicted would lead to the top. By 1992, seventy-three climbers had summited, compared to nearly twice that many who had been to the top of Mount Everest. The fatality rate on Everest hovered at about one death for every ten successful summit attempts. On K2, the ratio had been closer to one in four.

Scott and Ed intended to ascend via the Abruzzi Ridge. They would begin by going through a modest icefall, then climb a difficult section of rock that featured a near-vertical crack nearly 100 feet high called House's Chimney in honor of Bill House, a teammate of Paul Petzoldt who had been the first to scale it. They planned to establish their Camp I above the Chimney at 20,000 feet, then 2,000 feet higher put in Camp II. Next would come 1,000 feet of steep, difficult climbing on ice and rock to the top of the Black Pyramid, a geological feature where they hoped to pitch their Camp III tent. Climbing to the Shoulder, a hump on the ridge at 25,000 feet and the potential site of Camp IV, would involve steep snow slopes exposed to the weather, prone to avalanches, and almost impossible to navigate if visibility became poor. Assuming they made it that far, their bid for the summit would be challenged above Camp IV by a couloir called the Bottleneck.

The Mountain Madness trekkers settled in at the K2 Base Camp for a few days to enjoy the views of the Karakoram and the comforts that unfolded from the boxes the porters had hauled in from Askole. There was plenty of good food, a cook to prepare it, and a camp staff to see to the trekkers' needs. Scott dubbed their encampment next to the glacier the Baltoro Café, open to anyone stopping by for a visit and a cup of fresh-brewed coffee.

Among those who did show up with their coffee mugs in hand were the other members of the Russian-American K2 expedition, a loose confederation of climbers who had also had bought their way onto the permit. Four were from Russia and the Ukraine, one was British, and the dozen Americans included three Colorado climbers— Thor Kieser, Neal Beidleman, and Charley Mace.

A self-taught mountaineer introduced to climbing while a student at Colorado College, Charley had been working as a business consultant when his friend Thor, a Denver-based mountain guide, called to ask if he wanted to join the K2 expedition. "Let me think about it for five minutes and then call you back and tell you yes," Charley told him.

"I told my boss I was going to K2, and he said my job wouldn't be there when I got back," Charley told me recently. "That was the last time I've worn a tie."

Neal Beidleman had earned a degree in mechanical engineering at the University of Colorado. While the K2 expedition was his first trip to extremely high mountains, he had done plenty of climbing and trail-running in the Rockies. "I'd been around a lot of good athletes before," he told me of meeting Ed and Scott, "but that was the first time I'd been around Himalayan climbers."

Another group at base camp was the International K2 expedition led by Ricardo Torres-Nava who had summited Everest with the On Top Everest expedition. Scott had been the climbing leader, and Ricardo had felt with some justification that Scott had not respected his commitment or his alpine abilities. An exuberant Mexican, his stay at K2 was highlighted by a visit from his wife, a television broadcaster, who helicoptered in to base camp.

Two climbers with whom Scott did share a warm friendship were Rob Hall and Gary Ball. Gary and Scott had met in 1987 on Pik Kommunizma in the Pamirs. He and fellow New Zealander Rob

Hall had joined forces in the intervening years to complete a number of significant climbs. They had also shared time with Scott on Mount Everest in 1989 when none of them had reached the summit, and again in 1990 when Rob and Gary did succeed while Wally Berg and Scott were climbing Lhotse.

Having tried twice before to climb K2, Hall and Ball had bought onto Ricardo Torres-Nava's permit so that they could give the mountain another go. They were fresh from leading ten clients to Mount Everest with a company they had formed called Adventure Consultants, and had guided six of them to the top. It was a story they no doubt shared with Scott.

Camped a few minutes farther down the glacier was a team of four Swiss alpinists and French climber Chantal Mauduit. She and the Swiss intended to climb K2 alpine style, carrying as little as possible and relying on speed to see them through.

"I'd not been on a climb like that where most of the people didn't know each other and kind of got thrown in together," Ed Viesturs told me. "It wasn't my choice to do it like that, but Scott and I figured it was the one way we could probably go. We would do what we could for the group. We would carry loads for other people and help set up camps, but he and I would operate as a team."

Like Scott, Ed was soon connecting with climbers who would play important roles both on K2 and on other peaks. "Neal Beidleman and Charley Mace were strong, decent people, and I gravitated toward them," Ed remembered. "and I hooked up with Hall and Ball. It turned out all right."

Climbers from all the expeditions joined forces to push the route up K2, leaving ropes anchored in place so that on subsequent ascents they could clip their harnesses to the lines with ascending devices to make the next trips less difficult and to protect themselves from falling. Ed and Scott led much of the way, including working through House's Chimney. When they got as high as the Black Pyramid they were ready to descend to base camp and rest before going farther, though what happened on the way down threw into question whether Scott would go back up the mountain at all.

The icefall at the foot of K2 is modest compared with the Khumbu

Icefall guarding the way to Everest's Western Cwm, but not without danger. Maneuvering around crevasses and below cliffs of compressed snow, Scott felt a block of ice move beneath his feet. He leaned to counter the shift, lost his balance, and plunged into a crevasse, crashing to a halt as hot pain exploded in his shoulder. He knew he had dislocated the joint just as he had when he'd fallen into a crevasse on the Dinwoody Glacier in the Wind River Range two decades earlier.

"Almost déjà vu of the time in Wyoming," he wrote in a letter to Jeannie three days later. "An ice block broke away and I fell in the ice fall. My shoulder came out when I tried to catch myself." He explained that he had been with Ed. "We were roped up and doing everything right. Bad luck!" he scribbled.

"We hiked off the glacier with my shoulder out," he continued. "When we got to the moraine Ed ran for the Russian doctor." The physician had injected Scott with morphine and then cranked on his arm to pop the bone of his upper arm back into its socket. Ed helped Scott return to base camp where climbers shared their condolences. He would recover in his tent for a few days, they reasoned, and then would walk down the glacier toward Askole as he began the return to Seattle.

A few days passed, though, and then a few more, and Scott did nothing about packing up to leave. He had always loved being social when he was in camp and had always been motivated to press ahead when he was climbing, but now he was sidelined from the action. Incapacitated, he found himself in the unfamiliar role of being a spectator to others' activities.

Certainly he was a master at passing time in a tent. Stormed in on a high route, all he needed was a book, a chessboard, and someone to share a conversation, and the hours would roll by. But hanging around base camp to see if his body might heal required a different kind of patience than waiting for the weather to clear. He could feel himself losing strength and acclimatization. Even as his shoulder began to get stronger, he knew he was becoming weaker. K2 loomed overhead, and there wasn't a thing he could do about climbing it. Day after day his ice axe and crampons lay against a rock outside of his tent. They weren't going anywhere, and neither was he.

"It was frustrating for Scott," Charley Mace told me. "He was used to being strong and fit. Here's this dream of a lifetime, to climb K2, then he thinks he's lost it all by slipping and falling in that mellow ice field."

"When Scott dislocated his shoulder on that trip I was very impressed with how he waited it out and let himself heal," Neal Beidleman recalled. "Other people were going up and down the mountain, and I think your average person would have gotten frustrated. But he didn't. He hung in."

Scott's innate optimism got him through the first days of his recovery. "I'm not bumming," he told Jeannie. "My shoulder's going to heal enough for me to climb K2. It's going to. Really." He wondered if he would need surgery when he got home. He'd had his other shoulder worked on, and was not enthused about going under the knife again. "Right now I'm in a lot of pain."

He waited a week, finding in his inactivity plenty of time to put his thoughts down on paper. "This trip has been enjoyable for me because I have no responsibility and that's a big change from my normal life," he wrote. "I like most of the people. Before my little accident I was one of the stronger climbers. Ed is super strong. I could barely keep up. We're good partners, I think."

He was also keenly aware of the progress of the others. "Right now we have camps one, two, and three in. Camp four should go in in the next couple of days or so. I figure I'll be ready in a week or so . . . and then I'll try to charge this mountain."

More days passed. Scott was still in camp, unable to charge anything. "Now I'm bumming," he admitted. "Really depressed. I'm not convinced I'll get better and be able to climb this mountain. Here I sit, in pain, wasting my life away."

He turned to a clean page in his notebook, addressing his thoughts to his wife. "I do know what your advice would be: *come home*," he wrote, "but it's so hard for me. My self-image is so tied into my physical being and now I just feel worthless. Maybe I'm kidding myself to think that a guy with his arm all strapped up (even me) can climb K2."

Three more days dragged by. "God, I miss my family," he wrote. "What do I do this for? I am riding such an emotional roller coaster. When I started this letter I was doing great, and now I feel like crying. I know I shouldn't, but I'm afraid they are going to climb this mountain without me and then I'll think I've failed. Hate to fail!"

Scott waited two weeks, fighting off boredom and disappointment, pain and discontent, spending much of his time alone in his tent, embarrassed to have others see him with his arm in a sling. But then he'd had enough. He'd been hurt before and had mastered the pain. Didn't he always prevail? Hadn't the application of more energy, more of the old Bruce force, always been enough to see him through?

He told others he was done sitting around and that he was ready to get back on K2. Hearing that a group of climbers planned to ferry loads the next day to the higher camps, Scott offered to come along. Ed helped him secure a nylon strap around his wrist and tether it to his waist harness to prevent him from raising his arm high enough to dislocate his shoulder again.

The weather was so marginal the following morning that the other climbers postponed their carry, but Scott set out anyway. In the privacy of a snowstorm he would find out whether he could climb. He threaded his way through the icefall and past the crevasse where he had been injured. When he came to the first of the fixed ropes, he clipped his ascender to it and used his good arm to pull himself slowly up the slope. With excruciating effort he made his way 4,000 feet up to Camp I. Exhausted, he crawled into a tent, melted snow for water, and ate a little dinner.

The evidence of the day's effort told him what he already knew—that he was out of shape, still hurt, and no longer acclimated to higher elevations. He ignored the obvious, though, and the next day continued his solitary quest by dragging himself another 2,000 vertical feet to Camp II. If climbing higher would restore his energies and help him learn how to maneuver with one good arm, he was willing to put up with the pain. And if not? Well, that was out of the question.

Scott slept at Camp II and then for good measure stayed through the next day and another night. "I was up for four days (three nights) in real bad weather," he wrote after he had come down. "Now I've been in base camp for three days and I feel better all the time." He had passed his self-imposed test and concluded that he could no longer use his damaged shoulder as an excuse not to climb K2.

To others, Scott's recovery was nothing short of astonishing. "Scott was as strong as an ox," Charley Mace observed. "He bounced back from his injury much quicker than anyone expected and partied on."

Scott knew he could will himself farther up the peak, but there was more in play than just his ability to move. The expeditions had been in base camp for well over a month and the window of opportunity for climbing K2 was rapidly closing. Stretches of bad weather had demoralized some of the climbers and convinced them that this could be one of those seasons on K2 when nobody reached the top. A few had already packed their gear and started down the valley.

Then on the first day of August, Vladimir Balyberdin and his partner Gennadi Kopieka reached the summit without using supplemental oxygen. Their success sent a charge of excitement through base camp. If those guys could make it, the thinking seemed to go, then so can we. Scott wasn't about to argue with that logic. He and Ed Viesturs made ambitious plans to ascend 7,000 vertical feet from base camp to Camp III in one day, reach Camp IV the following afternoon, and then go for the summit.

The route up K2 was wide open, save for three climbers who had been high on the mountain when Balyberdin and Kopieka had gone to the top. Thor Keiser and Ukrainian climber Aleksei Nikiforov were on their way from Camp IV to the summit. They had been joined by the French climber Chantal Mauduit, whose attempt with the Swiss team to make a quick alpine ascent had been pounded so severely by the ruthless realities of K2 that the Swiss had gone home.

Scott and Ed climbed steadily to Camp III where they heard over their radio that Thor was in Camp IV after an unsuccessful summit bid. Chantal and Aleksei had reached the top of K2, but had been stranded overnight and had only returned to the Camp IV tents that morning. The three had been above 26,000 feet for the four days. They were cold and hungry and suffering from the altitude, and Thor reported that they were in desperate trouble.

Much of the route between Camp III and Camp IV cannot be protected with ropes, either to help climbers ascend or to find their way back down. Prone to avalanches, it is a portion of the mountain where many people have died. The two Seattle climbers set out to help those above them, but the weather kicked up and visibility became poor, forcing them to return to Camp III.

The air was clear enough the next morning to see Aleksei coming down the snowfield. Scott and Ed tucked him into a tent, then climbed again in hopes of finding Thor and Chantal. Scott was in the lead with Ed roped up below him, their progress slowed by deep, loose snow that had accumulated during the night. Suddenly the instincts honed during years on high mountains warned them that the steeply angled snowfield was about to slide out from under their feet.

With his ice axe Ed frantically began carving a burrow in the snow to shelter himself from the avalanche that he was certain was coming and that suddenly did break loose and roar toward them. Spindrift enveloped Scott, and then a turbulent wave of snow knocked him off his feet. He tumbled past Ed and when the rope between them tightened, the force of Scott's weight hitting the line yanked Ed out of his burrow and into a freefall of his own. Tons of snow thundered around them as they careened down the mountain, fighting to get their ice axes into the slope and bring themselves to a halt, Ed first and then Scott, the rope jerking Scott's harness tight up into his groin. "My balls!" he cried out. It may not have been the most memorable mountaineering quote of all time, but at least he was alive to shout something.

The avalanche rolled on below them, hurtling thousands of feet down K2. Scott tugged at his harness to relieve his pain, then he and Ed shook the snow off themselves and evaluated their situation. The release of the avalanche had cleared the slope of its loose snow and had somewhat reduced the danger of going higher. They climbed to Thor and Chantal and then dragged and belayed them down the mountain past Camp III, Camp II, and Camp I to base camp. At their high point, Scott and Ed had been within striking distance of the K2 summit, and now they were again by their tents on the Baltoro Glacier.

Everyone was off the mountain, and it appeared that the climbing was over for the season. Vladimir Balyberdin informed the remaining climbers on his permit that the Russian-American K2 expedition was disbanding and they should go home. Several of those who wanted to stay convinced the Pakistani liaison officers to shift leadership from Vladimir to another team member and keep the expedition going so that they could continue to try the mountain.

At first it didn't matter as three days of bad weather kept the climbers in base camp. Then the skies began to clear, and in twos and threes they bolted up the route. "When the weather breaks on K2, you go," Charley Mace told me. "It doesn't matter if you're Swedish or Mexican, from Seattle or Russia, we all work together to make it happen."

Scott adjusted the straps on his forty-five pound pack and climbed with Ed to Camp III one more time. They continued to Camp IV the next day, sticking thin wooden wands in the snow as they ascended to mark the route for their return. Late in the afternoon they were joined by Rob Hall, Gary Ball, three Mexican climbers, three Swedes, and Charley Mace.

"I was paired up with Hector Ponce de Leon, one of the Mexicans," Charley told me. "Scott and Ed were a team, Hall and Ball were paired up, and so were the other Mexicans and then the Swedes."

Camp IV was exposed to the brunt of winds slamming against

the mountain. There were no fixed ropes below it for more than half a mile. If a storm trapped them there, the climbers could perish from thirst, hunger, and cold. If they ventured down in poor visibility, they could simply disappear. All they needed was one day of reasonable weather to climb the final 2,300 feet to the summit, but conditions continued to deteriorate. The immediacy of their peril became even more apparent the next morning when several of the Mexican climbers tried to descend. One of them fell, plunging nearly a mile to his death. He had been a close friend of Charley's tent mate Hector Ponce de Leon. "We had some teary-eyed conversations," Charley recalled, "then Hector bailed and I was in the tent by myself."

Another day came and went as the wind tore at the camp and battered it with snow. The day after that was not much different, but the Swedes decided they'd had enough and started down the mountain. That left Rob and Gary, Scott and Ed, and Charley.

Three days into their stay at Camp IV, the five men decided the weather was improving enough for them to attempt the summit. "Hall and Ball were going to use oxygen," Charley recalled, "but Scott, Ed, and I were not." Charley's understanding was that the three Americans would leave camp at 11:00 p.m., an hour earlier than Hall and Ball, figuring that breathing bottled oxygen would allow the New Zealanders to catch up with them. Charley suddenly awoke at midnight.

"I'd expected Scott and Ed to roust me up, but I didn't hear them and they were already climbing," Charley told me. "Hall and Ball were still farkeling around, so I took off solo." He climbed fast, catching up with the other Americans at the Bottleneck, a very steep, narrow snowfield at 27,500 feet. Scott invited him to tie into the rope that he and Ed were sharing. Charley was grateful for the protection, though all three were aware that if one of them fell, he could easily pull the others down the mountain with him. They could not make a mistake. Charley led the way across the Bottleneck, and as they emerged above it they were aware of the profound distance between themselves and the fragile security of Camp IV.

"From there on up we swung leads," Charley told me. "The guy in front would plow through thigh-deep snow until he went hy-poxic while the guys in the back were just merrily chatting away." Snow began to fall as they rotated the lead from one to another, and they watched the weather with growing concern. "All of us thought it was okay to go up," Charley explained, "but we knew we were going to have to come back down into this maelstrom. It wasn't the best conditions, but we were willing to push on."

Ed would later remember the internal warning bells. There were so many ways to die on K2 and he wanted no part of them. Scott had already survived falling into the icefall, and he and Ed had used up a fair amount of karma coming away from an avalanche with-out much damage other than the kick in the crotch Scott had en-dured. Now the weather was bad and the air thin and the tremendous distance to safety growing greater with every step. Perhaps they should cut their losses, turn back, and reduce the risk of becoming lost or falling or being trapped by a storm. For Scott, though, the possibility of success overrode the danger. He was convinced they could reach the summit and return. It was the effort, the chance to extend, another opportunity to shove back the boundaries of what was possible. They were going to make it happen.

The three men plodded slowly through the deep snow. The over-cast became thinner and then they broke above the clouds and dis-covered they had run out of mountain. The sunlit summit of K2 gleamed beneath their boots.

They stayed long enough for a few celebratory whoops, then took photographs of one another and began their descent from the sunshine into the swirling snow. Their tracks were already being covered, and they had to find their way by trial and error. Spindrift sloughing around their legs reminded them of the increasing danger of avalanches, and they moved through the afternoon as quickly as they could. When they were sure they had descended far enough to reach Camp IV, they shouted into the whiteness and were relieved to hear Rob Hall and Gary Ball calling back, the sounds of the New Zealand accents guiding them to their tents.

"Hall and Ball had started out for the summit after I'd left camp," Charley recalled. "As I was trying to catch Scott and Ed I looked down and could see Hall's and Ball's headlamps falling back in the distance. They never caught up with us."

Completely spent, the Americans took shelter in their tents. The weather had not improved the next morning, but they knew they had to get down from Camp IV or risk being stranded. Enough snow had fallen to bury all but a couple of inches of the wands they had placed on their way up, but that was enough to guide them. They paused at Camp III to brew hot drinks, then clipped their harnesses to the fixed lines and dropped down to Camp II.

Darkness had fallen by the time Rob Hall and Gary Ball arrived. Rob was struggling with the altitude, but was in better shape than Gary, whose distressed breathing was an almost certain sign he was suffering from high-altitude pulmonary edema. His condition worsened through the night, and the next morning Scott, Ed, and Charley committed themselves to helping the Kiwis off the mountain.

"Getting Gary down was much harder than climbing to the summit and back," Charley told me. "We'd been above eight thousand meters and working our butts off for days, and now we're shouldered with the burden of helping another man down, yet being completely exhausted ourselves."

Rob Hall began recovering as they descended, but Gary Ball got worse. "He started off being able to clip on to a rope and tie a knot, but at the end we were literally carrying him and dragging him," Charley remembered. "It took two of us to carry Gary while the other guy trailed behind, and we traded out helping, just as we had swung the leads going to the summit. We definitely needed all three of us, plus Rob, to get Gary down."

The end of the day found them at Camp I, still high on the mountain. The tents there were inviting, but they feared Gary would not survive another night at elevation, and they continued to descend with him through the darkness. They were met at the bottom of the fixed ropes by climbers waiting with oxygen bottles and hot tea who took Gary the rest of the way to Base Camp. A helicopter flew Hall and Ball out of the mountains the next morning.*

*Rob Hall and Gary Ball recovered, though a year later while they were climbing the Himalayan peak Dhauligiri, Gary died from a recurrence of pulmonary edema.

Scott Fischer and Ed Viesturs were climbing again a month after their K2 expedition, only this time no higher than the rafters of the Fischer-Price house. There was a lot for each of them to think about as they nailed down plywood sheets and tacked new shingles in place. Andy was belayed with a mountaineering rope to the chimney, and it was great to see him running around and delighting in being again with his dad. Katie Rose was taking a nap and would soon be ready for Scott to cuddle her. He had an appointment for shoulder surgery, but first he and Ed needed to beat the rains by getting the new roof done.

Ed would say that the push to the summit of K2 was the biggest mistake of his climbing career. "What I learned from that episode has stayed with me for good," he wrote in his book *No Shortcuts to the Top*. "It can be summed up in a few words: *Your instincts are telling you something. Trust them and listen to them.*"

Scott probably would have agreed, though his instincts had always been tuned to a different frequency that could bring him to different conclusions. Make it happen. Go for it. Apply the Bruce force and difficulties will fall away.

The K2 climb may well have been the most daunting physical challenge Scott Fischer ever faced, and a tremendous test of his willpower. His accomplishments on K2 after tearing up his shoulder were beyond what would have been within either the abilities or the desire of most other climbers. Certainly the experience infused him with an even greater sense that by working harder he could overcome anything. In the years to come, he almost did.

CHAPTER 18

What Would Hillary Do?

How are you?
> —Sir Edmund Hillary mistaking me for someone else

Craggy, bushy, and even taller than I had always imagined him to be, Sir Edmund Hillary stepped away from the Sherpas and came toward me with his hand outstretched. It was a chilly evening in Namche Bazaar, the Sherpa village terraced into the steep bowl of a mountainside several days' hiking distance from Mount Everest. The center of Sherpa culture, it is a town of narrow streets winding among guest houses, shops, a clinic, and small homes constructed of stacked stone. Hillary had helicoptered from Kathmandu to Namche to take part in celebrations honoring the anniversary of the first ascent of Everest when, in 1953, he and Tenzing Norgay had stood together on the summit and revolutionized the mountaineering world. Forty years later, the highlight of the 1993 observance was a celebration for the Sherpa people and members of Hillary's party at the monastery overlooking Namche.

I was helping Scott Fischer square away the Mountain Madness camp in a small field in the village when we heard the monks blowing horns to summon Buddha, the deep sound resonating across the Khumbu and toward the peaks towering around us. We hiked up to the monastery in the last of the evening light to see what was going on, and stood in the darkness listening to the singing and laughter coming from behind the heavy wooden doors of the invitation-only party.

The gathering concluded and the doors swung open, spilling

light onto the stone walkway. Sherpas streamed past us, cheerful from the festivities. Then Sir Edmund Hillary emerged from the glow and the noise of the party, his neck draped with white scarves. He seemed completely at ease in that little mountain village and comfortable in his worldwide eminence. He caught sight of me as his eyes began to adjust to the darkness and his face broke into a broad smile. "How *are* you?" he asked warmly. He shook my hand vigorously and then suddenly looked confused, apparently realizing he had mistaken me for someone else and that he had not a clue who I might actually be.

"I'm very well, Sir Edmund," I told him as I returned his firm grip with my own, "and I am very happy to meet you."

"Yes, yes," he said, still puzzled as he let go of my hand. He peered closely at my face and then politely took his leave. "Good to meet you, then." As he turned to rejoin his party, he walked past Scott who was standing beside me. They were close enough to one another that they almost brushed shoulders, but Edmund Hillary, the most famous person ever to climb Everest, never noticed that Scott Fischer, who had yet to stand on the summit, was even there.

It was my first trip to Nepal, a Mountain Madness adventure Scott had organized with two peaks, Mera and Ama Dablam, as its goals. He wanted to re-create the energy of the successful Mera-Baruntse expedition two years earlier that had involved quite a few Bruces and Friends of Scott. This time he was trying to fit a two-peak trip into the tighter calendars of clients devoting their annual vacation days to an expedition in Nepal.

Frankly, I didn't care if I got to the top of anything, especially after I'd had the honor of shaking hands with Hillary. Everything I was experiencing was illuminated and new, and for several weeks I'd felt as if I were walking through the pages of *National Geographic*. It was good to be traveling again with Scott, to have him leading the way to a part of the world that was a mystery to me, and to know with a fairly high degree of certainty that he would get me safely home.

We had flown from Seattle to Bangkok and spent a night there, then continued to Kathmandu where we boarded a two-engine, eighteen-seat aircraft for the short flight to Lukla. An attendant on board gave us wads of cotton to stuff into our ears to muffle the engine noise, and pieces of hard candy to serve as refreshment while the plane gained elevation on its way to the Himalayas. I could look up the short aisle and through the cockpit windshield toward the enormous peaks looming ahead. The plane banked above a deep valley and aimed for a landing strip perched well up on the valley wall. One end of the short runway was at the lip of a cliff and the other near a cluster of buildings tucked against the mountain.

Edmund Hillary had overseen the construction of the Lukla landing strip in 1964 so that a hospital he had sponsored in Namche, a day's walk away, could receive medical supplies in a timely fashion. The village of Lukla was the closest location with anything approaching level ground. Even so, the runway rose at a steep incline and our plane didn't so much land as plow into the mountainside and, by sheer good fortune and the pilot's profound belief in the forces of gravity, physics, and Buddha, roar to a halt at the top of the runway in a swirl of dust and the acrid smoke from overheated landing-gear brakes.

We unloaded our duffels, grateful to be standing again on solid ground. Departing passengers took our places in the plane. The aircraft turned around and, with its engines at full throttle, rumbled down the runway and dropped out of sight over the edge of the cliff. It had several thousand feet of freefall to gain airspeed before hitting the river, and a few moments later we saw it rising above the terraced fields on the far side of the valley as it turned toward Kathmandu.

Air access had alleviated the need to make the four- to- six-day hike from the end of the road at Jiri and had transformed Lukla from a quiet farming village into the gateway for tourists and mountaineers trekking up the Khumbu Valley toward Mount Everest. Hillary may not have foreseen that thousands would fly to Lukla each spring and autumn to take advantage of decent weather to be among the highest mountains on Earth. He might also have been surprised how quickly the Sherpas adapted to the influx of foreigners and their money by catering to travelers' needs for lodging, meals, porters to carry gear and provisions, and guides to lead them to their destinations.

Yaks, dogs, and children wandered with me as I walked along the Lukla streets. The first toilet facility I found was an outhouse perched over a pile of straw. The first teahouse I passed had a satellite dish on its roof, and through a window, I could see the pop singer Madonna glowing on a television screen. I could cash a traveler's check almost anywhere in town, and credit cards were accepted for a night in a teahouse and an evening feast of rice and yak stew. There were no motor vehicles, and goods from salt and foodstuffs to firewood and beer had been carried from the valleys either on the backs of people or the backs of yaks. It was us, the visitors from afar, who utilized the airplanes that dropped out of the sky into the midst of Sherpa culture and mountains outrageous beyond belief.

Scott moved through Lukla with the familiarity of a man who had been there often. Everybody seemed to know him, and he greeted many of the Sherpas by name. Dawa, the sirdar for our trip, had organized the local logistics for the Mountain Madness team that included me and Scott's younger sister Lisa, and a group of more serious climbers who were hoping to make the ascent of Ama Dablam. Among them was Dale Kruse, veteran of many Mountain Madness adventures. Scott had also invited Charley Mace, with whom he'd summited K2 the previous summer, to help lead the expedition.

Dawa told us that porters were being hired to carry the expedition's food and camping equipment, and that they would take the bulk of our personal clothing and gear, too. I had always carried my own pack on backcountry journeys and it felt strange to expect others to haul my stuff for me, even if they were being paid. I tried to create as little imposition as possible by stripping my load to the bare essentials—a winter-weight sleeping bag and an inflatable pad, fleece and down clothing, a parka and wind pants, lots of sunscreen and camera film. A wide-mouthed plastic bottle insured that I could urinate in the middle of cold nights without leaving the warmth of my bed.

When I delivered my gear to Dawa, I discovered that each porter would carry about sixty pounds, jamming everything into a wicker basket that would be hoisted onto his back, the weight transferred to the muscles of his neck and shoulders with a tumpline across his forehead. My clothing and gear would be combined with that of others in our party to form a full load. By trying to take so little, I may in fact have been preventing an additional porter from getting to sign on to the expedition for a couple of dollars a day.

Scott's intent was to open the trip by repeating the Mountain Madness climb two years earlier of Mera Peak. The straightforward route up the 21,000-foot mountain had given Mera the subtitle of being the highest Himalayan peak suitable for trekkers, and was thus my idea of the perfect ascent. We would rope up for glacier travel, but there should be no serious challenges other than coping with the altitude and weather. Coming off the summit, Scott intended to have us continue to the pass at Amphu Labtsa and rappel into the Khumbu Valley not far from Mount Everest. From there he would take the more determined climbers to Ama Dablam while the rest of us eased our way down the Khumbu to Lukla.

When we set out the next morning, the dozen Mountain Madness team members were followed by forty Sherpas and porters. A couple of Sherpa women toting large backpacks seemed to have joined us, too. Scott mixed in with the climbers, encouraging them and exuding delight in the simple act of hiking in the Himalayas. We camped in a rhododendron forest, then climbed a snowy trail to Zetra La, a pass a thousand feet higher than Mount Rainier. I hurried ahead as we neared the top and looked back down at the line of porters, Sherpas, and climbers coming toward me. We were already far enough from more traveled routes that we were alone even though we were so many, and the skyline was crowded with huge peaks. It was a visual feast that was clear, simple, and overwhelming.

At each of our campsites the Sherpas set up the tents and cooked our meals. They awakened us in the morning by coming to our tents with mugs of coffee or hot, sweet tea. When we were ready to move on, we rolled up our sleeping bags and then the Sherpa staff took care of the rest, packing up everything and leapfrogging ahead of us to set up the next camp by the time we arrived. Having the camp chores done by others felt as strange to me as the fact that I was hiking with a light pack that contained only what I needed during the day. Part of traveling well is adapting, though, and I soon accustomed myself to having camp materialize before me and sitting down for meals at a makeshift table in a dining tent. Most of all I enjoyed staying cozy in my sleeping bag and, barely awake, sipping the morning's first tea.

Several days up the Hinku Valley we came to Tangnag, a few stone huts used in the summer by yak herders grazing their animals in the sparse alpine meadows. The Sherpa women with the backpacks had converted one of the huts into a little shop by setting out displays of chocolate bars, hard candies, and packets of nuts. For a few rupees they would heat water, brew a pot of tea, and enhance it with yak butter and rum.

We rested for a day at Tangnag to allow our bodies to adjust to the thinner air. Alan McPherson, a Scotsman with us who lived in Canada, unfurled a parasail and strapped himself into its harness. The afternoon winds held the canopy aloft and pulled him along the ground, the younger Sherpas running excitedly after him. Dale Kruse drew on his skills as a dentist to check some of the porters' teeth. Scott sat on his sleeping pad in the sunshine and read a book, relaxing as the Mountain Madness trip unfolded around him just as he had written it in a brochure in the West Seattle office six months earlier.

When the expedition got under way again, we left the valley to begin the ascent to Mera La, the pass where we would camp before climbing to the summit of Mera. The trail became steep and was covered with snow. Late in the day the porters dropped their loads at a campsite a thousand feet below the pass.

I was coming to realize that we were being accompanied both by Sherpas, mostly local men who had been involved in numerous expeditions, and by porters, many coming to the Himalayas from the lowlands of Nepal and India only during the climbing and trekking seasons to carry loads. Some of the porters were in their teens.

Quite a few were struggling with the altitude, and many had runny noses and persistent coughs. Not all of them were wearing enough warm clothing. For footwear in the snow they had thin green Chinese-made tennis shoes.

Those of us who wanted to climb Mera joined Scott, Dawa, Charley, and a few of the Sherpas to go up the next day and camp at Mera La, expecting the rest of the group to meet us there as we returned from the summit. Dale Kruse and I shared a tent, both of us awakening during the night trying to catch our breath, a sign that we had not yet acclimated to being above 17,000 feet. I was content as the sun rose to watch Scott get the others organized for their summit try. He was all business, concentrating on the work at hand. His humor of the hike and the lower camps was gone, replaced with an awareness of what needed to be done and leaving room for nothing else.

The day was clear but the wind gathered strength and kicked up spindrift on Mera's glaciers. The climbers found it hard going and the summit farther than they had expected, and by early afternoon they had returned to Mera La. The Sherpas laid out an aluminum platter covered with fry bread, boiled eggs, and cheese, but no one was hungry. Scott sat quietly on the snow, his face showing disappointment that only deepened when he learned that the rest of the expedition would not be joining us.

We packed our gear and returned to the lower camp. Dawa spoke with the porters and then explained to Scott that they were cold and some were ill. To reach the relative comfort of the Khumbu Valley, they would need to climb over Mera La, traverse above 16,000 feet for several days, then rappel off the pass at Amphu Labtsa. The drifts were deeper than Scott had remembered from his expedition two years earlier. Dawa added that many of the porters were worried that what lay ahead seemed too daunting, and they wanted no more of the cold and snow.

"Scott was gung ho," Charley Mace told me of the discussions. "He said let's do it, let's finish it up. But the sirdar was more prudent, saying no, those guys can't go any farther."

They explored ways to keep the Mountain Madness clients moving forward and Scott tried to infuse the expedition with his own enthusiasm, but at last he gave in to reality. We would need to abandon the plan of reaching the Khumbu by going over the Amphu Labtsa, retrace our steps to Lukla, and approach Ama Dablam by the traditional route up the Khumbu Valley. It could add four or five days of trekking time to our journey and there would be no chance for a second try at Mera. The detour might also shorten the time the climbers would have on Ama Dablam.

I saw Scott outside his tent the next morning holding a cup of coffee. The day was a stunning, perfect for hitting the Mera heights. I sat down beside him and offered him a cracker, but he waved it off.

"I can't eat anything yet," he told me. "I've been grinding my teeth in my sleep and it hurts too much in the morning to chew anything."

We talked about the porter situation and the need to retreat. We were drifting off schedule and a couple of the climbers were not happy about it. We had been honoring Buddhist traditions by walking on the correct side of mantra-covered mani stones along the trail, burning juniper branches in a shrine carved into a cliff, and pressing our hands together as we greeted the Sherpas by bowing slightly and saying *Namaste*. Despite all of that, the expectations of Western civilization still wound the clocks inside our brains. Everyone knew the departure time of our flights to America from Kathmandu. For some, the trip became back-dated from that moment, and they were anxious that they accomplish all they had been promised in the Mountain Madness brochure before the planes carried them away.

"Jesus," Scott said, "can't we just go climb and have fun? Does it have to be so complicated?"

I found it fascinating to watch Scott leading. So often when I had gone to the backcountry I was the one making decisions, but in Nepal I could observe him dealing with Sherpas, porters, and clients. "You know, Bruce, the adventure doesn't begin until someone loses the map," I told him, recalling an old saying I'd heard in other contexts. The Mountain Madness expedition was beginning to wing it, and some of those who had paid to come along didn't like the new dynamic. If I had been in charge, I probably would have been grinding my teeth, too.

We backtracked down the Hinku Valley, camping along the way, then climbed to the Zetra La above Lukla. The expedition moved out no faster than we had hiked in, though Alan McPherson did attempt to alter the time-space continuum by strapping into his parasail and launching himself off the pass. Those of us still earthbound watched the brightly colored wing drifting against a vast backdrop of rock and snow as Alan steered between the mountains, tracing in the air the shape of the terrain far below as he drifted around a distant ridge. When the rest of us reached Lukla many hours later, we discovered that he had landed on the airstrip where he had been surrounded and arrested by armed soldiers.

"It is not legal to jump out of an airplane over Nepal," they had told him.

He demanded that they present proof there had been an aircraft, then argued that in any case his documents were in order by showing them his membership card from a Canadian hang-gliding club. They had shrugged their shoulders and let him go.

Alan told us his story that night at a Lukla teahouse where we were gathered over bottles of beer. The Mountain Madness tents were pitched in a field near the airstrip, and we had taken advantage of being back among the guest houses to grab showers and enjoy meals that we ate while sitting at teahouse tables rather than on little stools in a dining tent. Whatever discontent had been growing on the trail seemed gone now, or at least tucked away.

Scott got a huge kick out of Alan's parasail tale. He showed no hint of the strain of keeping his expedition together and appeared to have put behind him the frustrations of coping with the porters. He was on the new plan now, and there was no reason to lament what might have been. The evening was full of sweetness and light, and even those who had been worried about the change in schedule were drawn into the fun of partying together in the heights of the Himalayas.

Wally Berg recently told me about a similar evening when, several years before that night in the teahouse, he and Scott had returned to Lukla after one of their attempts to scale Everest. The climbing season was coming to a close and many other mountaineers were in town, too, hoping to catch flights the next day to Kathmandu. A number of them gathered for the evening at a Sherpa hotel. Reinhold Messner was there, one of the world's most accomplished mountaineers. So was Dick Bass, the first to climb the Seven Summits.

"Bass is a wonderful man with a big booming voice and an amazing ability to tell a story," Wally recalled. "There were a lot of other characters there, too, drinking beer and sharing stories, and right in the middle of it all is Scott Fischer with his exuberance and his desire for acceptance in that world. He had that brilliant grin, and his laugh was so big he would lose track of his breathing a little bit. He was making sure everybody had a good time."

As Scott and Wally were sipping their coffee the following morning, a Sherpa from the hotel sought them out and presented Scott with the bill for the previous night's food and drink. It totaled hundreds of dollars. "It was a very innocent thing and a very accurate assumption on the part of the Sherpas that Scott should be the guy paying," Wally told me. "In a room full of large personalities that night, he had been the biggest."

The hike we made up the Khumbu Valley was a journey familiar to many Himalayan trekkers and climbers. In the warmth of sunny springtime days, we walked past terraced fields turning green and through villages with teahouses lining the pathway. Children inside peered through the small panes of windows with brightly painted sills. Menus tacked next to the doors offered tea, bottled beer and soda, and simple meals made of chicken, rice, potatoes, and eggs.

Our eyes were continually drawn to the peaks above us, but I was almost as fascinated by what passed beneath our feet. The rocky path had been worn smooth by centuries of soft pressure from calloused Sherpa feet and the pliant hooves of yaks. Even more remarkable were the bridges. Some were cantilevered arrangements of logs jutting out from either stream bank with enough rock piled on their butt ends to counter the weight of yak caravans. The worn wooden walkways of suspension bridges across deep gorges hung from rusty cables, flat rocks serving as makeshift patches to cover holes in the boards. A sign on one of the spans acknowledged the fragility of the structure by warning, in several languages, DO NOT WAG BRIDGE!

We spent a night in Namche Bazaar and had our Edmund Hillary moment at the monastery, then hiked the next day to the monastery at Thangboche. From there we could see Everest to the left and, to the right, the graceful skyward arc of Ama Dablam. Dawa explained that *ama* is a Sherpa word for *mother*. High on the mountain is a hanging glacier that to the Sherpas resembles a jewel box, a *dablam*, and thus Ama Dablam, the Mother's Jewel Box. It is modestly tall by Himalayan standards—just over 22,300 feet—but its striking appearance makes it a singular landmark in the Khumbu.

Those in our group who intended to climb Ama Dablam broke off from the main trail to get themselves onto the mountain and establish their first camp. Scott, Lisa, and I continued to the upper reaches of the valley, a broad width of terraced potato fields laid out beneath Island Peak. It was where we would have been a week earlier had we not turned back before going over Mera La and the Amphu Labtsa.

Just as Kathmandu can seem small to mountaineers who find one another in the restaurants and hotels, the Khumbu is a thoroughfare that many use during the climbing seasons. Ed Viesturs, who had been on K2 with Scott and Charley Mace the previous year, had been guiding Hall Wendel on Pumori, a peak near Everest. Wendel was CEO of Polaris Industries, a leading manufacturer of snowmobiles, who occasionally teamed up with Ed for mountain adventures. After Pumori, Wendel planned to join the Mountain Madness team to climb Ama Dablam. He and Ed had enjoyed their time on Pumori, but had encountered dangerous snow conditions and abandoned their climb. Knowing Scott was not far away, Ed hiked down to join us for the evening.

As the cold evening settled in, Scott led Lisa, Ed, and me to a little stone Sherpa house. The Sherpani greeted us by saying *Namaste* and pressing her hands together, then motioned for us to sit on benches around a rough-hewn table. She brewed tea over a small fire in the corner, the wood smoke rising through the dense thatch of the roof. Lacing the pot with rum and yak butter, she served the tea along with hot, yeasty cinnamon rolls she had just taken from an earthen oven heated by coals from the fire. The evening closed around us, our faces illuminated by the glowing embers and by a lamp on the table.

Scott told Ed that we had seen Edmund Hillary in Namche, and we talked awhile about the nature of mountaineering fame. The statistics are important, so much so that the journalist Elizabeth Hawley was devoting much of her time in Kathmandu to recording the accomplishments of every significant Himalayan expedition since the British had tried to scale Everest in the 1920s. It mattered to her and the mountaineering world that Ed Viesturs climbed Everest, and that he had done it without using supplemental oxygen. The route he had followed mattered, and the time of day he had reached the top. When Wally Berg and Scott had climbed Lhotse, it was important that they were the first Americans to summit. They had been confronted at the summit by a fragile fin of snow rising twenty-five feet above the highest rock, and they had gone up the snow, too, because they wanted to and, to the mountaineering record, it made a difference.

Documentation satisfies the climbers' need to know the edges of their game, to understand what has not yet been done, and to suggest where the boundaries can be stretched. Fascination with the record of what might be accomplished on Everest gained momentum early in the twentieth century after explorers reached the North Pole and the South Pole and then looked around for the next great challenge. Everest was seen by many as Earth's third pole, the only one still to be reached. Like the geographic poles in the Arctic and Antarctic, the mountain seemed to generate its own magnetic attraction, especially for those whose personal polarity was similarly aligned.

Scott had attempted to climb Everest from the north, the side the British had tried in the 1920s and 1930s when they were allowed to come into Tibet but forbidden from entering Nepal. Soon after the

Chinese took over Tibet in 1950 and closed off the country, Nepal opened its borders and expeditions began coming in from Kathmandu, hoping to climb Everest from what seemed a workable route through the Khumbu Icefall and up to Everest's South Col. A Swiss team pioneered much of the way in 1952. The following year a British expedition established camps along the route and stocked them with provisions and oxygen. A first team turned back at the base of a forty-foot cliff just below the top of the mountain. Edmund Hillary and Tenzing Norgay followed their footsteps a few days later. Hillary led the way up the cliff, now called the Hillary Step, and he and Tenzing managed to reach the summit.

To the record, what Tenzing and Hillary accomplished was a premier milestone of mountaineering. It was important worldwide as well, for their ascent had occurred just before the coronation in London of Queen Elizabeth II. The expedition relayed word of their success through Kathmandu and on to England, and the British Empire simultaneously celebrated the ascension of a new queen and the ascent of the world's highest mountain by Hillary, one of her subjects. He and Tenzing found themselves instantly famous.

Few today recognize the names of Swiss climbers Juerg Marmet and Ernst Schmied, the next to climb Everest. They matter to the record, but just as Buzz Aldrin, the second man to walk on the moon, will always be eclipsed by Neil Armstrong, those who followed Tenzing and Hillary to Everest's summit would never shine quite as brightly. (As if to tie up loose ends, Hillary traveled to the South Pole by dog sled and motorized vehicle in 1958, then twenty-seven years later joined Neil Armstrong himself to land a ski plane on the North Pole, thus making him the first man to summit Everest and reach both magnetic Poles. Armstrong has left his own matters unfinished by never setting out to climb Everest, but then Hillary has yet to fly to the moon.)

Before he had been there, Edmund Hillary must certainly have had a drive to try for the summit every bit as strong as Scott felt while we talked with Ed Viesturs and Lisa that evening in the Sherpani's house. Each climber drawn to a mountain is, in his or her experience, discovering it for the first time. It is a personal quest, an individual challenge. Those who are not attracted to the heights might question the motives of those who are, but if the magnetic pull is strong, a climber can find it almost impossible to resist.

Scott mentioned that several years earlier he had helped make it possible for Paul Petzoldt at the age of eighty-two to embark on a final journey into the world's highest mountains. The founder of the National Outdoor Leadership School had last been to the Asian mountain ranges in 1938 on the American expedition to K2. Coming through Tibet with Mountain Madness trekkers more than fifty years later to visit base camp on the north side of Mount Everest, Paul had relished everything about being in the high country where he felt he most belonged. His eyesight was failing and his mobility was limited, but at the Rongbuk Monastery he could hear the chants of the monks. He chewed on plants and tried to identify them by taste. He felt the wind coming off the glaciers and the chill of nights in camp. He enjoyed the hot tea brought to his tent in the morning, and for him the trip had been wonderful.

We savored our own cups of tea and the taste of the cinnamon rolls. A few evenings earlier at his event in Namche, Edmund Hillary had been celebrating friendships of forty years' duration. In the aromas of baked goods and the warmth of the fire, we were reveling in connections being forged in the mountains, too, and of memories that would stay with us for years.

I was the first to leave. As I neared my tent I looked back at the little stone house at the end of the world, lamplight shining golden through the narrow window. Behind it and all around, the world's biggest peaks soared into the night, the stars casting blue light upon their cold silhouettes. We were far from home, yet the place felt like home, or at least an extension of where I most wanted to be. It was a place of essential simplicity. There was up and down. There was light and dark. The edges were clean and defined, the clarity uncomplicated by the give and take of the world beyond the mountains.

Ed Viesturs was coming at a mountaineering career by leading private clients, by working with Rainier Mountaineering to take people up Washington State's highest peak, and by hiring on as a guide for expeditions organized by others. Scott was trying to make a success of his own adventure travel company, and the varied challenges of leading an expedition recommenced for him the next morning as he caught up with the Mountain Madness climbers at Ama Dablam Base Camp. Over the next twelve days the team would establish four camps on the mountain. Each climber would make carries of supplies as far as he or she felt prudent, and one by one they reached the limits of their comfort and chose to go no higher.

Ed accompanied Hall Wendel to the Mountain Madness Base Camp and spent a night there. Dinner consisted of small portions of peas, broccoli, and Spam, and it appeared that other supplies were also running low. "I don't think this is going to work for me," Wendel whispered to Ed, and by the next evening both of them had moved on to Namche Bazaar.

Scott was also discovering that the expedition didn't have enough new rope to anchor fixed lines up all the exposed sections of the route. He considered sending runners to Namche to buy more, but that would have added delay to the few remaining days. He used his remaining rope more sparingly and relied in places on ropes that had been left by previous expeditions.

"The schedule was too tight," Charley Mace told me of their time on Ama Dablam. "We couldn't do everything we wanted to do in the amount of days we had. With a couple of extra days a lot more people would have summited."

The plan to tailor an ambitious Mountain Madness expedition to accommodate the time constraints of clients' annual leave had collided with the vagaries of snow, cold, supplies, and the needs of porters and Sherpas. "Scott and I talked about this a lot before leaving Seattle," Charley Mace continued. "Say, three weeks of vacation a year, it made sense business-wise to fit an expedition into that time frame even though it pushes you and cuts down on acclimatization and rest days. To my mind, that was why that trip wasn't better."

"You know how Scott was," Ed Viesturs recently said as we talked about the Ama Dablam expedition. "He wasn't the most organized person, but he tended to surround himself with people who were. It was through his inspiration and his energy that things came together, and then you would go, Jeez, how did that happen?" If enough of those organized people weren't around, though, there might be not be enough broccoli and Spam.

As time on Ama Dablam ran short, Scott, along with Steve Schrader, a young Seattle climber, made a push to the top. "Scott felt he had to get to the summit in order to make it a successful expedition to drum up more business," Charley Mace observed. The climbing permit had included a deposit that would be returned only if the team brought down as much or more trash than they left behind. Charley and others on the expedition used the time Scott and Steve were gone to haul trash, tent remnants, and old rope down the mountain.

Despite only Scott and one other climber reaching the summit, the adventure did have much to recommend it. "It was a very cool trip because there was nobody else on Ama Dablam," Charley remembered. "I didn't realize at the time how good we had it. Today you have to fight over limited campsites."

Scott had great natural talent for energizing people and could inspire almost anyone to excel beyond his or her limits; however, the nuts and bolts of an expedition were not his forte. Simply applying more energy to a situation did not always overcome day-to-day problems better solved with careful planning and a clear series of steps. It could cause him to grind his teeth in the night.

Something about which he had no doubt, though, was his continuing desire to climb Mount Everest. As he stood atop Ama Dablam, he could look to the north and much farther into the sky and see an immense banner of snow being dragged off the heights of Everest by the jet stream. For Scott, the pull of Everest was palpable and ever-present. It was magnetic. He could not turn himself away, and soon he would be back in the Khumbu, trying once again to follow Edmund Hillary all the way up Everest.

The next time, though, things were going to be different.

CHAPTER 19

Everest with Good Style

It was a treat to be involved with that small team—low budget, five friends on a big mountain. Everest was empty and going off to climb it was still an incredible adventure.
—Steve Gipe, NOLS instructor and Mount Everest expedition physician

IT HAD ALWAYS been sweet when a bunch of Bruces had slung their packs over their shoulders and go off to the mountains in pure NOLS style. Sometimes the goal was the Grand Teton or a peak in the Wind River Range. This time it was the summit of Mount Everest, and what was there not to like about that?

The 1994 Sagamartha Environmental Expedition was the brainchild of Steve Goryl, a crusty instructor of the National Outdoor Leadership School famous in the NOLS community for having racked up 440 weeks in the field teaching courses, more than anyone else in the organization's history. That's eight and a half years of the man's life living out of a backpack in wilderness settings. When he wasn't in the backcountry, he devoted time to scuba diving and to parachuting out of airplanes, completing hundreds of dives through both water and air. He had been known to carry his own parachute on commercial airliners. He studied a NASA Space Shuttle manual to be ready just in case he got invited someday to participate in an orbital mission, and he listed as one of his goals in life, "to die on another planet."

When I sat down recently with Steve in his home near Boulder, Colorado, I told him I'd heard half a dozen NOLS veterans do their gravelly voiced impersonations of him as they had regaled me with some of his legends. He laughed and said with a remarkable basso profundo rumble, "I'm just not at all surprised to hear that." None of his imitators had come close to doing him justice.

He tempered at least one of the stories. Yes, he had carried a parachute on airliners, but not in anticipation of disaster. "I'm a skydiver and I don't want my 'chute damaged in the cargo hold," he explained. Then, after a pause, he added, "Of course, if there's ever trouble at thirty thousand feet I'm probably going to be the only passenger who's got any options."

Two years older than Scott Fischer, Goryl had been drawn to Lander by the 1970 *Alcoa Presents* television program "Thirty Days to Survival." NOLS founder Paul Petzoldt instructed his thirty-day student course. Despite his commitment to living in the backcountry, Steve became interested in high-altitude climbing much later than many of his peers, realizing as he reached his late thirties that if he were ever to climb Mount Everest, it had better be soon and he had better put the wheels in motion.

Steve applied to the government of Nepal for a 1992 Everest permit. As fellow climbers, he invited several other longtime NOLS instructors including Steve Gipe. A Montana physician, Dr. Gipe had been among the NOLS participants coming to Lander before the famous television program attracted so many others. In 1969, Petzoldt had assigned Steve Gipe to be one of ten young NOLS instructors to accompany the "Thirty Days to Survival" film team to keep them supplied with food, carry loads of camera batteries into the backcountry for the cinematographers, and haul out reels of exposed film.

Steve Goryl also penciled in Rob Hess, another NOLS veteran and professional guide with Jackson Hole Mountaineering, as a team member. Scott Fischer would be the expedition's climbing leader. The pieces seemed to fall into place until the permit negotiations became complicated.

After summiting Everest in 1990, Rob Hall and Gary Ball and the leaders of several other guide services began bringing clients to the mountain on a commercial basis. The demand for permits was intensifying, and the Nepalese government realized that increasing numbers of climbers eager to test themselves on Everest were willing to pay for the opportunity. Conversely, more people on the mountain meant adding to the mounds of trash polluting the camps, and more oxygen bottles discarded at the South Col and above. The Ministry of Tourism struggled to maximize income from permits without allowing the camps to be further buried by the garbage expeditions left behind.

Steve Goryl's first permit application required $5,000 payment, but the Nepalese government did not issue him the documents he needed. Nor did it return the money. Steve applied again the next year and discovered that the fee had increased to $10,000, so he passed the hat once more. Again the permit was denied and again the Ministry of Tourism in Kathmandu hung on to the cash. "There's no such thing as a refund once money goes to Nepal," Rob Hess told me. "It goes over there, it ain't coming back."

While raising the fees had brought in more revenue, the additional expense had done little to reduce the number of climbing teams. Twenty-one expeditions came to the Nepalese side of Everest in 1991. Twenty-four arrived in 1992, and the 1993 climbing seasons saw nineteen expeditions going up the Khumbu Valley to Everest Base Camp.

The Ministry tried a new strategy for the spring of 1994, announcing that only one expedition would be allowed on each Mount Everest route. To make up the revenue lost by drastically reducing the numbers of climbers, the Ministry increased the permit fee from $10,000 for an entire expedition to $10,000 for each climber. "In a three year period our team of five guys went from being charged five grand to fifty grand and we were pretty much stuck," Rob Hess said.

New Zealander Rob Hall's Adventure Consultants company and an Alpine Ascents group led by Americans Todd Burleson and Pete Athans had been issued their permits before the new restrictions went into effect, so were being allowed to bring clients to Everest under the old fee structure. A Japanese team had a permit to use Everest Base Camp as their staging area for a climb of Everest's

South Rib, a way up Everest that parallels the South Col route. It appeared that no other permits would be issued.

There was a loophole, though, that encouraged climbers with an environmental program to come to Everest. Goryl pitched his expedition as both a climb and a campsite cleanup effort. The Ministry of Tourism said if he could come up with the $50,000, a permit for five climbers was his. He decided he was still in. So did Steve Gipe. Scott had always been fully committed to the adventure. Rob Hess stayed with it, too. "I had already forked out all this money," Rob said, "and I figured, hey I'm a climber, I'm on this thing until somebody tells me I just can't go."

Through NOLS connections and mutual friends, Rob and Scott had known one another for a decade. Scott had engaged Rob to help lead a 1993 Mountain Madness climb for eight Princeton students wanting to go up Mount McKinley. The students called their expedition the Climb for the Cure and planned the ascent as a fundraising project benefiting AIDS awareness. As another guide, Scott hired Brent Bishop who for many years had also been guiding climbs in the Tetons.

"That Denali trip was a real turning point trip for Scott and me as friends and co-workers," Rob told me. "I felt we formed a very positive bond as guides. He was definitely the charismatic front man, larger than life, his reputation preceding him on the mountain. Not to say Scott didn't have good judgment and skills, but that was more my area of expertise. How to build snow shelters, set ropes, do logistics, and take care of the business of things, that's what I brought to the table."

Rob looked to Scott as both a friend and a mentor. "He had a way of bringing the best out of people, and he certainly did that with me. He was really encouraging and we definitely shined together." What really cemented their friendship, though, was the bottle game.

The Climb for the Cure Denali expedition proceeded smoothly until the team pitched their tents at 17,000 feet, 3,000 feet below the summit. A storm pinned them down for several days along with several other expeditions camping nearby. "It wasn't super bad weather," Rob remembered, "but it was bad enough that nobody was going higher for a while." The cramped tents were full of restless climbers.

Scott challenged Rob and a few of the Princeton students to come outside to play a round of the bottle game, a Fischer trademark not unlike his eagerness to take on all comers at arm wrestling. With the edge of his climbing boot, Scott carved a line in the snow. Keeping his feet behind the line, he leaned down to put his hands on two water bottles set upright ahead of the line, then worked the bottles forward as far as he could push them, his weight balanced on the toes of his boots and the two bottles. When he had reached out as far as he thought possible, he left one bottle as a marker and gripped the top of the other bottle to support himself while he scooted back toward the line and stood up, all the while touching the snow only with the bottle and his boots. Each person took a turn, trying to leave a water bottle farther out than anybody else had been able to place one.

"Scott started the bottle game at seventeen thousand feet on that stormy, nasty day on Denali and before long he had everybody out of their tents playing," Rob said. "Twenty, twenty-five people, the whole camp. It was amazing to see how Scott could get people motivated and psyched. Czechs, French, Americans, they all had to see if they could do it."

The Denali storm dragged on and several of the Climb for the Cure team became ill. Rob escorted them down the mountain while Scott and fellow climber Brent Bishop led the other Princeton students to the summit. "That all worked out real well," Rob says. "We got some publicity about that. Our photos were in *People* magazine. It was a pretty cool thing." Adding to the success was the fact that $280,000 was raised for the American Foundation for AIDS Research.

After working with Scott and Rob on Denali, Brent Bishop committed to the 1994 Everest journey, too. It would be a way for him literally to follow in the footsteps of his father Barry Bishop, a member of the 1963 American Everest expedition. Brent was completing two master's degrees at the University of Washington, one in business and one in environmental management, and could bring a commercial expertise to Steve Goryl's team that had been sorely lacking.

The expedition was budgeted at $150,000, a meager amount compared with most Everest trips of the time. The climbers began selling T-shirts, and Mountain Madness arranged for two groups of trekkers to visit base camp during the expedition, each trekker contributing a thousand dollars to the expedition. One of those groups would be composed primarily of administrators and board members from the National Outdoor Leadership School.

"Don't worry, we're going to make this happen," Scott kept telling everyone. "We're going to climb Everest."

The environmental cleanup angle that had allowed Steve Goryl to get the permit from the Ministry of Tourism proved to be the group's most effective fund-raising approach. Using the Nepalese name for Everest, they called themselves the Sagamartha Environmental Expedition and made the general promise to do something about cleaning trash off the mountain. There was precedent for that kind of effort. Bob McConnell, a NOLS veteran who had served as base camp manager on the 1987 American Everest North Face expedition, had returned to Everest several times to organize cleanup efforts on the Tibetan side of the mountain. As a true believer in the NOLS ethic of leaving the backcountry in better condition than you found it, Goryl loved that idea and was inspired by McConnell's success.

McConnell had been accompanied on one of his cleanup expeditions by Chris Naumann, a young Missouri native who had read about Himalayan expeditions and the trash being left on Everest. "Doing something about that interested me more than the climbing," Chris told me.

In 1991 Chris had gotten a Watson Fellowship and used the money to travel in the Himalayas to, as he put it, make his own observations. "The Watson family founded IBM," Chris explained. "They had a generous fund that gave students at small liberal arts colleges grants to do research that involved more than one country. I heard about a guy who got a fifteen-thousand-dollar Watson

Fellowship to study traditional beer brewing culture in England and Germany."

Chris came back from the Himalayas intending to study environmental law in Montana, and by chance ended up living in Steve Gipe's barn. He heard that Dr. Gipe had been invited to join an Everest expedition that would feature an environmental component. "I rolled out a proposal for becoming the base camp manager and environmental manager for the team," Chris told me. "I offered to do it just for a plane ticket." When he discovered the expedition was so strapped for cash that the climbers were paying their own airfare, Chris said he would get himself to Nepal, too, just to be part of the expedition.

"I told them that this could be the first truly environmental expedition," Chris recalled, "but that without me there, they weren't going to get the cleanup work done. The failure would not be from false intentions, but because their full-time job was going to be climbing the peak and getting down safely." The others bought the idea and Chris was in.

Chris Naumann and Steve Gipe organized an expedition fundraiser in Bozeman, arranging for food and beverages and silent auction items. Scott was to fly over from Seattle to be the featured speaker. Rob Hess and Brent Bishop would be there, too, and so would Brent's father. Scott waited to go standby for the last flight into Bozeman, only to discover that it was cancelled due to weather.

Barry Bishop got out a tray of slides from his 1963 American Everest expedition and filled in for Scott by giving an impromptu presentation built on the idea of environmental responsibility. "We left a junkyard up there," he explained to the crowd as he showed pictures of oxygen bottles, tent remnants, and trash abandoned on the South Col by the 1963 expedition and the several that had preceded it, "and now these guys are going to go clean up after us."

In fact, in the thirty-one years separating the Everest attempts by Barry Bishop and by his son, more than sixty expeditions had tried to climb the Nepalese side of Everest, and most of them had left behind gear and litter. In their defense, many climbers coming down the mountain had been struggling simply to stay alive, and they'd had little energy to devote to the ideals of responsible environmentalism.

The Bozeman fund-raiser was a success, but generating the remainder of the money continued to loom over the expedition members. "We hung in there on faith that Scott's willpower was going to get this thing out of the country and into Nepal," Steve Gipe said of the financial concerns plaguing them even a few months before departure.

"These were NOLS guys who never had any money, but they somehow were getting it together and they were certain they were going," added Steve's wife Pookie. "They called it the *Sagamartha Environmental Expedition*. I called it the *Expedition Sponsored by Your Own Personal Visa and MasterCards*."

Several days before departing for Nepal, the team members gathered in Seattle to buy food and sort equipment. Each man provided personal gear including goose down clothing and sleeping bags rated to forty degrees below zero. Scott contributed Mountain Madness tents, climbing hardware, and stoves. He knew that Rob Hall's Adventure Consultants company had arranged with the Sherpas to establish the route through the Khumbu Icefall and to install the fixed ropes to protect exposed portions of the route farther up the mountain. That meant Scott's team wouldn't need to bring much in the way of additional rope.

The team drove to a warehouse grocery store and purchased $3,000 worth of pasta, cheese, and other provisions, then stayed up nearly all night packing. Dr. Gipe asked the others to lower their shorts so that he could inject them with gamma globulin to ward off third world maladies. "It was just five guys in a garage getting their stuff together for a trip to Everest," Chris Naumann said. "Like that happens all the time."

Scott had obtained an exception from Thai Airlines that allowed each team member to check three bags rather than the customary two, a bag weighing a maximum of seventy pounds. The oxygen bottles were being shipped to Kathmandu from Russia, but aside from those and some fresh food they would buy in Nepal, everything they needed for their five-man Everest team weighed just over a thousand pounds, a featherweight figure compared to the tons of gear and supplies most expeditions were bringing to base camp.

"It's just camping," Steve Goryl said, and in many ways it had the feel of preparing for an ordinary NOLS course that happened to be a little more ambitious than usual. They had been awake for almost forty-eight hours when they boarded the flight to Bangkok. From there they flew to Kathmandu, took small aircraft to the landing strip at Lukla, and hiked up the Khumbu Valley to the base of the mountain they were hoping to climb.

Expedition Sherpas were already at Everest Base Camp staking out space. "Because of the environmental aspect of our expedition, the Sherpas called us the Clean Team," Chris Naumann told me. "They put our camp next to a big boulder and in three-foot-high letters in permanent green spray paint wrote 1994 AMERICAN CLEAN TEAM. Very environmental."

In addition to their Sherpa support staff, Scott's expedition had engaged the help of two high-altitude Sherpas, Sona Dendu and Lopsang Jangbu. Just twenty-one years old, Lopsang had climbed Everest the previous year with an expedition of women from India, and had reached the top of Cho Oyu while working with a Japanese team.

Brent Bishop panned around base camp with a home movie camera, the film first showing the tents of the Japanese in the distance. Closer in were the big, streamlined dining tents, cook shelters, and matching sleeping tents of the Alpine Ascents and Adventure Consultants teams. As Brent moved the camera, the Sagamartha Environmental Expedition came into view. There was a red-and-white-striped tepee tent to shelter the Sherpas who would be cooking for the team. An assemblage of mismatched tarps lashed down over boulders formed a dining tent. Nearby were the personal tents of the climbers, and that was all.

"It was the first year of this new permit system, and there were even fewer people than usual," Steve Gipe told me. "By today's standards there was nobody there."

The Japanese stayed mostly to themselves, but members of the other teams intermingled much of the time. Scott, Rob Hall, and

Pete Athans had known one another for years and had been to-gether at Everest Base Camp in 1989 and 1990. Ed Viesturs, who was working for Rob Hall, had climbed K2 with Scott two years earlier. Rob Hall's wife Jan Arnold, a physician, began sharing the medical duties of base camp with Steve Gipe. Most of the Sherpas knew one another, too.

"Rob Hall had a nice comfortable base camp and they were al-ways inviting us over," Steve Gipe told me. "We could leave our simple little place and go hang out in their luxury thing."

"Rob's camp had a solar shower, electric lights, satellite phone, stereo, three Honda generators," Steve Goryl remembered. "He had fifteen clients all paying him a lot of money to be there. His camp was a big event with imported food and liquor."

For all the congeniality, the mood at base camp could become strained, however. "Steve Goryl and Rob Hall would get into it about how the teams would set up the higher camps," Chris Naumann said. "Goryl was the expedition leader, but it was his first trip. Scott was the one that other people were looking to, and he made most of the critical decisions and negotiations with the other teams."

The Sherpas experienced tension, too. "Rob was paying his Sherpas six grand for their three months" Goryl explained. "We were pay-ing ours half that. I thought we really treated our Sherpas as equals. Everything they carried, we carried. Every time they picked up trash, we picked up trash. They felt that they were helping us, but they also suspected that we had more money than we said we did."

The Sagamartha expedition offered its Sherpas bonuses to carry trash and oxygen bottles down the mountain. That helped close the salary gap, and the Sherpas were quick to grasp the importance of the effort. "Rob Hall's Sherpas were watching our Sherpas picking up little pieces of trash and saying, yep, that's the right thing to do," Goryl said.

Climbers from the four expeditions shared the route that the Sherpas had established through the Khumbu Icefall, then made their way into the Western Cwm and up the Lhotse Face toward the South Col. They established Camp I at the top of the Icefall, Camp

II midway up the Western Cwm, and Camp III high on the Lhotse Face. Scott and Rob Hess made a carry to the South Col, touching down just long enough to leave a cache of gear and provisions for Camp IV.

With everything in readiness, the climbers returned to base camp to rest and wait for the window of clear weather that would signal the beginning of their summit attempts. And then Scott almost got himself tossed off the mountain.

The journey that had been marketed to the Mountain Madness trekkers included a visit to Everest Base Camp. The itinerary had been sweetened with the promise that several of the Everest climbers would then accompany the trekkers down the valley to climb Island Peak, a relatively easy climb frequented by trekkers coming into the Khumbu region. The round trip from Everest Base Camp to the summit of Island Peak would take four or five days. The side trip had seemed reasonable in Seattle when finding sources of funding was critical. By the time the trekkers reached base camp, though, the climbers had already spent a month on Everest and been as high as the South Col. Scott and the others were not enthused about spending the better part of a week trekking up another mountain.

"In the interest of getting to the summit of Everest, they thought their best option was to get some extra sleep and eat well in base camp," said Chris Naumann, "not put on any more miles than they had to."

Scott suggested that instead of Island Peak, he would lead the trekkers into the Khumbu Icefall even though the expedition's permit prohibited anyone not listed as a climber from going beyond base camp. The Nepalese liaison officer whose job it was to enforce the permit was staying in Namche, more than a day's hike away.

The icefall is a notoriously dangerous place. Encouraging trekkers to wander among the frozen cliffs and crevasses, especially in violation of the climbing permit, did not sit well with Scott's fellow expedition members. "We discussed the fact that taking trekkers into the icefall was not a good idea, but we'd promised them Island Peak and that wasn't happening," Chris Naumann explained. "We had to offer something other than just their trek to Base Camp."

In the end, Scott did take some of the trekkers into the icefall one day and several more the next. They got as high as the final obstacle—ten aluminum ladders lashed together and anchored against an eighty-foot wall of ice. Without scaling the ladder, the trekkers were satisfied with their tour.

News traveled quickly down the valley to Namche. The liaison officer learned of the illegal icefall trip and hurried to base camp an unhappy man. He warned Scott that he intended to radio a report of the transgression to the Ministry of Tourism, predicting that officials at the Ministry would be so displeased that they could fine the expedition $100,000 and ban Scott from Everest for the next five years.

Scott realized it was not an idle threat. Other climbers had been banished from the Himalayas for scaling Lhotse when their permits were only for Everest. Eight years earlier on Pik Kommunizma, Scott himself had refused to descend when Russian climbing officials had radioed that they wanted him and his Mountain Madness team to come down, and the next year he discovered that he couldn't get back into the Soviet Union to lead trips on Mount Elbrus.

Scott's team had no radio equipment to contact the outside world. The liaison officer went to the Adventure Consultants' camp and instructed Rob Hall to call the Ministry of Tourism in Kathmandu. "Rob was great," Chris recalled. "He told the liaison officer that for some reason the Adventure Consultants' satellite phone wasn't functioning. The liaison officer was never able to get his message out."

The officer warned Scott that he still might order the Sagamartha Environmental expedition off of Everest. "After these years of trying, Scott was finally poised to go to the summit and suddenly there's a chance he won't be allowed on the mountain," Chris said. "We ended up paying well over a thousand dollars to the liaison officer to get out of that jam." For a team short on money, it was an enormous penalty.

Scott and Rob Hall had picked the morning of May 9 to make their summit attempts. Their understanding of the records was that more people had reached the top of Everest on May 9 than on any other date. They also wanted to be on the high ridges of Everest at the same time, feeling that they were stronger going together than going separately. "There wasn't any rivalry between them," Steve Gipe said. "They chose to summit on the same day so that they could support each other."

On May 7, Scott, Rob, Brent, Steve Goryl, and Steve Gipe loaded their packs and, with Lopsang Jangbu and Sona Dendu, threaded their way through the Khumbu Icefall. They spent a night at Camp II, then moved up to sleep at Camp III. The following morning they clipped into the fixed ropes leading across the Geneva Spur and the Yellow Band toward the South Col. Rob Hess and Scott were in the lead, climbing easily and soon putting distance between themselves and the others. Steve Gipe and Brent climbed together until Steve stopped to make some clothing changes. The morning had been warm, and before they left Camp III, Steve removed off his down suit.

"Then the weather turned bad and it started snowing and blowing," Steve told me. "I was on the fixed line traversing over toward the Geneva Spur and Steve Goryl catches up with me. I decided maybe we were a little late in the day and the weather was too nasty, so we went back to Camp III." Brent continued his slow ascent and arrived at the South Col late in the afternoon where he rejoined Rob Hess and Scott. By evening Rob Hall and Ed Viesturs were also settling into their South Col camp with six Adventure Consultants clients and three high-altitude Sherpas.

The climbers rested, melted snow, checked their gear, and watched the questionable weather. The sky had cleared by midnight, and forty-five minutes later they left the South Col. Scott, Rob Hess, and Lopsang went ahead without supplemental oxygen and carried only fanny packs. "We figured we had to get up super early to try and get ahead of the people with oxygen," Rob told me. "It was super cold in the dark, but relatively straightforward climbing to the South Summit."

The sun came up and the wind stayed down. Clouds that had been lingering below them drifted upward and then dissipated into the Himalayan sky. Conditions were good, and Scott passed the high point of his previous summit attempts five years earlier when deep snow had turned him back along with Peter Jamieson and Wally Berg.

"I was ahead of Scott and I waited for him at the South Summit," Rob Hess remembered. Ahead was a fixed rope the climbers could use to protect themselves from a fall as they crossed the narrow, corniced ridge between the South Summit and the Hillary Step.

"I don't have anything to hook in with," Scott told Rob when he reached the South Summit, suddenly realizing he'd forgotten to bring the nylon sling and carabiner he would need to attach himself to the rope. "I'll just go for it."

"No, no, Scott, we've got to clip in," Rob told him. Rob had a sling tied to his ice axe as a leash to help him keep from losing it if he fell. He removed the sling and handed it to Scott who used it to secure himself to the fixed line.

"Scott was someone I wanted to look out for on the mountain," Rob told me, "and he looked out for me."

They scaled the Hillary Step and at about 8:30 in the morning reached the top of Everest. "Whooo-doggie!" Scott shouted. "Bruuuuuuce!" They were the third and fourth Americans to climb Everest without using supplemental oxygen. They had completed the climb with speed and, as climbers say of admirable ascents, in great style. Lopsang had done it, too.

"It was straightforward," Rob Hess said. "Scott was strong. He was psyched to be on the top. We all were very excited." In his laconic, laid-back style Rob added, "Not too much more to it than that."

Brent Bishop arrived on the summit and stood where his father had made alpine history more than three decades earlier. On the way down, the climbers passed Rob Hall on his fourth trip up Everest, and Ed Viesturs going up for the third time. With them were two Sherpas and six clients of Adventure Consultants.

"We were back down at the South Col by noon or 12:30," Rob Hess said. "It had all been just about perfect." They ate, drank tea, and watched the day unfolding around them.

"We entertained thoughts of going down farther, but our legs were really Jell-O-y. Super weak," Rob said. "A lot of the route from the South Col to the fixed lines over the Geneva Spur is unroped and it's best not to fall there. It was glare ice conditions. We probably could have gotten to the lower camps, but doing the summit without oxygen had been pretty much major."

Steve Gipe had brought a pulse oxymeter to Everest, a medical device for measuring the oxygen saturation in the bloodstream, and had sent it to the South Col with Scott and Rob. "Steve wanted to use it on us going up, but I told him no," Rob recalled. "I wanted to be true to how I felt and not have some external mechanical device clouding my thoughts. I didn't want it to be, *I feel good, but this instrument says my oxygen readings are low.* That might have led to self doubts instead of just going with how I really felt."

As they rested on the South Col after their Everest success, Scott and Rob did try out the oxymeter. A healthy person at sea level should register a blood oxygen level in the mid-90s. "Scott's was at fifty-eight and I was at sixty-four," Rob said. "At normal elevations people with those numbers are very, very sick. We weren't sick, we'd just gone to the summit of Mount Everest without oxygen and now we didn't feel all that good."

While Scott and Rob had been climbing that morning, Steve Gipe and Steve Goryl were again trying to get from Camp III to the South Col when they caught sight of their teammates high above, tiny dots against the whiteness of the mountain. "I saw them coming down and I knew they had probably summited," Steve Gipe told me. He also realized that having gotten to the top, Rob Hess, Scott, and Brent would be descending to Base Camp as soon as possible. There would be no one from their expedition in a position to help Goryl and Gipe if they ran into trouble.

"I didn't want to go up with just the two of us unsupported," Steve Gipe said. "I decided I had missed my chance to climb Everest."

Steve Goryl made the opposite choice, figuring he had come too far and invested too much to turn back. He pushed on to the South Col where he congratulated his teammates but found them less than enthused about his own ambitions.

"Steve, I've stayed up here before and not made it to the top," Scott told him. "You should come down with us."

"That's okay," Steve replied. "You had your chance, now I get my chance."

"You know, Steve, not everyone climbs Mount Everest. You've got to think about how much you're risking here."

"Well, you just climbed it," Steve argued. "I've been working as hard as you have and the summit's just right up there."

Scott made a final appeal. "Look," he said, "if you stay here and try to climb this thing by yourself, you're going to die. I know. I've been up there."

Steve needed to look no farther than a few yards from his tent to see what Scott was talking about. "There was a corpse not very far from me," Steve told me, "and I remember saying to myself that I definitely didn't want to end up like that. That would be a really stupid way to die."

"The next morning we got the hell out of there," Rob Hess said. High winds prevented Goryl from making a summit bid, but he had confidence in his ability to camp out anywhere and stayed in the shelter of his tent while the rest of his team went down the mountain. In keeping with the environmental ethic of the expedition, they brought with them all gear they had carried to the South Col that they were sure Goryl would not need.

They reached Camp II at noon where they visited with Steve Gipe, telling him that Goryl had stayed on the South Col and that bad weather was preventing him from going higher. Dr. Gipe told them he would stay at Camp II until Steve came down the mountain. The others wished him luck and continued their descent.

"When we got to base camp, I remember being as lethargic as I've ever been and stayed that way for three days," Rob Hess said. "I basically decided I'm not going up there ever again, ever."

For Scott, Rob, and Brent, the expedition was over. They had been living at base camp or above since the end of March, and now it was mid-May. They gathered their gear and headed for Lukla even though Steve Gipe was at Camp II and Steve Goryl was on the South Col. Their departure echoed the 1990 Everest-Lhotse expedition when it had been Wally Berg and Scott still on the mountain as some of those who had summited Everest packed up and left.

"Our expedition sort of just fell apart," Chris Naumann recalled. "I don't think it's all that uncommon, especially when it's not a commercial trip where people pay fifty thousand dollars and the boss says, *This is what we're going to do,* and everybody does it. I don't think a commercial trip would ever leave anybody on the mountain."

There was a commercial expedition at the South Col, the Alpine Ascents team of fifteen clients, guides, and Sherpas. But their primary concerns would be with members of their own group, not with the fate of a solo mountaineer who had insisted on staying behind against the strenuous concerns of his own team.

Paul Petzoldt had always admonished NOLS students that if they were going to climb big mountains they had to know how to camp in big mountains, and no one knew more about the NOLS way of camping in high mountains than Steve Goryl. He scavenged around the Col for oxygen bottles that weren't quite empty, testing them for gas and then attaching his breathing apparatus to one bottle after another to keep himself supplied with O_2. He dug through the shredded remains of tents left by expeditions long departed and found packets of tomato soup. For five days and nights he camped by himself on the South Col, trying not to glance at the remains of dead climbers.

"Steve had put together a lot of trips for NOLS," Steve Gipe said of Goryl. "He knew how to camp and he was very comfortable in a tent. He was mentally tough. He was at twenty-six thousand five hundred feet, essentially by himself in strong winds, and he was probably one of the few people who could have pulled that off."

Four days into Goryl's campout the weather began to improve. By sipping the dregs of nearly exhausted oxygen bottles, he had managed to reserve his own full canisters. He tightened his oxygen mask against his face, adjusted his headlamp, and climbed the peak. Along the way he mixed in with the climbers from Alpine Ascents, but in fact and very much in spirit he made the climb by himself.

"I was alone when I reached the top, and it was a little riskier than I had expected," Steve told me. "I spent ninety minutes up there taking pictures off in every direction, shooting self-portraits, and enjoying myself."

He was back at the South Col two hours later where he scavenged enough additional oxygen to get through the night. The next day he descended to Camp II and was greeted by Steve Gipe.

"I told Steve I'm beat, I'm hungry," Steve Goryl recalled. "He spent over an hour thoroughly assessing me in that professional physician's way he has. Very friendly, very detailed. I thought, this guy's above and beyond. He didn't want to be here all this time, but he stayed at Camp II for me."

Once he was certain that Goryl was okay, though, Gipe let his professional demeanor slip. He lit into Steve about the wisdom of staying on the Col for so many days. He also told him that he was ready to get out of there and would be leaving for base camp at dawn. The next day was Goryl's birthday though, and Goryl had decided he would sleep in.

"I didn't leave Camp II until 11:00 a.m., and when I got to the icefall it was the most melted out I had seen it," Steve Goryl told me. "Ropes were pulling, ladders were loose. If I'd gone early with Gipe when the ice was hard, I would have been down already and resting in base camp. You read about all these bad judgment calls people make, and I knew I had just made one."

When Goryl reached base camp, he discovered Steve Gipe had continued down the valley, eager to catch up with the others. Next to the 1994 AMERICAN CLEAN TEAM spray-painted boulder, there was nothing left of the expedition's camp except two duffel bags containing Goryl's personal gear.

Jan Arnold came over from the Adventure Consultants' tents and asked him how he was doing. She was waiting for her husband and Ed Viesturs to return from Lhotse, a climb they were attempting after having led their clients up Everest.

"I'm a little played," Steve told her. He'd not had a decent meal in days and had lost thirty pounds of body weight during his week above base camp.

"Scott said to watch out for you when you got back," Jan told him, and led the way to the Adventure Consultants' kitchen tent where she loaded a plate with food.

"Scott understood the big picture," Goryl explained to me. "When we talked on the South Col, once he knew I was committed to staying up there and climbing to the summit, he supported me completely. Even though he was in a big hurry to get out of base camp, he made sure that Jan would be watching for me and would take care of me when I came down."

The trash and the oxygen bottles that the climbers and Sherpas had brought off the mountain were also moving away from Everest. "We came back with three times as many yaks as we went up with, just to bring the garbage down the valley," Chris Naumann recalled. "These bags we had were probably three and a half feet tall and two or three feet in circumference. Sometimes two bags made up a yak load, sometimes four."

What could be burned went into an incinerator near Namche, but the metal and glass had to go to Kathmandu. The team wanted to bring the oxygen bottles to the United States where they were sure to sell some and give away others as thank-you gifts to expedition sponsors. A few of the bottles dated back to the 1952 Swiss expedition that didn't reach the top, and the 1953 British team that did. Brent Bishop kept several bottles he believed had been left by his father's expedition in 1963.

"We cruised on down to Lukla," Chris Naumann said. "The weather had been bad, so trekkers were backed up forever waiting for flights out, and we had to wait a few days, too." They had chartered a Russian helicopter, and when there was a break in the clouds it roared down onto the Lukla runway.

"It was huge, but with all the bags of trash and the oxygen bottles stuffed into it we could barely get in ourselves," Chris remembered. "As we were loading onto the helicopter, Goryl walks into town, comes straight to the airstrip, and literally gets into the helicopter still holding his trekking poles." The five friends were together once again.

Elizabeth Hawley met with the expedition members the next day at a rooftop restaurant in Kathmandu to document their accomplishments. Scott had fun trying to charm her, knowing she wanted only the facts of the expedition and the correct spelling of their names to file away with hundreds of other accounts of the Himalayan ascents she had recorded over the years.

"5,000 pounds trash off mountain and away from BC," she wrote of the expedition. "Got 100–150 bottles off mountain by Sherpas descending after carrying loads. Gave Sherpas income without making (them) go up just for trash."

To the small fraternity of elite climbers, Scott's success was something more. "In 1990 the business of guiding on Everest had been primed and ready to happen," Wally Berg told me. "A lot of climbers made it to the summit that year and Scott got left behind. By 1994 Pete Athans was going up Everest for the fourth time. I had climbed Everest twice. Rob Hall was ticking off summit climbs with clients every spring.

"So Scott did what he had to do, and he did it beautifully. He climbed Everest without oxygen and without any epics or problems. It was an exceptionally valid and impressive ascent of Everest. To the climbers, he more than redeemed himself for having gotten left behind in the big flurry of change and the commercial success that was happening on Everest."

Scott had arrived. After decades of striving toward the top of the world, he had finally reached the summit of Mount Everest, and he had gotten there in good style. The expedition had been, as Rob Hess said, perfect in all regards.

Now it was time to figure out what to do next.

CHAPTER 20

The Year Before the Year

You've climbed the highest mountain in the world. What's left? It's all downhill from there. You've got to set your sights on something higher than Everest.

—Willi Unsoeld, summiteer on the 1963 American Everest Expedition

LOOKING DOWN FROM a snow-covered cliff, Scott Fischer is wearing sunglasses, a helmet, and a blue parka with a Mountain Madness patch sewn on the pocket. His blond hair is pulled back into a loose ponytail. "I'm Scott Fischer, professional mountain climber and president of Mountain Madness," he announces. "I've climbed the highest peaks in the world, Everest and K2, without oxygen, and I think we can teach anybody to mountain climb!"

Upbeat music cues in the background and the latest episode of the locally produced 1995 television program *H2O,* "How to Outdoor," kicks into gear. With quirky camera angles, quick editing, and tongue-in-cheek humor, the program brings together unlikely characters for adventures in the outdoors. The host is Chip Hanauer, well known in the Pacific Northwest as a champion driver of hydroplane speed boats. Personable and engaging, Hanauer establishes the premise of the episode. Basketball player Shawn Kemp, the six-ten forward for the Seattle Supersonics, is going mountain climbing, and Scott will show him how.

Kemp and Fischer never actually appear together on camera. One suspects that the National Basketball Association all-star, dressed in a white T-shirt, reversed baseball cap, and baggy shorts more appropriate for sitting courtside than scaling a peak, has been escorted by the production team just far enough beyond a ski area parking lot to ensure a snowy landscape behind him as he delivers his lines. There is much lighthearted banter between Hanauer and Kemp about the challenge of climbing, then Kemp walks a few steps across a nearly level field of snow. Stopping to mop his forehead, he asks, "How far have we got left to go? Fifty miles?"

The camera returns to Scott on a much steeper mountainside. He shifts easily into the role of instructor, showing several novices the correct way to cross a steep mountainside that could be a potential avalanche path. "We're going to be aware, we're going to watch our partners when we cross it," he tells them. "The trick is never to be surprised." They find a campsite below a cluster of trees that Scott explains will anchor the snow and guard them from avalanches. He calls the place "an island of safety."

A recurring program theme is the matter of going to the bathroom in the woods, an issue that seems foremost among Shawn Kemp's concerns. Up on the cliff, Scott demonstrates how he can stay attached to a rope even as he loosens his climbing harness if he needs to relieve himself. The moment is ripe with comic potential, but Scott doesn't play it for laughs. "It's a little insignificant thing," he says of the technique he is explaining, "but if you've got to go sneak off into the bushes and get out of your harness, or go sneak off on a cliff, that could be the time that you fall."

He is all business, too, as he brushes away loose snow and explains the steps of setting an anchor for a rappel. With his ice tool he drives an aluminum stake into the snow, sinks another anchoring device next to it, and secures his rappel rope to them both. His hands move quickly and with no wasted motion. He has done this thousands of times. "In theory once I've got this anchor in it should hold me, it should hold my partner, it should hold my entire team," he tells the viewing audience as he tugs on the rope to test it. "This thing should hold a Volkswagen bus."

Scott backs over the cliff and slides slowly down the rope through midair toward the base of the cliff. "I'd like to see Shawn Kemp get this kind of vertical!" he exclaims.

I watched a tape of the "How to Outdoor" episode not long

ago, a dozen years after it had been made. Scott was at his relaxed best, enjoying himself in the mountains, having fun with people, and practicing his craft. He was unlikely to transform an NBA superstar into a mountaineer, but it was obvious that even in the contrived setting of a television show Scott delighted in sharing his passion for alpine adventure.

It is reassuring to be reminded how much enthusiasm and joy of the moment Scott exuded at a time when change was swirling all about. I try not to read too many of my own assumptions into his penultimate year, and yet I can't help wondering how he was thinking about all that confronted him. Even on the video he reflects on coming to see certain things differently.

"When I was young I climbed for the adrenaline rush, and when I got to the top I'd say, *Hooo! Good thing I got through that one!*" he tells the *H2O* audience. "Now days I want to climb with such control that I don't get scared."

Scott finally had an ascent of Mount Everest behind him. His fundamental life plan to be a climber and get others excited about the high country had guided him since he had been fourteen and at long last he had summited the world's highest peak. Good thing he'd gotten through that one, but it left him with a challenge that might have been even more scary. *What now?*

He wasn't alone in looking for an answer to that question. "I figured I could be a guide until I died or I could get into another field and have a better ending," Steve Goryl told me of his own career deliberations after he had climbed Everest with Scott. "I thought I might start using my mind more than I'd been using my body and probably end up wealthier. Both Scott and I'd had the central theme in our lives that being in the mountains is where it's at. After Everest, though, I was ready to move on."

Scott was on the cusp of turning forty. He knew climbers who had continued to excel into their fifties, and he imagined he would be one of them, but he was an athlete who had been at the top of his game for more than two decades, and the years had taken their toll. His body was scarred from surgeries on his knees, hip, abdomen, ankle, and face. Both shoulders had been dislocated, one of them numerous times, and both had been surgically rebuilt. He would sometimes awaken in the night as if from the effects of malaria. A nagging intestinal ailment that he told me he might have picked up years earlier in Asia persistently evaded cure.

The years accumulate for us all, and while our minds may continue to make promises, our legs and lungs will not always be able to fulfill those commitments. Scott might not have sensed it yet, but if not that year or the next he would surely begin facing the realities of growing older. For those whose lives are inherently physical, it can be difficult to accept that their powers may be slowly slipping away. That can be jarring for a professional athlete of Shawn Kemp's caliber. It can be difficult for elite mountaineers, too, as they begin to notice that their finely honed skills no longer hold quite so keen an edge.

On the record, at least, Scott seemed able to look beyond all of that. "Big mountains don't hold that much adventure for me anymore," he told a writer for *Northwest Wilderness Journal* soon after returning from climbing the world's highest peak. "Everest is pretty much the same experience as K2 and Broad Peak; I'll keep doing it, it's my identity, and I'm good at it, but I have other projects, adventurous ones."

He saw another fifteen years to his climbing career, then in his midfifties turning to professional photography, something he was already pursuing as an avocation. He wanted to spend more time in Alaska, travel to Baffin Island, and perhaps go to the North Pole. He envisioned a trip to Africa as well, one that would include his family. "If we're camping in the Serengeti, that's something I should do with my kids. God, what an experience that would be," he told the reporter. "You could bring horseshoes and badminton and it would just be a gas, to have lions and zebras around."

Even without the zebras and lions, Scott loved spending time with Katie Rose and Andy, and they reveled in the focused attention he gave them. But climbing at the highest levels of the mountaineering game still took him from his family for weeks and sometimes months at a time. In Andy's first nine years, Scott had been in Seattle only twice to celebrate his son's birthday in the middle of

May, the heart of the Himalayan climbing season. Jeannie would put together a special party for Andy when Scott returned from the latest springtime expedition, but it was never quite the same.

At age four, Katie Rose also continued to delight her father. She was as fearless as he was, and seemingly the one person in Scott's life who could defy him and carry it off. "Katie Rose!" he would say sternly, ready to correct her on some matter of errant childhood behavior. She would put her hands on her hips and stand her ground even though she was not much taller than his knee. Scott would break down in laughter and scoop his daughter into his arms.

To prepare them for their father's long absences, Scott and Jeannie helped the children construct calendar boxes. Each day Scott was gone, Andy and Katie Rose could peel back the paper marking another square on the calendar to reveal a small trinket or toy that would serve as a reminder of the passage of time and help them understand how many days were left before daddy came home. The children made prayer flags, too, featuring their hand prints and the totems they had chosen to represent themselves and their family. Scott would hang the flags on the guy lines of his tent in the Himalayas and would prop up photographs of Katie Rose and Andy next to his sleeping bag.

"I feel bad that my family misses me," he explained to the *Northwest Wilderness Journal* reporter, "but I'm really not pining away. I'm living right there where I am at that time." He concluded the interview by reflecting on the impact of his occupation upon himself and his loved ones. "The consequences of my actions have a lot more import these days," he said. "I always thought, 'I'm a climber, I'll die a climber.' Now I'd just as soon not die."

Jeannie was confronting changes, too, the most difficult of her career. She had flown for Alaska Airlines since 1982 and had become a captain in 1986, one of the first women in the company to achieve that rank. By early 1995, though, she had come to believe that the cockpit was a hostile environment for her gender, a concern she felt deeply enough to take legal action against the airlines. "I told Scott I wasn't going to do this if it was going to jeopardize our marriage," she explained to me recently. She said that Scott fully supported her through the legal process, though the ordeal became greater than either of them had anticipated. "I loved flying, but I couldn't fly anymore. I loved Scott and the kids more than anything, but I became very depressed throughout 1995 and I couldn't give him or the kids all the attention they needed."

Without Jeannie's income, the economic strain began to grow, too. It had been their understanding from the beginning of their marriage that while none of her earnings would go to Mountain Madness, she and Scott could rely on her pilot's salary to cover the family's living expenses. Scott's adventure travel company had always managed somehow to stay afloat, but what he could make with Mountain Madness wasn't enough to cover the family's financial shortfall. Being a mountain guide, even one with his own business, had seldom been a lucrative profession. Office manager Karen Dickinson stressed that fact when she fielded inquiries from people eager to work for Mountain Madness.

"We don't even think about hiring guides who aren't already guides," she would tell them. "You need tons of experience and it would be nice if you spoke a language or two. You have to know the place you're going inside and out, you need verifiable climbing skills and great people skills, and then we're basically not going to pay you."

The highest compensation Mountain Madness was offering at the time was a hundred dollars a day, and that was only for the days a guide was in the field. Some of the best climbers in the Northwest did sign on to lead Mountain Madness trips and climbing courses now and then, but as a full-time profession, almost any other career would have been more profitable. "If what you want to do is go climbing, you'll do a lot more climbing if you're not a guide but just go to the mountains for fun," Karen concluded. Her sobering words did not deter everyone. Tom Nickels, a young Seattle native returning to his hometown from extended travels around the globe, was interested enough in learning about the business of adventure travel that he volunteered to help out in the Mountain Madness office and gradually earned his way onto the tiny payroll.

Scott renewed his efforts to make his company more successful.

As he considered the trips Mountain Madness would run in 1995, he mulled over whether it was practical to offer a commercial expedition to Mount Everest. His friends Rob Hall, Pete Athans, Wally Berg, Ed Viesturs, and others would be guiding clients on Everest that spring, and seemed to be perfecting strategies for reaching the top. On the other hand, operating an Everest commercial trip required tremendous investments of time and money. There was a permit to buy, Sherpas and guides to hire, and thousands of pounds of gear and provisions to purchase and ship to the Himalayas. Getting enough bottled oxygen for the clients could eat up much of the budget. Even so, Scott applied to Nepal's Ministry of Tourism for a 1995 permit, but by the time he had gotten a positive response he felt it was too late to fill the roster and see to the hundreds of logistical chores he would have to complete before the expedition could begin.

Scott instead loaded the Mountain Madness brochure with trips to the mountains of the Pacific Northwest, East Africa, Argentina, and the Soviet Union, and rock-climbing seminars close to home. He intended to lead three of the bigger climbs himself—a springtime ascent of Alaska's Mount McKinley, a late summer climb of Broad Peak in Pakistan, and the Climb for CARE, a mid-winter fund-raising expedition on Kilimanjaro.

For the McKinley trip, Scott invited Rob Hess to come from the Tetons be one of his guides. Rob had helped Scott lead the Climb for the Cure on McKinley in 1993, and had summited Everest with him the following spring. Scott enjoyed climbing with Rob and saw their skills as well matched, especially with Rob's meticulous attention to the technical details of an expedition. In addition to several clients, Tom Nickels took time away from the Mountain Madness office to come to Alaska, too.

The Mountain Madness climbers were confronted by three weeks of McKinley's fiercest weather. They hauled their gear and provisions up the West Buttress Route, reaching a camp at 14,000 feet and waiting several days for a storm to ease. When it did, they climbed to 17,000 feet and set up their tents, the summit another 3,000 feet above them. They used blocks of snow to build walls around the tents to shield them from increasingly severe winds, and then storms pinned everybody down for five days. "It was really bad up there," Rob Hess told me. "Some Koreans hadn't made good snow walls and their tents were destroyed. They had to come and share our tents."

"Rob was great on that trip taking care of everybody, just amazing," Tom Nickels recalled. "He taught me so much—tricks, techniques, solutions for everything that happened on the mountain."

When the storm eased, the Mountain Madness climbers roped up for a summit try. The Koreans tied in with them, but soon the team was being beaten down by more bad weather. "It was very cold and very windy, and there was zero visibility," Tom said. "When we turned around, we weren't sure which way to go to get back to our camp." A guide from a neighboring camp realized the Mountain Madness climbers were overdue and left his tent to lead them in.

The skies were clearing the following day and Scott's climbers set off for the summit again, but their hearts weren't in it. "We were cooked and the clients were cooked," Rob Hess remembered. "It had been so brutal and so hard on us trying to keep people okay that we were maxed out. We got to talking about having a beer at the Fairview in Talkeetna and we were out of there."

They were met at a lower camp by the rest of the Korean team who treated them to hot tea and a meal of noodles and fish head soup. "The storms had been so scary loud that they were surprised that any of us who had been up higher had survived," Tom told me.

None of the Mountain Madness guides or clients had reached the top of McKinley, but there had been no fatalities among them, either. Others had not been so fortunate. As the team continued its descent, they saw a helicopter hovering over a glacier where rescuers were removing the bodies of three climbers who had taken shelter in a crevasse and succumbed to hypothermia.

"I am back from Alaska," Scott wrote to Lene Gammelgaard after he returned to Seattle. They had maintained a correspondence since meeting in the Himalayas several years earlier, and Scott knew of the Danish woman's continuing interest in mountain travel.

"Guess what? Mount McKinley beat me this time. It was the worst weather I have ever seen, anywhere."

Scott settled in to work at the office, saw to the logistics of upcoming expeditions, and spent time with his children. The money issues troubling the family were becoming increasingly acute as Jeannie's lawsuit ground slowly forward. As an economic measure, she and Scott discussed selling their house in West Seattle and moving to North Bend, thirty miles east of Seattle, where expenses would be lower. The town had the added appeal to Scott of being closer to the mountains. They went so far as to drive around North Bend neighborhoods looking at houses and property.

News from the 1995 spring climbing season on Mount Everest may have lessened Scott's disappointment about not marketing his own commercial expedition. The Adventure Consultants trip led by Rob Hall and Ed Viesturs had failed to reach the summit with any clients. An Alpine Ascents team that included Wally Berg as a guide had been turned back by deep snow above the South Col. Even so, organizing a 1996 Mountain Madness Everest trip was never far from Scott's mind.

By late summer Scott was ready to be on the move again. If he thought the storm on McKinley had been severe, he was soon to encounter weather even more deadly as he set out for Broad Peak, the world's twelfth highest mountain. At 26,400 feet it is one of the the peaks over 8,000 meters. While no 8,000 meter mountain is easy to climb, Broad Peak does not present the unrelenting demands of K2, its taller neighbor on the other side of the Baltoro Glacier.

Scott again enlisted Rob Hess as a second guide. He brought Lopsang Jangbu from Nepal, too, the young high-altitude Sherpa who had gone to the summit of Everest with Scott, Rob, and Brent Bishop the previous year. Two other Sherpas came with Lopsang to support the Mountain Madness effort. Scott's longtime friend Dale Kruse signed on as a climber, as did Peter Goldman, a friend from Seattle who had been with Scott on Baruntse in 1991 and on their attempt to climb the Everest North Face in 1987. A handful of other clients rounded out the team.

The Broad Peak climbers were joined for the ten-day hike from the end of the road to their base camp by a group of Mountain Madness trekkers led by Michael Allison, another of the Bruces who had been with Scott on many adventures. The trekkers were a mix of experienced travelers and several for whom strenuous mountain adventure was a relatively new experience. Lene Gammelgaard was among those who had been to the Karakoram before. She and Scott had plenty of time to talk during the long hike in, and Scott encouraged her to think about coming with him if he were to lead a Mount Everest expedition the following year.

Other climbers and trekkers were establishing their camps near Broad Peak, too, and the Mountain Madness camp soon became the latest edition of the Baltoro Café with Starbucks' coffee and good cheer for anyone stopping by. Keith and Christine Boskoff, a couple from Atlanta, Georgia, felt warmly welcomed. Trained as an aerospace engineer, Christine had been introduced to climbing by her husband and was relishing opportunities to travel to the great mountain ranges of the world. Now they had Broad Peak in their sights.

"I heard that Scott Fischer was going to be there with a Mountain Madness group, and I thought, wow, cool," Christine told me of her first meeting with Scott. "I knew about him but had never met him before. He was a good guy, nice, personable, and very approachable. He didn't know who we were, but there was no ego involved and he invited us over to his camp. He was handsome with long blond hair, and tall, but everybody's tall to me." Christine and Keith folded comfortably into the Mountain Madness energy, and were soon planning to join forces with Scott and his team for their Broad Peak ascent.*

The base camp at K2 was close enough for climbers preparing to scale that peak to hike over and enjoy the hospitality of the Moun-

---

*Keith and Christine Boskoff purchased Mountain Madness from the Scott Fischer estate a year after Scott died. Following Keith's death in 1998, Christine managed the company and led expeditions on many significant peaks including Mount Everest. In the winter of 2006, she and climbing partner Charlie Fowler were buried in an avalanche on the remote mountain peak of Genyan Massif in China's Sichuan Province.

tain Madness encampment, too. Among them was Peter Hillary, who had shared time with Scott on Everest in 1989 and 1990, and British alpinist Alison Hargreaves. Her children, home in England with her husband, were about the same ages as Andy and Katie Rose, who were with Jeannie in Seattle.

The Mountain Madness trekkers stayed a few days at Broad Peak camp and then departed with Michael Allison for the continuation of their journey. Rather than retracing their footsteps down the Baltoro Glacier, they planned to climb to Gondogoro La, an 18,000-foot pass offering spectacular views of Broad Peak, K2, and other giants of the Karakoram, then descend into the Hushe Valley and follow that drainage out of the mountains. The seldom-visited villages of the Hushe promised simple comforts, and the hike along the valley floor would take them between granite walls rivaling in height those of Yosemite. It was to be a magnificent conclusion to the trek, but also very demanding.

"The biggest problem I had on that trip was Scott not wanting to acknowledge the weakness of some of the clients we had," Michael recalled. "There was a lady with us who'd had a hip transplant, and I figured she had a fifty-fifty chance of dying up on that pass." He and Scott discussed the wisdom of allowing the woman to continue. Neither Scott nor Michael had been to Gondogoro La and so had not seen the other side, but Scott felt that since she had paid for the trip and had made it as far as base camp, the trekker should be allowed to continue.

"Scott was all for letting her go for it, but I had to tell her no." Michael sent the woman back down the Baltoro with some of the Mountain Madness support staff. "She was not happy at all, but I told her it was my decision." When he did reach the pass, Michael was convinced he had made the right choice. The trekkers had to rappel down the far side, then descend steep sections of loose rock. "It was like being in a bowling alley. If you fell, you were going to roll two thousand feet and you probably wouldn't survive it."

With the trekkers gone, the Mountain Madness climbers set about the business of establishing their intermediate camps on Broad Peak, and Rob Hess threw himself into solving the technical problems of the ascent. The first obstacle was getting everyone to the far side of a river near base camp. Sunshine warming the mountains each day caused the stream to swell with glacial melt and become a torrent that could sweep an unwary traveler into boulders downstream. Rob installed a Tyrolean traverse by stretching a rope above the river and tightening it so that climbers could use carabiners to attach their harnesses and then airmail themselves across.

"That went really well, and I was super stoked," Rob told me. He and the Sherpas took the lead in anchoring ropes on pitches of rock farther up the mountain and on steep snowfields. "We were setting it up for everybody that was there, not just our expedition," he continued. "We were successful, and in that regard it was really good. In other regards it wasn't."

For Rob, the other regards were that he felt Scott was distracted and not always fully engaged in leading the expedition. It was similar to the impression that Michael Allison had formed. Scott was there, but his mind could be elsewhere, his thoughts seemingly weighted with matters other than the mountain looming in front of him.

"Scott's presence and his energy were so strong that when he was off at all, I felt like I was off, too," Rob told me. "Scott was hanging back initially and I was by default thrown into the major leadership role of making lots of the hard client decisions with people."

One of the Mountain Madness clients climbed with difficulty to Broad Peak's Camp II. "He was barely able to carry his own load," Rob remembered. "The Sherpas who had come from Nepal to help everybody were putting all their attention on him."

Rob told the client he should return to base camp. "I basically cut him off. I laid it on the table, you can't go. I probably could have been nicer about how I did that, but it was clearly not appropriate for him to go on." The client gathered his gear and retreated down the mountain. "He got upset and he left," Rob concluded, "but I had to do what I had to do."

Scott had always tried to open the pathway for people to go as far as they could on a trip and to expand their sense of what was possible. His reluctance to turn climbers and trekkers around on Broad Peak seemed in keeping with that philosophy, though there were other ways to look at it. "Scott wanted to get everybody to the top of Broad Peak," Dale Kruse told me. "The more people he got on top of mountains, the better he would be able to sell his business, so instead of being the guy who wanted to be the first one to the top, he started pulling up the rear to make sure everyone was going forward."

Eventually Scott, Rob Hess, and Peter Goldman reached the Broad Peak summit along with the Sherpas and Christine Boskoff. The climbers could look across the Baltoro Glacier and see the huge pyramid of K2 rising a half mile higher than where they were standing. They might even have scanned K2's upper snowfields for a glimpse of Alison Hargreaves and three others nearing the summit by the same route Ed Viesturs and Scott had followed three years earlier. Peter Hillary had set out that morning with Alison, but had turned back. Five Spanish climbers were high up on another K2 ridge. The day was about to turn deadly.

"We reached the top of Broad Peak at ten in the morning, then descended to high camp and from there on down in a very vicious wind storm," Rob Hess told me.

"When we were coming off Broad Peak, the winds were brutal," Scott reported later, estimating the velocity at a hundred miles an hour. The Mountain Madness team managed to get to the lower camps, but three of the Spanish climbers on K2 perished. Alison Hargreaves and her team reached the K2 summit, then died in the storm. "The difference between Broad Peak and K2 is about 3,000 feet," Scott wrote. "That was the difference between life and death."

"We were actually listening on the radio to one of the climbers during his harrowing descent and ultimately collapsing and dying in camp," Rob Hess remembered. "It was an emotional, crazy situation."

The year had presented Scott with plenty of emotional, crazy situations, though as 1995 drew to a close, at least one of the stresses eased when Jeannie's lawsuit was settled out court. Scott could look ahead with growing optimism about Mountain Madness, too. Many of the trips the company had offered in 1995 had found clients, and he was putting together an ambitious schedule for the following year. He had not yet reached his business goals, but he was moving in the right direction.

Scott's self-esteem as a guide got another boost when representatives for CARE (the Cooperative for American Relief Everywhere) sought out Mountain Madness to organize and lead a Kilimanjaro expedition celebrating CARE's fiftieth anniversary as an international relief organization. The climbers were business executives, attorneys, and investment bankers enthused by the prospects of a successful ascent and the opportunity to use the Kilimanjaro ascent as a means to raise half a million dollars for their cause. Scott engaged Wes Krause and African Environments to provide logistical support in Tanzania, then flew to Africa to lead the climb himself.

Scott had predicted to the Seattle media that all of the climbers would reach the top of Kilimanjaro and fulfill their promises to those pledging donations to CARE. Privately he told the CARE team members that they would have one of the great experiences of their lives, and he was correct on both calls. Taking plenty of time to acclimate and to enjoy the journey, the team spent six days ascending Kilimanjaro's Western Breach route. At Arrow Glacier they tented with a view of the Breach Icicle that Scott and Wes had climbed together a dozen years earlier. They made their highest camp on the floor of Kilimanjaro's summit crater where, at close to 19,000 feet, the CARE climbers spun through the night as the highest humans in all of Africa. At dawn they bundled up in their warmest clothing, drank tea and coffee, then climbed the final few hundred feet to the very pinnacle of Africa.

When the CARE climbers were safely off the mountain, Scott accepted Wes's invitation to stick around Tanzania for a few days to go on a game-viewing safari in the Serengeti with him and his family. They bounced across open grazing lands in a Land Rover with the roof hatches open, watching elephants, rhinos, lions, and giraffes. Wes and Melly's children excitedly absorbed in the passing scene.

"Scott started talking about how it felt like he might want to chill out a little more and start doing more adventure stuff with his own family," Wes told me. "He was going to come back to Africa within the year and do some exploring with Andy and Katie Rose. I really felt that maybe by seeing Melly and me doing interesting and somewhat adventurous activities with our kids, he was seeing the possibilities. It's not the same high adrenaline type of adventure as climbing hard peaks, but it's equally rewarding."

It is tempting to look at 1995 as a year of foreshadowing for Scott. There were mountain storms and climbers lost in whiteouts. A guide left the safety of his tent to bring in members of a team struggling to find its way. Climbers had died. One might also make assumptions about the ways Scott was handling the challenges of balancing work and family, or to judge what, if anything, changed for him in the year after he had climbed Everest. Something that was never in doubt, though, was Scott's abiding pleasure in going to the high and windy places. He was in his element while he was in the mountains, doing what he most wanted to do.

The episode of the *How to Outdoor* television program closes with Scott Fischer in the mountains. He has just completed a rappel and is relaxing on the snow, his hands behind his head. He is in his island of safety, and appears to be completely at ease, happy with where he is at that moment and content with who he has become.

"I LOVE this stuff!" he shouts to the camera, his face breaking into a wide smile, and you know that he absolutely does.

CHAPTER 21

Last Climb

We were together for two months, and for all but the last few days, they were some of the best times of my life.
—Sandy Hill, *Outside Magazine*, September 2006

I WAS PACKING for the drive from Seattle to Wyoming to lead a trail crew working in Grand Teton National Park when the delivery boy hit the front door with the morning paper. A short article next to a thumbnail photo of Scott Fischer reported that his Mountain Madness team had reached the summit of Everest. I smiled with relief and satisfaction, and began stuffing my sleeping bag into my backpack.

Moments later the telephone rang and I answered to hear Scott's sister Lisa crying. "It's Scott," she sobbed. "He can't get down!" No, I assured her, the newspaper had already said that the climb was a success. "He can't get down," Lisa kept repeating, "he can't get down!"

I hung up and drove to the Fischer-Price home in West Seattle, as much out of my own need for understanding as from any expectation that I could be of comfort to Scott's family. Jeannie's sister Veda and their mother were in the living room, the walls covered with framed mountain landscapes Scott had photographed during his expeditions. Jeannie motioned for me to sit on the couch beside her, then drew my arm around her shoulders and leaned against me. Nine-year-old Andy crawled into her lap.

"Do you want to hear what's happening?" she asked.

"Only if you want to tell me."

"Andy, are you okay with this again?" He nodded, and cuddled closer.

Jeannie explained that the climbers had been to the top of Everest, but that during their descent they were hit by a storm. Sherpas had found Scott unconscious alongside another climber and had managed to rouse the second man, but had not been able to awaken Scott. "He was barely breathing when they left him, and that was a couple of hours ago," Jeannie said.

"Why can't somebody go get him?" Veda demanded. "Why isn't there a rescue? Bob, you've been in the mountains with Scott. Why aren't they doing something?"

I told her what I could about conditions so extreme that rescuers going that high on Everest would be risking their lives, too, and about air so thin that the rotor blades of a helicopter would have nothing to lift against. For Scott to be saved, he would almost certainly have to gather the strength to make it down under his own power.

Andy stirred uneasily. "Do you think Dad's eyes are open?" he asked.

"I don't know, honey," Jeannie told him. "Daddy probably got really, really tired and sat down to rest, and then he fell asleep and didn't wake up again."

More friends arrived and as the critical mass of support grew, I moved toward the edge of the room. Katie Rose was playing on the deck with her cousins, oblivious to the magnitude of the tragedy enveloping her family. When she saw me she raced up and repeated a knock-knock joke she and I had been sharing through the spring, then ran back to her games. It broke my heart to watch her, and tears streamed down my face as I drove away.

What was happening would become the subject of an avalanche of newspaper articles, magazine pieces, and website discussions. A shelf full of books would highlight the events on Everest in the spring of 1996, including Jon Krakauer's *Into Thin Air*, Anatoli Boukreev's *The Climb*, Lene Gammelgaard's *Climbing High*, and Beck Weathers' *Left for Dead*.

Some climbers who knew Scott tell me that they have never

looked at any of the accounts. They say that his earlier adventures were far more interesting to them than his last expedition, and I am inclined to agree. Even so, I have found myself compelled to read everything, hoping to piece together from all the reports a basic understanding of what happened to Scott Fischer during his final climb.

The seeds of a 1996 Mountain Madness Everest expedition were planted in 1994 as Scott came through Kathmandu after summiting Everest for the first time, and got together for a beer with Neal Beidleman, whom he had met two years earlier at K2 Base Camp. Neal had just climbed Makalu, the world's fifth highest mountain, on an expedition that had included Thor Kieser and Charley Mace from the same K2 trip, and Russian climber Anatoli Boukreev. Scott and Neal swapped stories of their recent ascents, and as they looked ahead to future adventures Scott said that he was applying to get a permit for a Mountain Madness commercial trip on Everest for the spring of 1995. He invited Neal to consider coming along.

"When I got back to Aspen I started getting e-mails from Scott about how to organize the whole thing," Neal told me recently, "but it became evident that he wasn't going to have enough clients and would have to postpone the trip."

A year later as he put together the 1996 Mountain Madness trip announcements, Scott included a description of an Everest expedition that listed as guides Neal Beidleman, Rob Hess, and himself. "Building on the success of 1994, the Sagarmatha Environmental Expedition is returning to the world's highest peak," the advertisement read. "Expedition leader Scott Fischer has designed the climb to get every member on the summit, using a pyramid of camps, each stocked from the one below. Climbers are welcome to assist in the cleanup effort, but their primary goal will be to stand on top of the world." Cost per person was listed at $65,000. The brochure also described a support trek that would allow trekkers to visit the Everest climbers and take part in environmental improvement projects around base camp.

"Scott showed up at the Mountain Madness office one day and said Neal was going to guide Everest," office manager Karen Dickinson recalled. "He said this guy is really solid and has great people skills."

Scott was also aware that Neal knew people who might want to be Mountain Madness climbers, and he offered to make it worthwhile for Neal to sign them on. "It was kind of commission based, but that was the only vehicle I had to get paid," Neal recalled. "I think I got $10,000 for the whole trip."

Neal encouraged fellow Coloradoan Charlotte Fox to come on board, and she in turn convinced Tim Madsen, her then boyfriend, that he should join them, too. A professional ski patroller, Charlotte had taken part in Himalayan expeditions to Cho Oyu and Gasherbrum II. "I'd been over eighteen thousand feet thirteen or fourteen times and was working into the eight thousand-meter peaks, so Everest didn't seem such a stretch," she recalled. Neal also invited Martin Adams, with whom he and Anatoli had shared their 1994 expedition to Makalu.

Dale Kruse was the first to write a check to hold a place on the Mountain Madness Everest team. He had joined Scott in recent years in the Himalayas for climbs on Baruntse, Mera Peak, and Ama Dablam, and on Broad Peak in the Karakoram. Though Dale had summited only Baruntse, Scott saw a try at Everest as a natural progression for the veteran Mountain Madness climber.

From her home in Denmark, Lene Gammelgaard had maintained a correspondence with Scott since meeting him in the Khumbu in 1991. She had come to Pakistan as a trekker on the 1995 Mountain Madness expedition to Broad Peak where Scott had shared with her his plan to climb Everest the following spring and convinced her she was ready for the challenge.

Pete Schoening and his nephew Klev were Seattle-area residents who pedaled their bicycles across town to meet with Scott. Pete had become a mountaineering legend more than forty years earlier while on an American expedition striving to be the first to summit K2. A teammate had become gravely ill at 25,000 feet and, in the face of a blizzard, expedition members began lowering their sick companion down the mountain. One of them fell, entangling the ropes of the others and dragging them toward almost certain death.

As their combined weight hit the end of the rope tied to his waist, Pete had the instinct to plant his ice axe and the strength to hang on and save them all. He had never been on a Mount Everest expedition, but at age sixty-eight was eager to try becoming the oldest person to reach its summit.

As Scott's Everest expedition took shape, Mountain Madness became involved in a drawn-out matter with the editors of *Outside Magazine* who for a time agreed to pay the company to accept Seattle-based journalist Jon Krakauer on the team. Scott offered to let him come at cost. Rob Hall's Adventure Consultants would also have a commercial expedition on Everest, the fifth in five years, and Karen Dickinson recalled that when *Outside* drew Rob's company into a bidding war, Hall came through with a lower quote. "If we had matched Adventure Consultants, we would have had to pay money to get Jon to go with us," Karen continued. "We figured that *Outside* at least had to cover his expenses."

The last to join the Mountain Madness team was Sandy Hill Pittman, a New Yorker setting herself apart from the upper circles of urban society by building a climbing resume that included summiting the highest mountain on six of seven continents. Among them was Mount Vinson in Antarctica where she had shared a camp with Charlotte Fox. Sandy had made several attempts to climb Mount Everest, the first in 1993 as a client of an expedition that had among its guides Wally Berg and Alex Lowe, a highly respected climber from Montana.

"Sandy was one of the strongest climbers that year," Wally told me. The expedition had sent two teams toward the summit. Alex and Wally led the first effort, reaching the top with three clients and three Sherpas. The subsequent team, composed of the expedition's stronger clients, was turned back by difficult conditions. Sandy was included on that team but had withdrawn before the final attempt. She returned the next year to try a route on Everest's Tibetan side with a small group that included Alex Lowe and Everest filmmaker David Breashears. Avalanche danger brought an early end to that expedition, and she was still without her Everest summit.

Sandy intended to write a book about climbing the Seven Summits, and would be bringing a computer and a satellite phone to the base camp so that she could post messages on a website. She provided Mountain Madness a potential for publicity Scott felt he had lost when Jon Krakauer switched to Rob Hall's expedition, and he knew that coverage was vital if commercial trips on Everest were to flourish. Media exposure could bring the possibility of climbing Everest to the attention of a much larger pool of potential customers with the interest and the resources to join a guided Everest expedition.

Publicity was nothing new to Himalayan mountaineering, but the speed of disseminating information had increased dramatically since the 1920s when it could take weeks for anyone not on an expedition to discover what had happened during an attempt to climb Everest. By 1953 as Hillary and Tenzing succeeded on the mountain, written messages could be sent by runners from base camp to Kathmandu and then shared with newspapers abroad. In 1990 Peter Hillary patched through a call from the Everest summit to his father in New Zealand. Rob Hall took a satellite telephone to base camp in 1994, but at a cost of twenty-five dollars a minute, using it for anything other than vital communications was prohibitively expensive.

In addition to the eyewitness reporting of Sandy Hill and Jon Krakauer, an expedition led by David Breashears and aided by Ed Viesturs planned to carry a wide-screen IMAX movie camera to the summit, filming all the way. MountainZone, a fledgling Internet site, was hoping to satisfy an increasingly computer-savvy audience with timely accounts from base camp and above, drawing on sources that including Mountain Madness. The Internet had not yet evolved to include real-time links from remote locations, but technology did exist for news of Everest to be uploaded and posted on the World Wide Web within a few hours of an event.

In the Mountain Madness office, Scott, Karen, and Tom Nickels realized that if all went well for the Everest expedition, media coverage could be a boon for the business. On the other hand, if clients felt they weren't being treated in the right way or believed they hadn't gotten full value from their considerable financial investments, negative reports might damage Mountain Madness.

Both Karen and Tom counseled Scott to select as a guide someone other than Rob Hess. Karen had not been a fan of Rob since the weeks after the 1995 Mountain Madness Broad Peak trip when a disgruntled client had complained to her that Rob had turned him around in a manner the client found abrasive. Tom had been on Mount McKinley with Rob the previous year and respected his considerable strengths, but agreed with Karen. "Rob was capable, strong, and technically skilled, but he could be blunt," Tom recalled.

The debate was taken up by others within the Mountain Madness circle. "Rob had a tough moment with a client, but for the rest of the trip, I thought he was great," argued Michael Allison who had been with the Mountain Madness trek to Broad Peak. He reminded Karen and Tom that Rob was technically excellent in the mountains, that he and Scott had worked well on McKinley, and that the two had climbed together to the Everest summit.

"Before 1996, if you turned a client around, basically it was the guide's word that it needed to be done," Neal Beidleman told me recently. "There hadn't yet been a real incident where a guide could tell a client, *Look, this is what can happen if you keep going*. So guides felt there had to be a very obvious cause to turn clients around." Clients who were sent down when they weren't doing well at altitude could later reconsider the matter in the comfort and richer air of base camp and might come to believe they had been robbed of their summit opportunity.

"After 1996 there was the precedent of what happened on Everest that could be used as an example of what could go wrong while guiding," Neal continued. "From then on you would be much less likely to second-guess the decisions that a guide like Rob Hess had made up high."

Scott was back in Kathmandu in October of 1995 to work out the details of the Everest permit, and ran into Anatoli Boukreev, the mountaineer he'd heard about from Neal Beidleman and others.

Anatoli had just climbed Dhaulagiri, the world's seventh highest mountain where he had gone alone from base camp at 15,000 feet to the summit at nearly 27,000 feet and back again in twenty-five hours. "The Russian moved with his crampons like he was born with them on his feet," one of his teammates told Elizabeth Hawley, the Kathmandu-based chronicler of Himalayan climbing. "He used his crampons so easily, so smoothly." Anatoli had also been in the Himalayas the previous spring to climb Everest from the Tibetan side.

Scott told Anatoli he had been pondering the matter of who would be the best fit for guiding a 1996 Mountain Madness Everest climb, and offered him a place on the team. The Mountain Madness guides would be Fischer, Beidleman, and Boukreev. "If something goes wrong with this expedition," Scott told Jeannie, "we've got Anatoli."

"Scott recognized the strength of Anatoli and he liked the idea of having this guy along who was as strong as Superman," Michael Allison told me. "Of course, Rob Hess was super strong, too."

Scott also met with his Kathmandu business associate P. B. Thapa to put together the expedition's support team. As sirdar they chose Lopsang Jangbu, the young Sherpa who had summited Everest and Broad Peak with Scott and had been on other Everest expeditions including one with Rob Hall. Lopsang's father and an uncle also signed on along with several other Sherpas.

With the roster of guides and Sherpas determined, the issue of money to pay the expedition expenses came into sharper focus. Scott struggled to keep his Friends of Scott attitude out of it as he negotiated with interested climbers, though Karen Dickinson would report that ultimately only Sandy Hill Pittman paid the full fee.

I dropped in at the Mountain Madness office to see Scott before he left for Everest. He was sorting gear and topping off a heavy cardboard crate with equipment to be shipped to Nepal. Since coming back to Seattle in January from leading the Climb for the Cure on Kilimanjaro, he had been running at full throttle to organize the Everest expedition and manage the rest of his business. He seemed weary, a fact that other friends would also later recall, and he'd not had time to do much training.

"The thing about Scott was that he had that physique that made him always look like he was built," Ed Viesturs reminded me recently. "He wasn't as strong as he could have been if he'd put more time and energy into running and biking. He could have made himself stronger for climbing, especially at altitude." That wasn't necessarily a worry since alpinists can sometimes climb their way into better shape during the weeks on an expedition leading up to a summit attempt. Like everyone else, I'd always known Scott to overcome any obstacles in his path, and I didn't express concern.

The Mountain Madness team arrived in Kathmandu in late March and enjoyed the color and culture of the city while Scott tied up dozens of loose ends, then helicoptered with his climbers to a landing area above Namche Bazaar. At long last they were all together, all hiking toward base camp, and all eager to get up Mount Everest. "Scott was great to travel with," Neal Beidleman recalled. "We had a really good time on the way in."

Fourteen expeditions were establishing their camps at the foot of the Khumbu Icefall with dozens of tents and hundreds of people. Beneath a Starbucks banner lashed to a boulder, the Mountain Madness camp featured a mess tent, a cook tent, and a tent to house communications equipment. The camp staff served big meals of Nepalese versions of American dishes supplemented with powdered drinks, energy bars, and Tillamook cheese Scott had shipped from Seattle. The compound was a far cry from the make-shift encampment that Scott and his four friends had established near the icefall two years earlier.

Seeing to the details of the expedition required much of Scott's time, but he was glad to be in the Himalayas. He was also happy to be among mountaineers he had known for years. He could get together with Ed Viesturs and Rob Hall to discuss their plans to climb Manaslu, an 8,000-meter Himalayan peak never summited by Americans, as soon as the three of them were done with their current responsibilities on Everest. Climbers from other teams dropped in at the Mountain Madness camp to fill their mugs with coffee and socialize. In many ways it was the same engaging camp scene that Scott had always encouraged and enjoyed when he got to the high country.

Base camp was full of people with big plans. For nearly everyone, the chance to climb Everest was shaping up to be a remarkable endeavor. Those who were new to the Everest scene found themselves among veteran climbers who could seem bigger than life because, in many ways, they were. At the center of much of the energy was Scott Fischer. "He had so much magnetism, and he made base camp really fun for everybody," Charlotte Fox told me of people wanting to be around him. "Men in a nonsexual way were attracted to Scott as much as women were in a sexual way."

For the first time in Scott's experience, members of expeditions were filing daily reports of the events at base camp and using satellite telephones to contact journalists, website managers, and family and friends on the far side of the globe. Scott could call Jeannie in Seattle and hear what Katie Rose and Andy were doing even as they were doing it. He was able to dial the Mountain Madness office and catch up on business matters. While it was reassuring to keep track of much that was happening beyond the Khumbu, the communication link worked both ways. The outside world was looking in. People far away were watching. The privacy of an expedition, so long one of its basic aspects, was about to disappear.

The Icefall Doctor and his Sherpa team completed the route through the Khumbu Icefall in mid-April and the way was open into the Western Cwm. "We'll have fun in Kathmandu, we'll have fun on the trek, we'll have fun at base camp," Scott had written to Lene Gammelgaard before the expedition, "and from then on, it will be one and a half months of extremely hard struggling."

The hard struggling was about to begin, though what constituted struggle depended on the person. "The reason you go out there is because you really love to climb," Charlotte Fox told me. "I feel bad for these people who come to Everest just because they need to say they've climbed it. It's not fun for them, whereas it's really fun for the rest of us. We love that sort of suffering. It really doesn't have to be fun to be fun."

The climbers began their trips up the mountain, climbing higher each time to acclimate to the thinning air and to the exertions of the ascent. Scott and Neal mixed easily with the Mountain Madness group, and Scott granted them a large degree of freedom to set their own agendas. "What I really liked was that Scott let us know that he thought of all of us as competent climbers," Charlotte explained. "If we wanted to be guided, he would guide us. But Scott was there to assemble a game plan and see it through, and we went climbing. Our team did not feel guided."

Whatever the selection process had been, Ed Viesturs viewed the Mountain Madness team as composed of mountaineers who would be able to manage pretty well even without Scott around. "Rob Hall as a guide was very nurturing," Ed told me, "and so people became dependent on him. On Scott's team they had to take care of themselves, and in the end I think they were stronger, more independent climbers."

Even so, Scott was concerned about how his team was responding to the leadership they felt they were receiving. Anatoli Boukreev concentrated on pushing the route, helping anchor the ropes that would protect climbers on the steeper pitches above the icefall. There were differences in expectations between him and the Mountain Madness climbers, and language barriers that created distance, but he felt confident that he was contributing to the team's success and fulfilling his obligations to Scott. He was startled to discover that Scott was frustrated with him for not being more supportive of the climbers.

"Scott was upset with Anatoli when I was there," Brent Bishop told me of what he saw when he led the Mountain Madness trekkers to base camp. "Anatoli wasn't willing to hold hands and be counselor and motivator and friend. It just wasn't in his cultural makeup."

A much more serious concern was the illness of Lopsang's uncle Ngawang Topche Sherpa of the Mountain Madness staff. Showing symptoms of altitude sickness above Camp I, he had continued to climb to Camp II only to be evacuated to base camp with a rescue effort organized by Klev Schoening and Tim Madsen and then joined by Neal Beidleman for the descent through the icefall. Ngawang was diagnosed with high-altitude pulmonary edema severe enough that he was carried to a village farther down the Khumbu with the hope that he would improve at lower elevations. As his health continued to decline, Lopsang helicoptered with him to a hospital in Kathmandu.[*]

The illness of Ngawang Topche Sherpa and Lopsang's absence for nearly a week from Everest left the Mountain Madness team short-handed. Scott worried about getting the upper camps established on schedule and stocked with provisions and oxygen canisters. He understood it was a necessary expense, but he also realized that the fee Mountain Madness was being billed for the helicopter evacuation could have a serious impact on his dwindling budget.

"For him it was probably a bit overwhelming to run a big trip like that," Ed Viesturs told me. "We'd sit by the tent and drink beer together. He would come on his own and not bring his entourage. He was escaping a little from them, and he would tell me what was going on and his woes."

"Scott was under the limelight and the pressure," Brent Bishop observed. "He was having to organize and manage, something he would rather have delegated to somebody else."

Guides and Sherpas from several teams joined forces to fix the ropes in place up the Lhotse Face to Camp III at nearly 24,000 feet, and then to chop tent platforms into the steep ice. Scott had told his team members they should be able to reach Camp III without oxygen if they expected to be included on a summit attempt. Dale, Lene, Klev, Martin, and Sandy made it that high and settled in for a night, though by the next morning Dale was having serious difficulties adjusting to the altitude. Scott and Anatoli descended with him, and Dale seemed recovered by the time they reached Camp II. The next morning Scott continued his trips up and down the route by returning to Camp III with Pete Schoening for his chance to acclimate to the higher elevation.

---

[*]Ngawang died two months later.

With the Camp III ascent behind them, all the Mountain Madness climbers returned to base camp to rest for three or four days before going for the Everest summit. Scott met with other expedition leaders to determine a schedule for attempts. The IMAX team wanted to summit on May 9, hoping to find both good weather and high ridges uncluttered by other climbers who might spoil the backgrounds of their camera shots. Scott and Rob Hall favored May 10, a date close to the time they had found earlier success. Scott also believed from his previous Everest expeditions that there was strength in numbers. If the Mountain Madness team ran into trouble, it would be good to have mountaineers nearby as skilled as Rob Hall and his guides Michael Groom and Andy Harris.

On one of their rest days, Neal Beidleman and Scott laced up their running shoes and set off toward Pumori, the graceful peak across the Khumbu Valley from base camp. Carrying rucksacks with only their sleeping bags and pads, some dinner, and their camera gear, they cruised above Pumori's lower reaches and bivouacked for the night. Leaning against a boulder, they sat in their sleeping bags and watched the golden glow of a gorgeous Himalayan evening illuminating the mountains around them. They could see the lights of base camp far below, and took pictures of the full moon coming around Everest.

"We're in the mountains at altitude, and it was really cool," Neal remembered. "People weren't bugging Scott. We were just there, and we had some really deep philosophical talks. He told me about his plans for his business and his life." Scott shared his hope of putting together a strategy for Mountain Madness with Everest expeditions as an important piece of the company's future.

"On Pumori we also hatched the final plan about who would do what and how we would manage our ascent of Everest," Neal recalled. "If clients or other people missed some of the points later it's not because it wasn't talked about in full, but because Scott didn't relay all the details to everybody."

Neal said that they discussed where the oxygen bottles were cached, who would take on various tasks, and how people would be organized on summit day. They talked about the fact that Anatoli wanted to climb without oxygen, but that they needed to tell him it wasn't going to happen that way. They also agreed that Lopsang and another Sherpa would leave Camp IV ahead of the team to anchor fixed ropes higher up.

"Basically Scott and I went over all the fundamental elements of our Everest plan," Neal explained. Of course, drawing up a plan while relaxing on Pumori on a calm, moonlit evening could be very different from putting the steps into motion on Everest's windswept heights.

The Mountain Madness team departed from base camp the morning of May 6, intending to bypass Camp I at the top of the Khumbu Icefall and reach Camp II by mid-afternoon. After resting there for a day, they would ascend the Lhotse Face to sleep at Camp III. The following morning they would climb to the South Col at 26,000 feet, and on May 10 head for the Everest summit, another 3,000 feet higher. If all went well, everyone would be back in base camp a few days after that, celebrating success.

The climbers spread out as they went through the icefall and ascended into the Western Cwm. Scott and Neal were the first to arrive Camp II. Despite some breathing difficulties he had been experiencing, Pete Schoening kept pace with his nephew and with Lene Gammelgaard, and Scott cheered them as they reached their tents.

Another climber coming from below told Scott that Dale Kruse had become ill above the icefall and taken shelter in a tent at Camp I. Dale wanted Scott to know that he would stay overnight at the lower camp and then hoped to catch up with the team the following day as they rested at Camp II. The group debated what should be done, realizing that while Dale's condition might improve overnight, the altitude sickness causing his struggles could become much worse.

Scott had always been extremely loyal to his friends. He had enjoyed his times with Dale from the days a dozen years earlier when the Coloradoan began showing up at Mountain Madness ice-climbing seminars near Ouray, and had convinced Dale to come on the Everest expedition. Dale had done everything asked of him except have a constitution that adapted well to the high altitude's thin air.

"Dale is my friend," Scott told Lene Gammelgaard when she suggested he send a Sherpa to descend with Dale rather than burning his own energy by going down the mountain himself. "As expedition leader, I want to be the one to tell him that his Everest trip is over."

Neal accompanied Scott as far as Camp I, then the Mountain Madness leader went through the icefall with Dale, arriving at base camp late in the day. Scott relaxed, visited with friends, and had a beer. He called Jeannie in Seattle and they talked about Andy and Katie Rose, then Jeannie asked, "What's the deal, why are you back in base camp?" He told her how bad he felt that Dale's Everest climb had come to an end. The rest of the team was just where he wanted them, he reported, and he would soon be heading back up the mountain to go with them to the summit.

"He was in a really good mood when he called and I didn't try to change his mind about anything," Jeannie remembered. "I'd asked him one time if he couldn't just stay in base camp and use the radio to guide the climb from there, but he'd said no, he couldn't do it that way."

Scott climbed through the icefall the following morning, making the 4,000-foot ascent to rejoin his team. "We were going to go over our final plans during that rest day at Camp II," Neal told me, "but Scott arrived late and tired. The timing of having a relaxed day to go over everything and get organized was shot. I had tried to relay the story to everybody as best I could, and then Scott finally got there and we talked through it, but it was probably not as organized as it could have been."

Neal had also spoken with Anatoli about the importance of using oxygen higher on the mountain, and had given the Russian climber a regulator and a mask so that he could use oxygen cylinders cached at the South Col. "He sort of reluctantly took them," Neal remembered.

In 1996 the protocols of being a commercial guide on Everest were still being figured out. Most guides were using supplemental oxygen above the South Col in the belief that it helped them stay warmer and function more efficiently. Anatoli knew that climbers using bottled air could perform well, but if their canisters ran dry, exposure to thin atmosphere could cause their bodies to crash from suddenly breathing air with only a third the oxygen content as at sea level. He had long believed he was at his best going to high elevations if he didn't breathe supplemental oxygen, and his successes on Everest, Makalu, and Dhaulagiri were evidence of his ability to climb without it. By not relying on supplemental oxygen, he felt he would never suffer the debilitating effects of exhausted air canisters.

Another climber making decisions was Pete Schoening, who told Scott that he'd had a great adventure on Everest and had felt strong climbing to Camp II, but realized that he wasn't adapting well enough to the altitude to go much higher. He bade his teammates farewell and the next day returned to base camp.

Scott and his team were on the move again, too. As they climbed the fixed ropes on the Lhotse Face toward Camp III, they intermingled with Rob Hall's Adventure Consultants' group going up and the IMAX film team coming down. Ed Viesturs and David Breashears told Scott that winds roaring across the South Col had not been conducive either to climbing or to making a movie, and they had broken off their summit attempt. The upper slopes of Everest were also about to become crowded with climbers they didn't want intruding on their film, so the IMAX mountaineers had decided to return to base camp and wait for the weather and the route to clear.

In the early light of May 9, more than fifty climbers left Camp III and crossed the Yellow Band on their way to the South Col. Neal stayed with Scott near the end of the long line. "He was really lagging," Neal recalled. "When you're following a group that big, though, somebody will be moving at a glacial pace and even if you're not feeling your greatest, you can go slowly and deal with it."

All the Mountain Madness team members arrived at Camp IV by late afternoon and themselves and their gear inside their tents. Neal and Scott were among the last to arrive. Scott congratulated everyone for reaching the Col and predicted they would soon be standing on the summit, then he crawled into a tent with Neal and Charlotte.

"I thought he was taxed," Neal told me. "He was really tired, but Scott was such a tough s.o.b. it wasn't the kind of thing you worried about."

Scott laid back in his sleeping bag to rest, listening to the wind buffeting the nylon tent fabric. When the wind diminished a few hours later, he unzipped the door of the tent and looked out to see a calm night and a sky filled with stars. He turned on his headlamp, adjusted his goose down suit and insulated plastic boots, and went to the other Mountain Madness tents to tell his teammates that the climb was on. It took more than an hour to get dressed and ready, and then they were standing outside the tents, moving around in the bitter cold and feeling their crampons crunch on the frozen stones of the Col.

The summit plan Scott and Neal had discussed a week earlier on Pumori had been that Lopsang would take the lead and carry one of the Mountain Madness radios while Anatoli and Neal would travel among the climbers. Scott would bring up the rear and have the team's other radio. If he determined there were climbers who should go no farther, he would send them down.

"He insisted that we go to the summit 'like a Cub Scout troop marching in formation,'" Sandy would later recall. "He said, 'We go up together and we come down together.'"

Some climbers were under the impression that Scott had set a turnaround time for anyone who had not reached the summit to begin descending, but others understood it would be at Scott's discretion when a retreat would begin. Some also thought that Sherpas from both Mountain Madness and Adventure Consultants would leave the South Col several hours ahead of everyone else in order to fix ropes on exposed sections of the route above, but there had been no early departures.

An hour before midnight the Adventure Consultants team of fifteen people walked across the South Col. Thirty minutes later the Mountain Madness climbers set off in their tracks. The last of them to leave Camp IV was Scott Fischer.

Hearing the sound of his breathing through his oxygen mask, Scott would have stepped around the shredded remnants of old tents, the bits of trash, and the discarded oxygen bottles still littering the Col. When he looked up he could see his team crossing the gradual rise of the Col to its intersection with steep, hard ice that would take them 1,200 vertical feet to the crest of the Southeast Ridge at a place called the Balcony. He might have noticed that Lopsang had tied a rope to Sandy's harness and was using the line either to guide her or to pull her along.

Scott undoubtedly saw the string of headlamps of the Adventure Consultants team moving toward the Balcony, the points of light separating from one another in the darkness as the faster climbers pulled ahead. He reached the edge of the Col and felt his crampons biting into ice bulging at a more severe angle. Using the rest step, he locked his knee and breathed several times before moving his other leg forward.

After a few hours of steady ascent Scott would have seen that the Mountain Madness climbers had closed the gap between themselves and Rob Hall's clients, members of the two teams becoming indistinguishable from one another as they climbed through what little was left of the night. If he glanced down, he probably noticed the headlamps of three members of a Taiwanese expedition, Makalu Gau and two Sherpas, about thirty minutes behind him.

The Balcony was in sunlight when Scott reached it. Most of the climbers of Mountain Madness and Adventure Consultants were moving up the Southeast Ridge, though Scott would have seen Adventure Consultants' client Beck Weathers sitting on the snow. A Texas pathologist on his first high-altitude climb, Weathers's bid to scale Everest had ended when vision problems began to plague him. Rob Hall had instructed Weathers to stay near the Balcony and wait for Hall to return from the summit to lead him down, and Weathers had agreed.

Scott climbed slowly up the Southeast Ridge. In the brilliance of the morning light, climbers farther up the ridge appeared as bright shapes of red, blue, and yellow. Several were coming toward him, members of Rob Hall's team returning to Camp IV after making the difficult decision that it wasn't their day to summit. They talked with Scott for a few moments, recalling that he did not seem to be struggling more than anyone else up so high. If he had looked down a little later, Scott might have seen them visiting with Beck Weathers, too, and then continuing their descent as Beck waited near the Balcony for Rob Hall's return.

Fixed ropes appeared before him, though Scott probably did not know who had put them there. Nor would he have realized that several hours earlier there had been debates among climbers and Sherpas about who should take the initiative to install the ropes on the steepest pitches of the ridge. He would not have known that Anatoli had given Neal the oxygen mask and regulator that Neal had provided him at Camp II, or that Neal had taken a coil of rope from Lopsang, who was no longer tied to Sandy, and gone ahead to start anchoring the lines.

The sky had become a radiant blue, and he saw the shapes of the giant peaks around him, their summits lower than he was now, their dazzling whiteness tinted by the dark shading of his goggles. He could look down for nearly two miles on either side of the ridge, and while he may have paused to take in the enormous vistas, his focus would have returned to lifting a foot and putting it back down and then taking another step. He concentrated on breathing, on overcoming weariness, on the simple act of staying in motion. He might have been startled as Makalu Gau and his Sherpas overtook him and passed by, leaving him as the final climber that morning ascending above the South Col.

Where the Southeast Ridge goes no higher, Scott reached the small promontory of the South Summit and looked across the knife-edged traverse of broken rock and corniced snow to the forty-foot rib of the Hillary Step. Anatoli had scaled the Step and anchored a rope at the top for those who followed to protect themselves as they searched for footholds and handholds. Scott saw nine or ten climbers waiting at the base for their turns to clip into the rope. Several climbers on top of the Step had been to the summit and were waiting for the Step to clear so that they could come down.

Scott crossed the traverse, attached himself to the rope, and climbed the Hillary Step. "Nobody discussed Fischer's exhausted appearance," Jon Krakauer would write of seeing Scott. "It didn't occur to any of us that he might be in trouble." Jon had reached the top of Everest and was on his way back to the South Col. Anatoli Boukreev was there, too, descending from the summit. He would later recall discussing with Scott his intention to descend quickly to Camp IV and ready himself to come back up to help any climbers who might need it.

Continuing up the last of the ridge, Scott saw the rest of his team on the summit along with Rob Hall, Rob's client Yasuko Namba, and several of the Adventure Consultants Sherpas. Scott toiled on. His teammates were coming toward him now with Neal leading Sandy, Lene, Charlotte, and Tim.

"Scott and I kind of reached out to touch mitts or do a high five as we passed," Neal remembered. "We said a few things, just sort of congratulations. My impression was hurry up, get to the top, turn around."

It was 3:30 p.m., very late for anyone to be so high on Everest with so far to go to reach camp. There was no need for Scott to climb higher. His teammates were below him now, headed down the mountain. Lopsang was still on the summit but would have seen if his expedition leader were to turn around and descend in the company of the others.

But Scott was nearly there. Ten more minutes to reach the top of Mount Everest, maybe ten minutes to take a few photographs, then another five or ten minutes back to this point. Half an hour, at most. If he thought about it at all, could he even have imagined not completing the ascent?

Putting one foot in front of the other, waiting to catch his breath, taking another step, Scott overtook Doug Hansen. Hansen had been close to the top of Everest the previous year on another expedition with Adventure Consultants, but with concerns about the lateness of the day, Rob had turned Doug around. This time he did not.

When Scott reached the summit, there was no exuberance, no shouting a celebratory "Bruuuce!" down the valleys, none of the joy of the first time he had been there. He took off his oxygen mask and sipped a little tea from a vacuum bottle cup Lopsang handed him, then radioed his support team at base camp and reported that he was weary and felt ill. They joined Lopsang in urging him to get off the mountain. Lopsang would later recall that as Scott began his descent, he had not put his oxygen mask back over his mouth and nose.

Makalu Gau and the Sherpas with him arrived as Scott started down, and then Doug Hansen got to the top, too, helped the last few steps by Rob Hall and Lopsang. At the Hillary Step, Scott paused to lift his camera and photograph Neal and the Mountain Madness climbers just ahead of him crossing the traverse toward the South Summit, the sky below them becoming dark with the rising swirls of a late-afternoon storm. The rope hanging down the Step was empty. Scott had only to descend it and he would be only a few minutes behind his team. A little infusion of the old Bruce force and he might have rejoined them for the rest of the way to Camp IV. But even though the others would be delayed on the South Summit while Neal and those with him sorted through a scattered pile of oxygen bottles in search of some that were full, Scott never caught up.

The Mountain Madness team was laboring down the ropes on the Southeast Ridge as Scott reached the South Summit. He continued to descend alone, trying to concentrate through the dull lethargy of exhaustion and oxygen depravation. Clouds were engulfing the mountain and the wind increased. As he neared the Balcony, he saw that it was empty. Two hours had passed since he had left the top of Everest and come down 1,600 vertical feet of treacherous terrain, two hours since he had spoken with anyone, and perhaps that long since he had last breathed supplemental oxygen.

Lopsang rejoined him above the Balcony and realized with alarm that Scott was in worse shape than when he had been on the summit. The Sherpa tied a rope from Scott's harness to his own and as he urged him to keep moving toward the South Col, the storm that had been building through the late afternoon slammed against the peak. Makalu Gau and his Sherpas emerged out of the whiteness, passed Scott and Lopsang, and were swallowed again by swirling snow.

Battling wind and darkness, Lopsang and Scott stumbled another 300 feet down the mountain and again came upon Makalu
Gau, now by himself and unable to continue. It was as far as Scott
could go, too. Lopsang pleaded with him not to stop, but Scott was
slipping deep into the confusion of hypoxia and what could have
been cerebral edema. He urged Lopsang to get Anatoli, and at last
Lopsang agreed that was what he should do, promising to have
Boukreev come with hot drinks.

Scott lay on the snow in the dark and the cold, the storm howl-
ing around him. Time seemed to stand still as the hours slipped
away, and then Scott Fischer slipped away, too.

Acts of heroism and episodes of tragedy were playing themselves
out higher on Everest and below. In horrific circumstances climbers
did the best they could for their own survival and that of others. In
some cases there were miracles.

Before the storm had unleashed on Everest, the fastest summit
climbers and those who had turned back early collapsed into their
tents at the South Col, some of them too exhausted to move. Anatoli
arrived to rest, and then as the storm gained ferocity, started back
up the mountain to assist climbers who had not yet returned. The
wind and driven snow were too much, though, and after several
hours of fruitless effort to find anyone he was forced back to his tent.

The Mountain Madness climbers Anatoli was searching for had
descended below the Balcony as the weather worsened, and come
upon Yasuko Namba. Neal had taken her by the arm and insisted
she stay with them. The group passed Adventure Consultants' guide
Mike Groom, too, who had persuaded Beck Weathers to come
down with him.

"When I grabbed Yasuko, everything slowed down a bit and
everybody accordioned together," Neal told me. "We descended to
the South Col and were in a full storm with seventy-mile-an-hour
winds. We had a big group and we're screaming at everybody to
stay together. The wind was veering us off course, and no matter
how hard we tried to keep going in the right direction, it was just
impossible."

Fearing they were dangerously close to the east edge of the Col and a two-mile plunge into Tibet, they huddled long into the night a few hundred yards from their tents. Klev Schoening glimpsed mountain silhouettes during a brief break in the storm and, realizing which way to go, set off with Neal Beidleman, Mike Groom, and Lene Gammelgaard toward Camp IV. They were too spent when they reached their tents to venture out again, and could find no one other than Anatoli able to go very far beyond the camp to attempt a rescue. On several forays into the resurgent storm, Anatoli found the stranded climbers and brought Sandy, Charlotte, and Tim to safety. He was unable to do the same for Namba Yasuko, who would not survive, or Beck Weathers. Remarkably, Weathers got to his feet the following afternoon and stumbled to the tents, his limbs and face badly frozen.

Higher up, Rob Hall and Doug Hansen had managed to get as far as the South Summit where they tried to shelter themselves from the wind and cold, but then Hansen was gone. Hall's guide Andy Harris disappeared, too, perhaps while attempting to bring oxygen to Hansen and Hall. Ed Viesturs and others in base camp were in sporadic radio contact with Rob, pleading with him to descend, but he was freezing and could no longer move. His last radio contact was a heartbreaking conversation patched through the base camp communications system to his wife in New Zealand.

The morning of May 11 dawned windy and cold, but the storm had passed. Sherpas climbing from the South Col found Scott where Lopsang had left him. Although he was unresponsive, the Sherpas detected shallow breathing and placed an oxygen mask over his face. Makalu Gau did stir, and the Sherpas helped the Korean climber descend to Camp IV. Later that day Anatoli climbed to Scott's side, then came down to report that the leader of the Mountain Madness expedition had died.

Members of several other expeditions abandoned their itineraries and threw their resources and energies into evacuating those on the South Col. Beck Weathers and Makalu Gau were brought almost to Camp I where a helicopter flying at the limit of its altitude capacities touched down to pick up Gau, then returned and carried Weathers to safety, too.

When the Mountain Madness climbers reached base camp, they discovered that news of the tragedy was already being broadcast around the world. The *Seattle Post-Intelligencer*, the paper where I had read about the success of Scott Fischer's expedition, published an article two days after the first, this time reporting that eight climbers had perished on Mount Everest and that Scott had been among them. The article closed by quoting Scott's answer to a question of what scared him most, posed months earlier on the website Outside Online.

"Making a bad decision and dying in the mountains, to be perfectly honest," he had said. "Not coming home from a trip, leaving my kids without a dad. That scares me. We can control a lot of things (on expeditions) but even so, things happen."

Things happen. Among them is the fact that all of the climbers who had put their trust in Scott Fischer returned from Everest alive and without significant injury. By instinct or luck or both, he had organized and conducted the Mountain Madness expedition in ways that resulted in the survival of his team. He had pushed himself to the limit, given it his all, and become one with the mountain that long ago had become one with him. There was a clarity to his passing, a simplicity on the clean edges of the mountains where there is up and down, storm and calm, dark and light, and life and death.

Things happen, and at the top of the world they can happen with devastating finality. In the end, perhaps that is explanation enough.

CHAPTER 22

After the Storm

SAY WHAT YOU will about the guy, he always attracted a crowd, and the last crowd included just about everyone. Three weeks after Scott Fischer had died on Mount Everest we gathered for his memorial service. It had taken that long to make the arrangements. It had taken that long for the people who felt the need to be there to travel to Seattle from around the globe and to compose themselves behind their dark glasses and subdued demeanors.

"Right after Scott died, I had no idea how many people would want to come together," Jeannie told me. "Then Larry our milkman asked if he could attend whatever service we were planning, and I realized it was going to be big."

In fact, there were two gatherings. The first, open to the public, was held in a city park near the Fischer-Price home. Hundreds of people came to sit for an afternoon in a grassy vale, share stories of Scott, visit with friends, or simply satisfy their curiosity about a man they had never known but with whom they were feeling a compelling connection.

The second memorial was a few days later on Bainbridge Island. I took the same ferry across Puget Sound that I had ridden with Scott years earlier on our way to Mount Olympus for our first climb together, then drove down the island to Kiana Lodge, an Indian cultural center tucked in a forest of cedar and Douglas fir. The airy main building was set up for a banquet. Rows of white folding chairs filled the lawn leading down to the water. The sun broke through the clouds as I arrived, and a breeze rich with the smells of the woods and the sea fluttered the strings of yellow, red, and green Buddhist prayer flags hung between the trees. There was nothing vertical anywhere, nothing frozen, nothing that could even remotely invoke mountain tragedy save for the awareness of the death that was bringing us together.

The event on Bainbridge had been intended for Scott's family and close friends, and 300 people arrived, most including themselves in one or both categories. Many who had accompanied Scott on mountaineering expeditions comprised a who's who of American climbers of the 1980s and 1990s. Murray the Fisherman busied himself grilling salmon he had brought from Alaska to feed everyone, a gracious act that allowed him to focus his attention on something other than the profound sadness of the moment.

A generation of instructors from the National Outdoor Leadership School visited among themselves, the dozens of Bruces from the years Scott had worked for NOLS. Wes Krause had traveled from his home at the foot of Kilimanjaro, bringing his wife Melly with him and his children and a Tanzanian nanny who spoke softly in Swahili with several of the climbers who had extensive African experience. Scott's buddies from his high school days in New Jersey mixed easily with the climbers. The Fischer family was there, too—parents, siblings, Jeannie and Andy and Katie Rose—the only group dressed up in a gathering where most people were wearing loose, casual clothes and where so many moved with the easy assurance of mountaineers walking on flat ground.

The faint outlines of their glacier goggles were still burned into the faces of the Mountain Madness climbers who had just been with Scott on Mount Everest. It was almost surreal to see them so soon after their struggle to survive high in the Himalayas. They had about them a distance and a wariness, as if they were not yet fully back from the heights or quite in command of the expedition stories as they would be telling them in the months and years to come. What had happened was still too fresh to have manageable shape, though its form was already gaining permanence.

Among the Sherpas who had flown from Nepal was Scott's logistics manager P. B. Thapa, who recognized me from my own travels with Scott in the Himalayas, and Lopsang Jangbu. "We summit Everest together, but the gods did not help," Lopsang told me. "I am so sorry."

"It is very sad, this thing that happened to Scott," P. B. added, "but this is what was allotted to him. In Nepal we know he is always with us."

As I moved toward my seat for the beginning of the service, I introduced myself to Anatoli Boukreev and shook his hand. I knew just enough Russian from a Mountain Madness trip to Mount Elbrus to greet him in his language rather than mine. He gave me a little smile and gripped my hand firmly in his.*

A minister read remembrances of Scott from family members. Neal Beidleman gave Andy and Katie Rose a pocketknife that Scott had carried with him on his last trip to Nepal. Jeff Long and Peter Goldman told about their adventures with Scott in the way-back days when they had been young and a world of possibilities lay open before them.

Then Wes Krause stepped to the lectern, bringing with him a flash of the charisma and charm that he and Scott had always exuded, a powerful surge of the Bruce force missing from everyone's lives in the weeks since Scott's death. Wes talked of coming to the National Outdoor Leadership School as a young man and hearing about this Scott Fischer who was supposed to be such a hot climber. It had taken them a siege of arm-wrestling contests and pull-up competitions to mesh their strengths and become an inseparable team.

It's hard to explain the essence of Scott, Wes told us, hard to figure out just what made him so dynamic. "One time Scott and I were in the Wrangell Mountains in Alaska," Wes said, then told the story about being charged by a grizzly and Scott's insistence that surely the two of them together could take on one solitary bear. "The moral of the story was that if Scott told you he had a plan, you'd better pay attention because the guy had a plan."

*Six months after Scott's memorial, Lopsang Jangbu Sherpa died under an avalanche on Mount Everest. On Christmas Day of 1997, Anatoli Boukreev perished in an avalanche while attempting to climb Annapurna I.

Wes could have added that Scott had also been among the rising cadre of young climbers who had found themselves and one another at NOLS and Outward Bound and become committed to mountaineering. Climbing and guiding had been Scott's passion, his profession, and what gave meaning to much of his life. He had been central to a remarkable era of Himalayan mountaineering when he and a core group of climbers eager to summit the world's great peaks had accomplished what they set out to do and then made it possible for others to have that dream come true for themselves. Scott had done it with grace, boundless enthusiasm, and joyous optimism. He had lived his life, as his fellow climbers said of his first Everest ascent, with good style.

The service closed with a ceremony of reunification as we opened small cardboard boxes and released a swirl of butterflies. The Sherpas lit bundles of incense and led us in a Buddhist chant while the scented smoke followed the butterflies up through the prayer flags and the boughs of the trees and into the open sky.

I visited with friends the rest of the afternoon as we feasted on Murray's grilled salmon. People were reluctant to leave. Having come together in this safe and comforting gathering, they didn't want it to conclude, but at last it was time to go. As I waited in the traffic line at the ferry terminal, I watched some of the people who had attended the memorial as they melted into the throng of weekend travelers. Scott's people were dispersing again. The Bruces were going back out toward the far corners of the world.

I had trouble falling asleep that night and when I finally did, I dreamed that Scott's son Andy had come to stay at my house near Puget Sound. The boy in my dream tells me he wants to swim in the Sound but I say no, the water is too deep and too cold. He dives in anyway, only now it isn't Andy, it's Scott, and though I shout for him to come back, he swims away with strong, sure strokes until he is far from shore. Then he begins to struggle. I see him gasping for breath and fighting to stay above the water. I dive in and try to swim out to him, but he is at too great a distance and the water is freezing, and even as I top each wave I can no longer see where he had been. Scott Fischer is gone and there is nothing I can do to bring him back. I awaken suddenly and it takes me several moments to realize I am still in my bed.

The next morning I loaded my backpack with camping gear and drove to Grand Teton National Park where I had agreed to supervise a work crew for the Student Conservation Association. It was the fourteenth summer that I had worked for the SCA, and while I had always been enthused about leading backcountry programs, I was reluctant to embark on this one. Scott's death had left me emotionally drained, but more to the point was the fact that as a young NOLS instructor Scott had rambled all over the Tetons. He had climbed the Grand Teton in the summer and in the winter. He had scaled it with NOLS students and with his best friends. Early in their relationship he had taken Jeannie Price to the summit. My head was so full of thinking of him that I didn't want to spend the summer in a landscape that would constantly bring him to mind, but the wheels were already in motion and it was easier simply to go to Wyoming than to figure out a way to go somewhere else.

I picked up my trail crew at the bus station in Jackson and at the Jackson Hole airport, three boys and three girls ages sixteen to eighteen, eager to volunteer the upcoming weeks to live deep in the backcountry and do something good for the land. Drawn to Wyoming from all over America, they were bubbling with enthusiasm. They had learned of the SCA from reading about it in magazines or hearing of it from high school classmates or seeing a television news story featuring environmental opportunities for teens, and it had struck all of them as exactly what they wanted to do.

We drove to a campground and I spent the afternoon getting them outfitted with clothing made of fleece and wool. We sorted provisions and measured rice, beans, flour, and the other staples into plastic bags that we closed with loose overhand knots. The next morning a Park Service boat dropped us on the far side of Jenny Lake and we hiked into a valley near the park's northern boundary. We pitched our tents and set up a tarp to protect our camp kitchen from inclement weather. A line stretched high between two trees allowed us to hoist our food bags off the ground and protect them from the bears.

The teenagers took charge of the camp, cooking big meals, baking biscuits in a Dutch oven, and having as much fun as they could possibly stand. Each morning we set out with shovels, axes, and cross-cut saws to clear and repair another section of trail. At first my heart wasn't in it, but I had supervised crews so many times I could do it almost with my eyes closed. I passed the days working by myself a short distance from the others, and at night I crawled into my sleeping bag and fell into a deep, dreamless sleep.

The weeks passed, and despite the sadness of Scott's loss, I could feel the power of the mountains seeping back into my bones. Life slowed and simplified. The present moment became more important than preparing for the next day or worrying about the past. The world beyond the Tetons faded and then seemed to disappear.

Slowly I began to connect with the youngsters on my crew. My sorrow was not theirs, and while they listened with interest as we sat by the campfire and I told them about Scott, they were building their own backcountry reality. They were forming friendships and having joyous adventures full of exuberance and teenaged excess, and I found myself being drawn in. I spent more time cooking with them, swimming in a nearby stream, and playing chess badly on a little board I'd brought along. I eased in among them as they worked, the swinging of tools paced by the conversations of young people reveling in the satisfaction of hard physical labor. They were about the same age Scott had been when he discovered NOLS and found the mountains. They were the age I had been when I had gone to New Mexico with the Boy Scouts and fallen in love with trails. They were thriving on being in the wilderness and celebrating the freedom they were finding there. Their lives were changing and so, I was discovering, was mine.

With summer drawing to a close and our trail work nearly done, I felt a growing need to be in motion. We studied topography maps and sketched out a route that would lead us to the crest of the Tetons and then keep us near the high divide for a run down the range's center. After loading our packs with our camping gear and a week's worth of provisions, we hiked toward the head of the valley. The forests shrank around us and then fell away as we climbed above tree line into meadows awash with alpine flowers, the crew sharing my compulsion to keep climbing higher. They tucked in behind me and stayed close as we ascended beyond the meadows and entered a world of rock and wind and open sky. The great peaks of the Tetons lifted all around us, the terrain seeming to leap straight out of the prairie far below. We were above everything, above complexity, beyond complication. There was nothing manmade, not even a pathway, and no one but us as far as we could see. Everything felt clean, angular, open, and spare. It was a simplicity I had been yearning for, an immediacy of experience that I had always found in the mountains but that had been lacking for me since Scott had died.

The sun pounded us as we hiked, and the wind beat against us. Each afternoon we dropped off the crest and took shelter from thunderstorms crackling across the highest ridges, then we hiked fast to get up high again and unroll our sleeping bags under skies ablaze with stars. We were traveling swiftly and self-contained along the crease between earth and sky. The teenagers with me were feeling the joy of devouring great expanses of wild country, the earth turning beneath our feet as the horizon rolled toward us. They wanted more open space, more elevation, and they were eager to follow me wherever I was willing to go.

As we neared the park's center, we needed to traverse the crest of the Tetons a final time and descend to a trail leading to a road. With an early start and using a compass to set our course, we made good time. By mid-afternoon we had come to the far edge of a high plateau. Threading along the lakeshore far below us lay the trail we had to reach. Beyond the lake was the immense granite monolith of the Grand Teton, Scott's mountain, rising far above us against a darkening sky. Clouds were moving up behind the Grand, heavy with a foreboding afternoon storm.

The descent looked much steeper than our map had suggested, but we had no choice but to proceed if we were to get away from a place so exposed to the potential of lightning. I led the teenagers through a boulder field and into a rocky, snow-filled gulley, keeping an eye on the weather and hearing distant thunder moving our way.

Our backpacks made us ungainly, and while the youngsters with me were strong from their weeks of work on the trails, they were not experienced mountaineers. Moving on precipitous rock did not come naturally to them and it demanded the most of their abilities.

With 500 feet to go, the gulley tilted from steep to vertical, and without belay ropes or the hardware to set anchors, we could go no farther. The thunderstorm welling up behind the Grand crackled with electricity, and the beat of thunder became more powerful and insistent. Taking care to find good holds for my hands and feet, I eased around a rib of rock into an adjoining gulley only to discover that it was also too steep for us to descend.

We had been traveling since dawn. I could feel myself tiring from the effort of leading novices through serious terrain, a weariness compounded by my acute awareness that we were now fully exposed to the approaching storm. I climbed around another rock band but could still not see a way down. Black clouds wreathed the summit of the Grand, and a cold fear gripped me as I realized the increasing danger and my responsibility for the well-being of these young people. Looking down the cliffs below me, I could see only places they might fall.

"*You know, Scott,*" I said aloud without knowing why, "*I could use a little help here.*"

Suddenly I sensed the wind warming and shifting direction, and I felt myself being held more securely against the rock. The storm that had been ready to break across the valley and engulf us seemed to pause, as if hung for a moment against the back of the Grand. I looked down again, studying the rock face under my feet as if through the eyes of a better mountain guide than I could ever hope to be, and a route seemed to materialize. It was tenuous and getting down it required all of our concentration, but then the teenagers and I were at the base of the cliffs and running across the valley floor, and as we reached the shelter of the trees by the lake the storm unleashed its lightning and rain. The concussions of thunder nearly drove us to our knees.

The storm moved on. The teenagers were alive with the power of having been in the heart of the storm, their eyes wide and bright.

They were shaking with excitement, and so was I. We dug into our packs for dry clothing and then swung our packs to our shoulders and hiked a few miles down the trail before making camp. Our provisions were nearly gone, but we had enough left to cook a pot of macaroni and cheese. We were going to be fine. We were okay.

The sky slowly cleared and I sat in front of my tent watching the Grand Teton becoming a silhouette as the evening settled around us. I opened my journal and wrote about the day. When I got back to Seattle in a week or two, I would put the notebook in the box I store under the stairs, the box with all the other Mountain Madness journals.

And now I'm sitting again on the steps with that box open beside me as I read the pages I scribbled in the Tetons the evening after the storm. This is the last of the notebooks that I've taken from the box in my journey to find the Scott Fischer I had known so long ago. I've read through them all, discovering some of him in each one. I'm finding myself in them, too, and I think back to where this began, next to Scott on Kala Patar as we had looked toward Everest and he had described for me the route his expedition would follow. He had been fully engaged with life, filled with the Bruce force, energized by the simple, uncomplicated joy of climbing.

That is how I remember him best. It was a good place to begin finding him as I started tracing his steps down from the snows of Everest and back through the years of his life. It is a good place for me to leave him now. The mountains endure, but the footprints in the drifts hold only a little while, and then they melt away.

Notes

Chapter 2: Thirty Days to Survival

00   The article described Petzoldt—Jane Howard, "Last Mountain Man? Not if He Can Help It," *Life* (December 19, 1969).

00   **"We did everything wrong"**—Molly Absolon. "Paul Tells His Story," *The Leader* (Fall 1995).

Chapter 3: A Bunch of Bruces

00   *First Bruce: G'day Bruce!*—"The Bruce Sketch," *Monty Python's Flying Circus,* Episode 22: 24 November 1970.

Chapter 6: The Fallingest Man in Climbing

00   **"Every so often, if we were camped"**—Sebastian Junger, "Large as Life," *Outside Magazine* (August 1999), 50.

Chapter 8: Mountain Madness

Portions of this chapter first appeared in Robert Birkby, "A Walk on the Hot Side." *Seattle Weekly* (April 30–May 6, 1986), 63.

00   "His motto for Mountain Madness"—Ed Viesturs, with David Roberts, *No Shortcuts to the Top: Climbing the World's 14 Highest Peaks* (New York: Broadway, 2006), 19.

00   "Since 1978, 35,000 people have strolled"—Nancy Griffin, "Charismatic Kid," *Life* (March 1985), 42.

00   "I was always going to have a company"—Tina Kelley, "Scott Fischer . . . Reaching Beyond Everest & K2," *Northwest Wilderness Journal* (November/December 1994), 40.

Chapter 9: Kilimanjaro the Really Hard Way

00   "The risk had been incalculable"—Reinhold Messner. *Free Spirit: A Climber's Life* (Seattle: Mountaineers Books, 1998), 204.

Chapter 10: Annapurna Fang

00   "The mountain is considered to be very difficult"—Elizabeth Hawley and Richard Salisbury. *The Himalayan Database: The Expedition Archives of Elizabeth Hawley*, CD-ROM edition (Golden, CO: American Alpine Club, 2004).

00   "Krause twisted ankle"—Elizabeth Hawley and Richard Salisbury. *The Himalayan Database: The Expedition Archives of Elizabeth Hawley*, CD-ROM edition (Golden, CO: American Alpine Club, 2004).

00   "The Fang got the better of us"—Scott Fischer. "An Expensive Education: Our First Himalayan Climb," *Rock and Ice* (January/February 1986), 29.

Chapter 11: Rockin' with the Ruskies

00   Portions of this chapter first appeared in Robert Birkby,
     "Rockin' with the Ruskies," *Rock and Ice* (March/April
     1986), 28–32.

Chapter 12: It's All Fun Until Somebody Dies

00   **Stacy noticed that Steve Monfredo was having a little
     difficulty**

00   Stacy Allison, with Peter Carlin. *Beyond the Limits: A
     Woman's Triumph on Everest* (Boston: Little, Brown
     1993), 109–10.

00   **"Three metres below the surface"**—Colin Monteath. *Hall &
     Ball: Kiwi Mountaineers: From Mount Cook to Everest*
     (Christchurch, N.Z.: Hedgehog House, 1997), 60–61.

Chapter 13: Everest North Face

00   *Hundreds of Sleepy Sherpas*   Gary Synder, "For George
     Leigh-Mallory." *Left Out in the Rain: Poems* San
     Francisco: North Point, 1988).

Chapter 14: The Nutrition Expedition

00   **Sergio Fitch-Watkins was a seasoned guide**—Elizabeth
     Hawley and Richard Salisbury. *The Himalayan Database:
     The Expedition Archives of Elizabeth Hawley*, CD-ROM
     edition (Golden, CO: American Alpine Club, 2004).

00   **Hall and Ball piled into a vehicle**—Colin Monteath. *Hall &
     Ball: Kiwi Mountaineers: From Mount Cook to Everest*
     (Christchurch, N.Z.: Hedgehog House, 1997), 88.

Chapter 16: F.O.S.

00 "Even then, in the midst of expedition"—Phil Powers. "Scott
Style: Adventure Student Makes Good" *NOLS Leader*
(Winter 1992). Reprinted at www.nols.edu/
alumni/leader/92winter/scottfischer.shtml.

Chapter 17: K2 in '92

00 "It can be summed up in a few words"—Ed Viesturs, with
David Roberts. *No Shortcuts to the Top: Climbing the
World's 14 Highest Peaks* (New York: Broadway, 2006),
34.

Chapter 19: Everest with Good Style

00 "5,000 pounds trash off mountain"—Elizabeth Hawley and
Richard Salisbury. *The Himalayan Database: The
Expedition Archives of Elizabeth Hawley*, CD-ROM edi-
tion (Golden, CO: American Alpine Club, 2004).

Chapter 20: The Year Before the Year

00 You've climbed the highest mountain in the world.—
"EverestHistory.com: Willi Unsoeld," at
www.everestnews.com/history/climber/unsoeld.htm

00 "Everest is pretty much the same experience"—Tina Kelley.
"Scott Fischer . . . Reaching Beyond Everest & K2,"
Northwest Wilderness Journal (November/December,
1994), 40.

00 "I feel bad that my family misses me"—Tina Kelley. "Scott
Fischer . . . Reaching Beyond Everest & K2," *Northwest
Wilderness Journal* (November/December, 1994), 40.

00 **"I am back from Alaska"**—Lene Gammelgaard. *Climbing High: A Woman's Account of Surviving the Everest Tragedy* (Seattle, WA: Seal Press, 1999), 19–20.

00 **"When we were coming off Broad Peak"**—Paul Roberts. "Scottish Climber Alison Hargreaves and Six Others Killed on K2," Outside Online internet posting at outside.away.com/news/specialreport/alison/w01.html

Chapter 21: Last Climb

00 **"We were together for two months"**—Mary Turner. "Sandy Hill, 51," *Outside Magazine* (September 2006), 84.

00 **"Building on the success of 1994"**—Outside Online. "Back to Summit Journal '96," at outside.away.com/outside/disc /features/fischer2.html#africa

00 **"The Russian moved with his crampons"**—Elizabeth Hawley and Richard Salisbury. *The Himalayan Database: The Expedition Archives of Elizabeth Hawley*, CD-ROM edition (Golden, CO: American Alpine Club, 2004).

00 **"We'll have fun in Kathmandu"**—Lene Gammelgaard. *Climbing High: A Woman's Account of Surviving the Everest Tragedy* (Seattle, WA: Seal Press, 1999), 166.

00 **"Dale is my friend"**—Lene Gammelgaard. *Climbing High: A Woman's Account of Surviving the Everest Tragedy* (Seattle, WA: Seal Press, 1999), 145.

00 **"He insisted that we go to the summit"**—Mary Turner. "Sandy Hill, 51," *Outside Magazine* (September 2006), 84.

00 **"They talked with Scott for a few moments"**—Anatoli Boukreev and G. Weston deWalt. *The Climb: Tragic Ambitions on Everest* (New York: St. Martin's Press, 1997), 142.

00 **"Nobody discussed Fischer's exhausted appearance"**—Jon Krakauer. *Into Thin Air: A Personal Account of the Mount Everest Disaster* (New York: Villard, 1997), 211.

00 **"He would later recall discussing with Scott"**—Anatoli Boukreev and G. Weston deWalt. *The Climb: Tragic Ambitions on Everest* (New York: St. Martin's Press, 1997), 154–155.

00 **"Lopsang would later recall"**—Jon Krakauer. *Into Thin Air: A Personal Account of the Mount Everest Disaster* (New York: Villard, 1997), 236.

00 **"Making a bad decision"**—Rob Taylor. "Everest Turns Ugly on Climbers," *Seattle Post-Intelligencer* (May 13, 1996), A1.

Selected Bibliography

Allison, Stacy, with Peter Carlin. *Beyond the Limits: A Woman's Triumph on Everest.* Boston: Little, Brown, 1993.

Bates, Robert H., et al. *Five Miles High: The Story of an Attack on the Second Highest Mountain in the World by the Members of the First American Karakoram Expedition.* New York: Dodd, Mead & Company, 1939.

Boukreev, Anatoli, and G. Weston deWalt. *The Climb: Tragic Ambitions on Everest.* New York: St. Martin's Press, 1997.

Gammelgaard, Lene. *Climbing High: A Woman's Account of Surviving the Everest Tragedy.* Seattle, WA: Seal Press, 1999.

Hall, Lincoln. *White Limbo: The First Australian Climb of Mt. Everest.* Seattle, WA: Mountaineers Books, 1987.

Hawley, Elizabeth, and Richard Salisbury. *The Himalayan Database: The Expedition Archives of Elizabeth Hawley.* CD-ROM edition. Golden, CO: American Alpine Club, 2004.

Jordan, Jennifer. *Savage Summit: The True Stories of the First Five Women Who Climbed K2, the World's Most Feared Mountain.* New York: Harper-Collins, 2005.

Krakauer, Jon. *Into Thin Air: A Personal Account of the Mount Everest Disaster.* New York: Villard, 1997.

Messner, Reinhold. *The Crystal Horizon: Everest—the First Solo Ascent.* Translated by Jill Neate and Audrey Salkeld. Seattle, WA: Mountaineers Books, 1989.

Messner, Reinhold. *Free Spirit: A Climber's Life*. Seattle, WA: Mountaineers Books, 1998.

Monteath, Colin. *Hall & Ball: Kiwi Mountaineers: From Mount Cook to Everest*. Christchurch, N.Z.: Hedgehog House, 1997.

Potterfield, Peter. *In the Zone: Epic Survival Stories from the Mountaineering World*. Seattle: Mountaineers Books, 1996.

Ringholz, Raye C. *On Belay! The Life of Legendary Mountaineer Paul Petzoldt*. Seattle, WA: Mountaineers Books,1997.

Viesturs, Ed, with David Roberts. *No Shortcuts to the Top: Climbing the World's 14 Highest Peaks*: New York: Broadway, 2006.

Weathers, Beck, with Stephen G. Michaud. *Left for Dead: My Journey Home from Everest*. New York: Villard, 2000.

Acknowledgments

I am deeply indebted to the Fischer family for sharing so much of Scott with me—Scott's parents Gene and Shirley Fischer, sisters Lisa Fischer-Luchenbach and Rhonda Fischer, wife Jeannie Price, and children Andy and Katie Rose Fischer-Price.

I am also grateful that so many who found adventure with Scott have told me about their experiences. Of great assistance, too, have been those who helped me understand the significance of what I was hearing, and those who helped me find the words that matched the subject:

Michael Allison
Stacy Allison
Helen Andersen
Pete Athans
Randy Aton
Neal Beidleman
Leila Berg
Wally Berg
Brent Bishop
Craig Birkby
Jeff Birkby
Christine Boskoff
Melany Brown
Nathan Byers
Page Byers

Mike Burns
Sarah Calhoun
Patty Calver
Paul Calver
Dana Carver
Bruce Cartwright
Randy Cerf
Michael Crehore
Karen Dickinson
Kathleen Digre
Jennie Douglas
Polly Fabian
Charlotte Fox
Pookie Gipe
Steve Gipe

Steve Goryl

Mark Gunlogson

Molly Hampton

Wayne Herzog

Rob Hess

Peter Jamieson

Mary Jensen

Wesley Krause

Dale Kruse

Jeff Long

Charley Mace

Luanne Mannon

Greg Martin

Walt McConnell

John McIntosh

Dan McHale

Veda Price Moretti

Pat Morrow

Chris Naumann

Laura Naumann

Maggie McManus

Carol Munch

Jeff Murray

Jim Nelson

Bruce Newell

Liz Nichol

Tom Nickels

J.D. Owen

Len Pagliaro

Glenn Porzak

Phil Powers

Joel Rogers

Rod Replogle

Melly Reuling

Robert Reynolds

Nelljean Rice

Paul Rice

Bobbi Robinson

Jay Satz

Craig Seasholes

Diane Shoutis

Dawa Geljen Sherpa

Laurie Skreslet

Bonnie Stenehjem

Scott Stenehjem

Caroline Smith

Ingrid Stokes

Ed Viesturs

Dorothy Warren

Tom Warren

Dana Welch

Steve Wennstrom

Finally, my deep love and thanks to my own base camp staff—
the Birkby family for their constant support, the Rice family for
their encouragement, the Satz family for always setting a place for
me at their table, and Seattle's Teahouse Kuan Yin for keeping me
caffeinated throughout this long and rewarding expedition.